LIVE THE

LET-GO

LIFE

—

ALSO BY JOSEPH PRINCE

—

The Prayer of Protection

The Prayer of Protection Devotional

Grace Revolution

Glorious Grace

Grace Revolution Study Guide

Reign in Life

The Power of Right Believing

100 Days of Right Believing

Destined to Reign

Destined to Reign Devotional

Unmerited Favor

100 Days of Favor

Healing Promises

Provision Promises

Health and Wholeness through the Holy Communion

A Life Worth Living

The Benjamin Generation

Your Miracle Is in Your Mouth

Right Place Right Time

Spiritual Warfare

For more information on these books and other inspiring resources, visit JosephPrince.com.

JOSEPH PRINCE

LIVE THE
LET-GO
LIFE

Breaking Free from Stress,
Worry, and Anxiety

New York   Nashville

FaithWords

Hachette Book Group

1290 Avenue of the Americas, New York, NY 10104

faithwords.com

twitter.com/faithwords

First Edition: October 2017

FaithWords is a division of Hachette Book Group, Inc.
The FaithWords name and logo are trademarks of Hachette Book Group, Inc.

The publisher is not responsible for websites (or their content) that are not owned by the publisher.

The Hachette Speakers Bureau provides a wide range of authors for speaking events. To find out more, go to www.hachettespeakersbureau.com or call (866) 376-6591.

Library of Congress Control Number: 2017942517

ISBNs: 978-1-4555-6133-9 (hardcover), 978-1-4789-2395-4 (large print), 978-1-5460-3283-0 (intl. pbk.), 978-1-4555-6135-3 (ebook)

Printed in the United States of America

LSC-C

10 9 8 7 6 5 4 3 2 1

CONTENTS

INTRODUCTION

It feels like our world today is spinning faster on its axis than ever before and picking up momentum with each passing day. One moment, we are wishing each other "Happy New Year!" and before we know it, we're preparing for Thanksgiving. The parade would be back on television and we would be heading back up to the attic to get the box of Christmas decorations that it seems like we had just put away yesterday. Where did all that time go?

Many factors add to this frantic pace of life. New demands are arising in a rapidly changing workplace, and almost every industry has been confronted by disruption. Many are struggling with the need to keep up with new knowledge and to be retrained or redeployed in order to stay relevant, while juggling the demands of marriage, parenting, and church. And all this is happening amid a backdrop of political turmoil, economic uncertainty, currency fluctuations, the very real threat of terror in our everyday lives, natural disasters, and new strains of deadly viruses. The immediacy of real-time communications through various mediums such as text messages, Snaps, and WhatsApp group chats has also created a new normalcy where any person, regardless of their hierarchy of importance in our personal lives, has the power to place an immediate demand on our time and possibly distract and even derail us from our plans.

It is easy to see why so many people today are experiencing stress, worry, and anxiety attacks. Unfortunately, these aren't simply innocent states of emotion—they can insidiously develop into chronic depression, psychosomatic illnesses, and even suicidal tendencies. Studies have shown that people who are under high levels of stress tend to engage in unhealthy behaviors to cope. These behaviors range from spending excessive time surfing the Internet or watching television to overeating, binging on alcohol, smoking, depending on drugs, and even viewing pornography. Stress could also end up being a gateway to sin, as someone who is under tremendous pressure may make irrational and even morally questionable decisions in a bid to escape the realities confronting them.

Do not underestimate the destructive power of stress. Stress, which has been called a "silent killer," can affect our immunity and lead to serious consequences, including insomnia, depression, bulimia, stomach conditions, and even cancer. Stress can paralyze us and render us incapable of functioning normally in society. Stress is depleting and can completely wipe out our energy reserves. Stress can render us powerless, with no strength or resolve to say no to temptations. Stress can be debilitating and cause us to completely self-destruct.

That is why I wrote this book with a great sense of urgency in my heart and spirit. At its very core, stress is about demands—demands that we can neither keep up with nor satisfy. But the Lord's grace is all about supply! In this book, I want to teach you how to walk in a greater measure and depth of the Lord's supply, and practical ways to allow His supply in your life to flow unabated. Stress, worry, and anxiety choke God's supply of favor, wisdom, and good success. The more you learn to let go of your anxieties, the more you will see His supply flow. This is why I have titled this book *Live the Let-Go Life*. I have no doubt that you will be greatly encouraged and strengthened by this book as you learn powerful scriptural truths that deal with stress.

I understand what it means to be under tremendous pressure. Being the senior pastor of a church that has an average attendance of over 30,000 every Sunday definitely comes with its demands. There was a period in my life when I developed symptoms in my body that doctors told me were caused by stress.

But the Lord is so good. He patiently showed me how His Son has already paid the price for our peace. Because of His sacrifice, you and I can live a victorious life free from stress and worry today, even when we are faced with overwhelming demands. I pray the truths and practical tools in this book will set you free in the same way the Lord has used them to liberate me and many others.

Here are just some of the themes that I cover in this book:

- Discover the power of letting go
- Tune in to the wavelength of peace
- Learn the richness of His *shalom*
- Know how to guard your heart
- Step into the rhythm of rest
- Find the right tempo for your life
- Receive healing when you are relaxed
- Walk in restful increase
- Experience days of heaven

I have received so many testimonies from precious people who have received breakthroughs that they never thought were possible. Their stories might be different, but they all point back to the same God who broke them out of their depression, the same

God who took away their anxieties and gave them His peace, the same God who has given them joy and put a song of praise in their mouths. I share their stories in this book because I want you to see that if God can do it for them, He can also do it for you.

My dear reader, you were not designed by God to live under stress; you were called to live the life of rest. The life of rest is a life of victory. Come with me, my friend, and let's start living the *let-go life*, a quality life free from stress, worry, and anxiety!

See you in the first chapter.

LIVE THE
LET-GO
LIFE

—

I.
LET GO

Are you feeling overwhelmed? Bombarded by unending demands, responsibilities, and deadlines? Assailed by bills to be paid, credit card debts to be cleared, health issues to attend to, troubled children who need your immediate attention, and endless mountains of emails and text messages that need to be answered?

Perhaps everything seems to be screaming at you and calling your name. Perhaps you are left breathless by the half-formed thoughts that await completion and demand answers:

What needs to be done?
Why should that be prioritized?
Whom did I forget to call?
Where do I have to be?
When does this need to be completed?

Your unfulfilled to-do list pulls you in twenty-five different directions.

When night comes, it is hard to shut all those swirling thoughts and burdens out. Sleep becomes elusive, and when you finally drift into a fitful slumber, you are startled awake time and again, your heart racing with anxiety.

With so much already going on, I know you are probably thinking, *I don't have the time to read another book!*

Trust me, I understand. With all the demands that I am confronted with in my world—from church to television recordings to speaking engagements around the world to my precious family—I honestly don't have time to work on another book. Yet, here I am.

Why? Because I believe that we all need to hit the Pause button.

We need to pause, step back from all the hustle and bustle, and *listen*. Listen to the sound of birds singing their greetings to the morning sun. Listen to the sound of waves gently embracing the shore. Listen to the sound of rain dancing through the treetops.

Most importantly, we need to pause and listen to the everlasting words of the One who loves us. This is not about reading another book. This is about being refreshed. This is about taking a cool evening walk with our Lord. This is about hearing Him whisper to us today:

Be still, and know that I am God.

—*Psalm 46:10*

There is a modern minimalist movement today that is all about simplifying and decluttering your surroundings. The premise behind the movement is, if you can tidy up your *outside*, you will find peace on the *inside*.

This book you hold in your hand takes a contrarian approach. The premise of *Live the Let-Go Life* is, if you can declutter what is *inside* you—in your heart, your soul, and your mind—the clutter that is on the *outside* will be taken care of.

The Spirit of the Lord works from the inside out. Yes, you might be faced with a mountain of demands that would make Mount Everest look like a molehill. But when there is a song in your heart, any mountain can be surmounted. Take care of the knots on the inside, and the knots on the outside will be super-naturally untied.

> *Take care of the knots on the inside, and the knots on the outside will be supernaturally untied.*

Letting Go

Would you believe that the answer to all your problems is found in letting them go? Letting go of your worries is not an irresponsible act. In fact, it is the most powerful thing you can do when you let them go into the hands of the One who created the universe. You are acknowledging that you cannot, *but He can*, and stepping aside so that His supply can flow into every area of your life. You are making the decision to be still and to let Him be God (see Ps. 46:10), to stand still and to see His salvation (see Ex. 14:13)! When you let go, you are effectively saying, "Lord Jesus, I put my faith in You to take over. I cannot, but You can. I trust in You. I choose to let go and release all my stress, worries, fears, and anxieties into Your hands because I know You love me."

The Scriptures say it this way:

Casting all your care upon Him, for He cares for you.
—1 Peter 5:7

I want you to see this verse in the Amplified translation:

Casting all your cares [all your anxieties, all your worries, and all your concerns, once and for all] on Him, for He cares about you [with deepest affection, and watches over you very carefully].

Beloved, you can cast *all* your cares on Him *once and for all* because He cares for you. It doesn't matter what you are anxious about. Whether you fear becoming irrelevant in the marketplace, or are stressed about the upcoming interview, or are worried you might end up unloved and alone, you can take that care and put it in His hands. Your Father loves you with the deepest affection and watches over you so carefully. He is waiting for you to let Him take over.

Many times, we struggle to let go because we think that if we let go, nothing will happen. We think that not worrying about something is to be irresponsible. So we hold on so tightly our knuckles turn white. We agonize and worry because we think we are being *responsible*! But our Lord Jesus posed a very important rhetorical question for us all:

> *And which of you by worrying can add one hour to his life's span?*
>
> —*Luke 12:25* AMP

Our Lord was telling us *not* to hold on to our worries because all our worries and anxieties cannot change any situation. No amount of worrying on our part can cause us to live even a little longer. In fact, worry and stress can be detrimental to us and shorten our lives!

According to researchers at the Mayo Clinic, chronic stress puts us at increased risk of numerous health problems, including anxiety disorders, depression, digestive problems, headaches, cardiovascular diseases, high blood pressure, sleep problems, weight gain, and the impairment of memory and concentration.[1] If you are suffering from these symptoms because of stress, then you are not living the abundant life that our Lord Jesus came to give us. He came that we might have life and *life more abundantly* (see John 10:10). God doesn't want us to just have a trickle of life or just enough life. He wants us to have overflowing life! Being bowed down with cares, fighting chronic fatigue, or battling stress and sickness is not living life more abundantly. Our Lord Jesus loves you so much and He wants you to cast *all* your cares to Him because He does not want you to live a life of worry!

> *Our Lord Jesus loves you so much, He wants you to cast all your cares to Him.*

Let Him Take Care of Your Journey

Some years ago, when I was on a domestic flight in the United States, I sat beside a lady. She was dressed like a top-notch executive—she looked poised, capable, professional...and then I realized that her face was wet with tears. Alarmed, I started to ask her if she was all right and noticed she was also trembling and clutching her armrests so tightly all the whites of her knuckles were showing. She looked at me and said, "I'm sorry, I'm just afraid of flying. I always go through this before I fly."

I told her I was a minister of the gospel and asked if I could pray for her. "Yes, please," she said. So I prayed for her and shared the gospel with her. I told her how wonderful it is to know God not just as God Almighty, but as our Father, and how there is no Father like Him in the way He watches over His children. And thousands of feet up in the air, I had the awesome privilege of leading her to the Lord and seeing His peace come over her. Immediately after she prayed to receive Jesus as her Lord and Savior, she began to let go and relax her tight grip on her seat.

Dear reader, I share this story to tell you how many of us are like that precious lady. No matter how poised, cool, and collected we may seem on the outside, we all have problems that only Jesus can handle. And no matter how tightly we clutch and hold on, all our holding on is not going to keep the plane up in the air or safe through a patch of turbulence. We forget that if God doesn't lift our "plane," no amount of us trying to "lift" it is going to help. Today, let me encourage you: When it comes to Jesus, you can let go. You can relax completely. You can lean back in your seat, push it back all the way, cover yourself with the blanket, and just relax because He will carry you through. You can let go, trust His piloting, and enjoy the journey.

Let Go and See His Supply Flow

Some time ago, I had an inner vision from the Lord. In my vision, I saw soft, pliable golden pipes coming down from heaven and pouring out golden oil on a believer, every pipe bearing constant supply for different areas of the believer's life. Soon after I had that vision, I asked the Lord for confirmation from the Scriptures and He led me to Zechariah 4:12, where the prophet Zechariah saw golden pipes from which golden oil flowed. In my vision, one of the golden pipes ministered to the believer's health, another golden pipe ministered to his finances, while yet another golden pipe ministered to his marital well-being. Another golden pipe ministered to his walk with God, with *charismata*, anointings, and spiritual gifts flowing down from heaven. Another golden pipe ministered to his sense of peace.

All of a sudden, I saw the believer getting worried about a particular area of his life and squeezing the end of the golden pipe that was ministering to him in that area. The supply was still flowing from heaven, but his worry had constricted the pipe on his end. To the believer, it looked like the supply had stopped, but all he had to do was stop worrying and let go…and the supply would flow out again.

When our Lord Jesus died on the cross, He paid for our healing. He paid for our provision. He paid for our peace. He paid for our marriages to be blessed. He paid for the well-being of our children. He paid for heavenly supply to flow into *every* area of our lives—for golden pipes filled with golden oil to flow unabated over us, bringing supply constantly into our lives.

Our heavenly Father is ever supplying. He is the God who rained bread from heaven and brought water out from the flinty rock. He is the God who multiplied a little boy's lunch to feed five thousand, with twelve baskets full of leftovers. He is the God who turned water into wine and gave a net-breaking, boat-sinking haul of fishes to a fisherman. My friend, there is no problem with the supply! The problem is at the receiving end—when we worry, we end up constricting the flow of His supply to the area we are worried about. We end up like the believer I saw in my vision, gripping the pipe so hard that the flow of oil is choked. God does not stop supplying; He is always supplying by His grace. Our part is to let go and let His supply flow!

> God is always supplying by His grace. Our part is to let go and let His supply flow.

Take No Thought

I would like to share with you a precious testimony that we received from Anita, who lives in Virginia:

I worked in a manufacturing plant as a production supervisor and was laid off in January. As I was led into the human resource office to be told the news, I heard in my heart, "All things work together for my good." After the news was delivered, I rose up and told them that this was going to work together for my good. I am a divorcée and mother of two teens. I was the sole provider for my household, or so I thought.

I continued to concentrate on the grace of God that has been given to us as believers. I taped your program every day and watched it nonstop. I even kept it going while I slept. **The love of my heavenly Father and Jesus became so true in my heart that I just knew everything was going to be fine. Whenever the bills were due, I would hear Him tell me, "Take no thought for tomorrow; My grace is sufficient for you."** Sure enough, everything always worked out fine.

In July, I was offered a position as a manufacturing supervisor for about the same pay as I was making in my last assignment, but I just knew in my heart that that was not the position I wanted. I had prayed and asked the Lord for a position as a human resource manager, so I turned the position down.

In November, the CEO of that organization called me and stated that she was looking through the former human resource manager's desk and came across my résumé. She said that she knew it was a divine appointment because she had decided that she was not going to fill the position until the following year, but she wanted to interview me. At the interview, she hired me on the spot—she said the Lord had sent me to her. When she asked about my salary expectations and I answered, she responded by saying she was going to **give me significantly more than what I wanted.** Praise the Lord. I am now employed in my dream job and I know the Lord sent me here. It's wonderful.

I just wanted to share my testimony to encourage those who are unemployed that they should truly make their requests known to God and let the peace of God guard their hearts and minds in Christ Jesus. May our heavenly Father continue to bless your ministry.

Praise the Lord! Notice that Anita's breakthrough did not come immediately. In fact, it took almost a year before she received her dream job. But through it all, the Lord kept reminding her to trust Him and to "take no thought." Through it all, He kept supplying by His grace. As a single mum who had to take care of the needs of two children, it would have been so easy for Anita to allow the stress to consume her, but instead she chose to focus on the Lord's love for her. She chose not to worry about how she would provide for her family and believed that all things would work together for her good. And as you just read for yourself, God didn't just give her what she asked for. She was given a position with a salary that was "significantly more" than what she asked for!

Beloved, whatever trial you might be faced with today, I want to challenge you to let go and stop worrying about it. Your God is big enough, and He is just waiting for you to allow Him to take care of your need. I declare to you that He will provide for you the same way He provided for Anita—exceedingly, abundantly above all you can ask or think!

Choose Not to Worry

Perhaps you might not be trusting God for a job, but for healing. A health issue has been weighing on your heart and you are troubled by the symptoms that you have been experiencing in your body. If so, please allow me to share another testimony with you that I believe will bless you. Belinda from California wrote:

> *Some time ago, I went to my doctor for my regular checkup after my mammogram because I had an early detected case of breast cancer five years ago. The doctor who had examined me said she had felt a lump. She proceeded to conduct an ultrasound on me but because the scan wasn't very clear, she requested that I stay on to have a further scan done by the radiologist.*
>
> *I agreed but I began speaking Scriptures over the lump and refused to give in to fear. As I was waiting, I received your Daily Grace Inspiration email titled* Choose Not to Worry *on my phone.*
>
> *The message encouraged me not to worry and quoted the verse from Matthew 6:27—"Which of you by worrying can add one cubit to his stature?" In that message was also the testimony of a woman in your church who was diagnosed with lumps in her breast after a mammogram. She believed that she was healed and even wrote on her medical report that Jesus is her healer and that she had received her healing. And a subsequent ultrasound scan the very same day revealed no evidence of any lumps!*
>
> *I almost burst into tears because I knew that the message was for me. I claimed it and also pulled out other Scriptures from 1 Peter 2:24 and Nahum 1:9 to meditate on. And even though I wanted to call my husband and friends to pray for me, I didn't because I felt that God was telling me to trust Him.*
>
> *An hour later, I was scanned twice. However, the radiologist who conducted the scan was unable to find the lump and I had to point out the location to her. However, all she*

said was, *"I can't find anything! There's nothing on the film and I can't find anything!"*

Praise God for His healing hand and touch on my life that morning and for the encouraging message from your ministry! In between scanning and checking, I had continued to believe for my healing, laid hands on the affected area, and claimed victory in Jesus' name. I also spoke over the lump, all the time remembering the testimony shared in your email.

THANK YOU!

We rejoice with Belinda at the Lord's healing in her life! Worrying about the lump that her doctor had found would have done nothing to it. She chose instead to let go of that worry and to put her trust in the Lord, and He accomplished a miracle for her. Hallelujah!

Did you notice that both Anita and Belinda chose not to worry even though they faced challenging circumstances? They were heeding the voice of their Savior. They were letting go of their challenges and holding on to His promises.

I'm not telling you to stop worrying and God will supply. That would be an untruth. I am telling you that God *has* already supplied and He is *still* supplying. Your worrying is hindering your receiving.

Let go.

Your worrying is hindering your receiving. Let go.

Let Go and Let God

I once heard the story of a young Christian college student who was greatly stressed, as he did not know if he would have sufficient finances to finish his studies.[2] During one of the lectures he

attended, the professor told the class, "If you let God do everything for you, it'll be perfect. Let God do it. Let God supply for
you. Let God bless you. Let God feed you. Let God heal you. Let
God do everything." This greatly inspired the young man.

When he got back to his dormitory, he took six postcards and
wrote a letter on each of the cards, spelling out the words L-E-T
G-O-D. "Let God." He then stuck them on the wall where his
study table was as a daily reminder for himself. From that day, he
tried his very best to trust the Lord and to let God do everything
for him and be everything to him. However, nothing seemed to
change. He didn't know what he was missing. The supply wasn't
coming in and he didn't seem to have the breakthrough he was
hoping for.

Finally, he prayed and told the Lord, "I don't understand.
What is happening? I'm trying to let You take over and let You
bring the provision, but nothing seems to be happening and I
know something is wrong. So show me, Lord."

After he had finished praying, a wind blew into his room and
knocked off one of the cards. It was the card with the letter *D*.
The letters on the cards now spelled "Let Go." The student took
that as the answer from the Lord—the reason God did not seem
to be making any inroads in his life was because he was still holding on! He had to *let go* and only then could he "let God"!

In the midst of your worries, let go and let God be God in
your life. Let go and allow His abundant supplies of health,
strength, victory, peace, provision, and so much more to flood
your life. Whatever you might be praying for, I am believing
together with you for miracles and breakthroughs to happen as
you put your trust in Him!

2.
JUST LOOK AT
THE BIRDS

There was once a Christian archaeologist who discovered an abandoned well in the wilderness. The mouth of the well seemed to have been deliberately covered by some large rocks, which suggested that it was not just another well, but a well that possibly contained ancient treasures waiting to be discovered.

When the archaeologist threw some stones into the well to gauge its depth, he heard the distinct clink of stone hitting metal and thought, *Could it be that I have struck archaeological gold? Could it be that precious artifacts lie at the bottom of the well?* The archaeologist was so excited about the possible magnitude of his discovery that he decided to climb down the well to investigate, even though he did not have the proper equipment with him.

Gripping a long rope, he lowered himself into the musty opening. He did not have his torch with him, but he figured that the sunlight filtering through would be enough to illuminate some of his way. Gingerly, he went deeper and deeper into the bowels of the earth, full of anticipation at the discovery that awaited him. But the well turned out to be much deeper than he had thought. He had lowered himself as far as the rope allowed, but still he had not reached the bottom. He peered into the abyss beneath him, but all that stared back at him was thick blackness. He had no way to tell how much farther the bottom of the well was or what lay beneath him. So the archaeologist decided to return to the well again when he had more tools with him and a much longer rope.

But when he tried to hoist himself up, he realized he had no more strength. By now, he was dangling from the end of the rope, his hands clasping it tightly over his head. Rivulets of sweat trickled down his face, his arms burning from the exertion of bearing his weight the entire way down. In his eagerness to uncover what lay at the bottom of the well, he had used all his strength to make his way down and had no reserves left to manage the arduous climb back up. Mustering all that was left of his strength, he cried out for help even as he realized the futility of doing so—there was no one around to even hear him. All he could do was cling on as tightly as he could for as long as possible and hope that somehow, someone would come to his rescue before the last ounce of his strength fizzled out.

Time passed agonizingly slowly. His voice had grown hoarse from crying out for help. Painfully raw from gripping the coarse rope, he felt his fingers weakening. In spite of the suffocating heat that wrapped itself around him, his body turned cold with fear when he realized he could no longer hold on. He imagined how his body would hurtle into the chasm below, smashing his bones to pieces as he hit the bottom of the well. When the last ounce of strength had been spent, he cried to God, "Let me drop into eternity!" and finally allowed his trembling fingers to let go of the rope. Down he fell. After hanging on for dear life for what had felt like forever, he landed—and discovered that he was actually just three inches from the ground!

Many of us are like the archaeologist in this story. We are

so afraid to let go, thinking that if we did, we would fall into a bottomless pit. We hold on to our worries, stress, and anxieties the way he held on to his rope with all his might. We hold on by worrying about our health, worrying about our finances, worrying about our families, worrying that every worst-case scenario that can happen in our lives will happen. But that's *not* how God wants us to live. He wants us to let go! When we let go and release our worries to Him, He will catch us and uphold us with His everlasting arms of love. As the Bible declares, "Whoever believes in Him [whoever adheres to, trusts in, and relies on Him] will not be disappointed [in his expectations]" (Rom. 10:11 amp).

> *When we let go and release our worries to Him, He will uphold us.*

What's Your Recurring Theme?

Whenever I am in Israel with my "band of brothers" (some of the pastors from my church), one of my favorite places to visit is the Mount of Beatitudes. In fact, Wendy and I have a large, framed photograph of the mountain beautifully taken from the summit. It captures the panoramic splendor of the lush mountainside with the Sea of Galilee glistening in its foreground. Today, there is a plantation right at the foot of the mountain, which serves as a spectacular visual aid for us to imagine the multitudes that once gathered there to hear our Lord Jesus speak.

Near the summit of the mountain, you can also find a large rock. The Bible tells us that Jesus went up the mountain, sat down, and taught the people (see Matt. 5:1). So who knows, that could have been the very rock that our Lord Jesus sat on! In any case, whenever we are there, my pastors and I always take the opportunity to sit on that rock and read aloud portions from the Sermon on the Mount.

In this chapter, as we embark on our journey of learning how to let go, I want to draw your attention to one of the things that our Lord Jesus said on that very mountain:

> *Therefore I say to you, do not worry about your life, what you will eat or what you will drink; nor about your body, what you will put on. Is not life more than food and the body more than clothing?*
>
> —*Matthew 6:25*

Are you living your life based on how our Lord guides us in Matthew 6:25? Or are you living your life based on your own principles? Perhaps this is what you are *really* saying:

> *Therefore I say to myself, worry about my life, what I will eat and what I will drink; and about my body, what I will put on. Life is all about food and clothing, and unless I worry nothing will happen.*

God does not want us to worry. In fact, the central, recurring theme in Matthew 6:25–34 is "Do not worry," as the Lord Jesus tells His listeners this over and over again. He knows we have our legitimate reasons to be stressed because we live in a real world. There is no denying that practical matters such as what to eat, drink, and wear concern us daily. Our heavenly Father knows we have need of such things. But even when we have such needs, He does not want us to worry. He wants us to *let go* of our worries.

When we worry, we are saying, *"I've* got this!" When we let go of our worries, we are saying, "God, *You've* got this!"

> When we worry, we are saying, "I've got this!" When we let go of our worries, we are saying, "God, You've got this!"

What is the central recurring theme of your life today? Is your life characterized by you *holding on* to your worries? Or is it characterized by you *letting go* of your worries to the Lord? In the name of Jesus, I pray that before you are done with this book, you will have learned to release your grip on those areas in your life that you are stressed and anxious about. You can let go because *He* will uphold you. You can let go because you are releasing them into the hands of One who loves you with an everlasting love!

Look at the Birds

I started the previous chapter of this book by asking you to hit the Pause button and to take time to listen to the birds. Did you know that our Lord Jesus had the same conversation when He was on the Mount of Beatitudes? Let's eavesdrop on what He said as we continue reading from Matthew 6:

> *Look at the birds of the air, for they neither sow nor reap nor gather into barns; yet your heavenly Father feeds them. Are you not of more value than they?*
>
> *—Matthew 6:26*

This is the ultimate illustrative sermon. Imagine our Lord Jesus smiling with affection at the people gathered before Him at that mountain. He would have pointed at the birds as they flew over Him and told the people, "Look at the birds of the air." But how many of us have actually stopped to observe the birds around us? I challenge you to take some time this week to go for a walk in the park and to simply look at the birds. See them take flight, soar in the sky, sing in the trees, and bathe in the water fountain. Watch how free and untroubled they are—they show us the care-free life that God intends for us to live.

Birds don't sow nor reap, nor gather into barns, and yet our heavenly Father feeds them. He provides even for the birds—how much more will He provide for you, oh child of God! In the wild, you will seldom see birds die of starvation. You will only see a bird die of starvation if it is caged up and neglected by its captor. Now, who catches birds and cages them up? A fowler. And do you know what are some of the snares that the fowler (the enemy) uses? He uses stress, worries, and anxieties to trap us.

The devil knows that in the very area that you are worried about, that's the area that God's grace doesn't flow. Hence, if the devil can keep you full of worries, he has succeeded in keeping you in a place of defeat. You must understand this: A worried, stressed-out, and anxious believer is a *defeated* believer. That's not the life of faith, victory, abundance, favor, and good success the Lord came to give us. But praise the Lord, there is a promise in Psalm 91 that I want you to read for yourself:

He who dwells in the secret place of the Most High shall abide under the shadow of the Almighty. I will say of the LORD, *"He is my refuge and my fortress; My God, in Him I will trust."* **Surely He shall deliver you from the snare**

of the fowler and from the perilous pestilence. *He shall cover you with His feathers, and under His wings you shall take refuge.*

—Psalm 91:1–4 (boldface mine)

God promises to deliver us from the snare of the fowler.

Wow! I am not sure if you caught what I just shared. If you did, you would be doing cartwheels in the spirit! Let me ask you this: What is the very first thing that the Lord promises to deliver us from in Psalm 91? He promises to deliver us from the snare of the fowler!

Beloved, if you are feeling defeated today, I urge you to go back to dwelling in the secret place of the Most High. Go back to abiding under the shadow of the Almighty. Go back to declaring that the Lord is your refuge and your fortress. Go back to acknowledging God as God and trusting in Him. Go back to taking refuge under His wings of protection. Better yet, don't just go back, but stay there—in the secret place of the Most High God.

In that place, the Word of God promises you that God Himself will *surely* (not maybe) deliver you from the snare of the fowler— from all stress, all worries, and all anxieties. What an awesome place to live in! What a great way to live the carefree, let-go life. In the secret place of the Most High, you can live like a bird that soars freely in the sky, not like a bird trapped in the snare of the fowler!

Let's look at Matthew 6:26 again:

Look at the birds of the air, for they neither sow nor reap nor gather into barns; yet your heavenly Father feeds them. Are you not of more value than they?

I just felt I had to highlight this: When our Lord Jesus pointed out that the birds neither sow, nor reap, nor gather into barns, He was not saying that we should all quit our jobs, spend our money unwisely, and forget about any form of savings. Of course not! We are called to be diligent in our work (see Prov. 10:4; 21:5), and the Bible also says, "Whatever your hand finds to do, do *it* with your might" (Eccl. 9:10).

So lean on His wisdom, be a good steward of your finances, don't spend more than you make, clear your credit card debts, be generous yet prudent with your money, have savings, and plan for the future. However, you can do all of the above *without* stress! God wants you to be occupied in a career but not be stressed by it. Your supply does not come from your job; your heavenly Father who feeds the birds of the air is your source and your supply!

He Will Provide for You

Pastor Prince, you don't understand my financial situation. It's impossible for me not to be stressed about money!

You are right, my dear reader, I don't understand your situation. I really don't. But I know Someone who *does*! He knows how dire and difficult your situation is, and how pressing your needs are. He knows about the cash-flow problem in your business. He knows about the payments you need to make this week. He knows! He does have intimate knowledge of all that you go through and the pressures you face, but He is telling you that you have a heavenly Father who wants you to release your worries to Him because *He will provide for you*!

I imagine that as our Lord Jesus taught from the Mount of Beatitudes and directed the people to look at the birds flying overhead, He would have then turned to them and pointed at them before saying, "**Your** heavenly Father feeds them" (boldface mine).

He did not say, *"My* heavenly Father feeds them." He deliberately chose the word *your.* This word is so beautiful and important in our understanding of what Jesus was trying to convey here.

You see, for the Jewish people, the idea of God being their *Father* (or in their vernacular, *Abba*) was a very foreign concept. They knew God as *Elohim*—the all-powerful being—and not as a loving, affectionate, and caring Father. But Jesus came to reveal the name *Father* to the people! He came to show us that God is not just a powerful God, but also a *Father* who loves us dearly. He's our Papa, our Daddy, our Abba (see Rom. 8:15). Our Lord was unveiling to the people then and to us today that we have a heavenly Father who cares even about feeding common birds. Our Lord Jesus then posed an important question that I encourage you to meditate on today: *Are you not of more value than the birds?*

I love how our Lord Jesus used examples that the people could easily understand. During His time, birds were cheap. In fact, He even tells us that you could buy two sparrows with just one copper coin. They were of little value. And yet, our Lord tells us that not even one of them is forgotten before God—not a single sparrow can fall to the ground without God knowing it.

> *What is the price of two sparrows—one copper coin? But not a single sparrow can fall to the ground without your Father knowing it.*
> —*Matthew 10:29* NLT

In case you still aren't sure if you are of more value than the birds, He adds, "You are more valuable to God than a whole flock of sparrows" (Matt. 10:31 NLT). You are worth much more than the birds of the air. If your heavenly Father feeds them and watches over them so carefully, how much more will He provide for you and take care of your practical needs!

God Values You

The question remains: What is our value? How much are we worth?

I want to share a simple illustration with you. A woman goes to a boutique and finds a dress that costs $200. If she decides to pay $200 for the dress, it means she values the dress enough to give up the $200, right? Now I want you to think about how much God values *you*.

What was the price He was willing to pay to purchase your forgiveness and your salvation (which includes your health, your peace, your wholeness, and your mental soundness)? The Bible tells us that God did not spare His own Son. But do you know who God did not spare His own Son for? Who He gave His own Son up for? *You* (see Rom. 8:32)! Our Lord Jesus was God's only begotten Son, the Son whom He loved, the Son who was daily His delight (see Prov. 8:30). And yet, God loved *you* so much that He gave His Son up for you (see John 3:16). God paid for your redemption with the blood of His Son. That is how much God values and loves you!

> *God paid for your redemption with the blood of His Son. That is how much He values and loves you!*

God Loves You

I love my children intensely. I love to bring them close and kiss them. I love to watch them grow. I cannot get enough of them and will find every reason to be with them. Yet, despite all my love for Jessica (who will always be my baby girl) and Justin, I have never once taken the time to count the number of hairs on their heads. But do you know that your heavenly Father loves you so much He even numbers the very hairs on your head (see Matt. 10:30)?

Don't make the mistake of thinking that God loves you only in a general sense. Some years ago, I was in New York and decided to take a cab to visit a church there. The driver asked me if I was a Christian. I took the opportunity to share God's love with her and said to her, "Do you know that Jesus loves you?" She responded by saying, "Yeah, yeah, He loves all of us." So I told her, "No, He loves *you*. *You*, lady."

Too often, people generalize God's love like how this lady did, by thinking that God loves everybody. But when you do this, you fail to recognize the impact of His very personal love for *you*. God's love is not general. And neither is He only involved in the "big things" of life. His love for you is intricately detailed and He is intensely involved in the day-to-day minutiae of your life. Like I mentioned earlier, not a single bird falls to the ground without His knowledge. *How much more* do you think He cares about every detail of your life?

Don't Allow Past Hurts to Stop You from Letting Go

I believe the degree to which we worry about provision today is directly related to how much we believe we are loved and valued by our heavenly Father. We can't let go of all our worries because we find it hard to truly believe that God is upholding us. That's our struggle.

> *The degree to which we worry about provision today is directly related to how much we believe we are loved and valued by our heavenly Father.*

It's so much easier for a young child to receive and depend on God's love. But as we grow up and become jaded with negative experiences, disappointments, and setbacks, our hearts are conditioned to be less trusting and less believing. So we hold on. We hold on to our stress, hold on to our burdens, and hold on to our worries, not realizing that holding on to all that is destroying us from the inside out.

If that describes you, I pray you will experience healing in your heart for every bad experience and disappointment you have had. Release the wounds, hurts, and bitterness into His loving hands. Your heavenly Father is not the author of your pain. He is the author and finisher of your amazing future in this life (see Jer. 29:11). He values you so much He sent His own Son to ransom and redeem you. Let this be the day where you make the decision to let go of your fears to your heavenly Father and trust Him to provide for you!

Couple Blessed by the Gospel of Grace

I want to share this testimony that Casey from Tennessee sent us:

> For twelve years, my husband and I were financially challenged and were never able to make ends meet. We never once stopped tithing or giving sacrificially, but we were always faced with lack and extreme stress. Our hearts were at a loss as to what to do since we'd tried everything we knew to do spiritually and financially.
>
> About two years ago, I started watching Joseph Prince on television and received a true revelation of grace. Then, I started watching tons of his podcasts and YouTube videos so I could **learn how to stay at rest.**
>
> My husband and I finally got the revelation! In the last two months, my husband got a great-paying position he didn't apply for. We have a contract to sell our home, which

we had tried five times to sell in the past without success. And we are now living in a bigger house in a safe, family-friendly neighborhood.

*We are forever changed **knowing that Christ has paid for our needs and that we don't have to make things happen for ourselves!***

Isn't this amazing? Notice how God's supply began to flow unhindered in their financial situation when they began to live the let-go life and release to God what Casey described as "extreme stress." Her husband got a great-paying position he didn't even apply for and they are now living in a bigger house after struggling financially for many years. Praise the Lord!

Now, how did all that happen? Unlike the cheesy infomercials you see on television, there is no catch here, no terms and conditions to fulfill, no steps to follow. This is all about a Person! This is the love of your heavenly Father—the same heavenly Father who provides for the birds of the air—in action here. The more Casey and her husband received an abundant supply of His grace—His unmerited, unearned, and undeserved favor—the more they made the shift from extreme stress to His rest. And in that rest, God's supply of provision flowed unhindered without their stress and worries. My prayer for you is that you will also learn to rest in your heavenly Father's love for you and experience breakthroughs in every area of your life!

Beloved, you are loved and you are valued by your heavenly Father. I pray that this revelation will burn deep in your heart today, because when you know how much God loves and values you, you will never again fear that your needs will not be provided for. You will never again be worried about your health or stressed about your future or the well-being of your children. How can you, when you have a heavenly Father who loves you so much? You can stop holding on and start living the relaxed, carefree, let-go life!

3.

EXPERIENCE HIS QUALITY LIFE AND HEALTH

—

Many people have asked me what I like to do to unwind and destress after a long day. My first answer is always to be with my family. I love being with Wendy and the kids. It's just so replenishing for me. They are the joys of my life and my heart overflows with thanksgiving to the Lord whenever I get to be with them. The other thing I really enjoy is taking walks in the evenings. After all the hustle and bustle and the many demands of the day, I like to go out to a lovely park close to my home. I love taking in the crisp, fresh air and having quality conversations with my Lord Jesus while strolling amid the lush greenery.

During one of my evening walks, I had a really unique experience. As I was walking, the Lord began to give me an entire message. For an hour and a half, the Lord opened up a whole passage from Matthew 6 that I had memorized. Verse by verse, He began to open my eyes to new insights and revelations. It was like a conversation between us—I would ask the Lord a question, and He would answer me. I heard His voice inwardly and clearly as He patiently broke down the truths for me and taught me from His Word.

Let me be the first to tell you that this is not normally how I receive or prepare my messages. Most times, I would prepare my message in my study, my ideas and thoughts in bits and pieces as verses, Bible aids, and references would be scattered everywhere. However, for this particular message, He gave it to me line upon line. Whenever I was dull of understanding, He would clarify it further for me and ensure that I grasped what He was showing me. I wish it were like that every time I prepared a message, but this was really an exception and not the norm.

I believe the message the Lord has for us from Matthew 6 is of such critical importance that He wanted to make sure I got it! Before this experience, I had preached extensively from the same portion of Scripture and I truly thought that I had mined all it had to offer. However, the Lord opened my eyes to some really powerful truths that day and I can't wait to share them with you!

"Do Not Worry"

Matthew 6:25–34 is one of the most beautiful passages you can ever read in the entire Bible, spoken by our Lord Himself on the Mount of Beatitudes. I have committed these ten seemingly straightforward but profound verses to memory, and if you are struggling to live a carefree, let-go life, I strongly encourage you to get these words into your heart. They will change your perspective and change your life! The power to live the let-go life is in these words spoken from the very mouth of our beautiful Savior. Whatever giants might be before you today, listen to these words:

Therefore I say to you, do not worry about your life, what you will eat or what you will drink; nor about your body, what you will put on. Is not life more than food and the body more than clothing? Look at the birds of the air, for they neither sow nor reap nor gather into barns; yet your heavenly Father feeds them. Are you not of more value than they? Which of you by worrying can add one cubit to his stature?

So why do you worry about clothing? Consider the lilies of the field, how they grow: they neither toil nor spin; and yet I say to you that even Solomon in all his glory was not arrayed like one of these. Now if God so clothes the grass of the field, which today is, and tomorrow is thrown into the oven, will He *not much more* clothe *you, O you of little faith?*

Therefore do not worry, saying, "What shall we eat?" or "What shall we drink?" or "What shall we wear?" For after all these things the Gentiles seek. For your heavenly Father knows that you need all these things. But seek first the kingdom of God and His righteousness, and all these things shall be added to you. Therefore do not worry about tomorrow, for tomorrow will worry about its own things. Sufficient for the day is its own trouble.

—Matthew 6:25–34

In this chapter, I want to share with you what the Lord revealed to me in this passage about the correlation between stress and our health. Medical science has demonstrated that a large percentage of physical illnesses, including hypertension, heart troubles, stomach ulcers, and in some cases even cancer can be traced back to chronic stress. As a pastor of a large church, I have lived many lives. Having worked with and counseled many precious people from around the world in the last two decades of ministry, I've had front-row seats to observe how people choose to live their lives and what those choices resulted in. I have seen people who have fought and struggled, allowing themselves to be consumed by stress—and this often led to very dire and complicated physical conditions in their bodies. At the same time, I have also watched those who started letting go of their worries to the Lord by faith—and they began to walk in greater levels of victory and peace, and for some they even experienced healing of chronic health problems.

Perhaps you are thinking, *Stress is irrelevant to me. I'm doing okay.* Well, let me just say that's what I used to believe as well. Years ago, I began to experience symptoms in my body related to irritable bowel syndrome, and I went to consult a doctor about it. After examining me, the doctor asked me, "Are you under stress?" I felt somewhat insulted by the question. In my mind, I was thinking, *What is this doctor talking about? I am a believer of Jesus. I am God's beloved, a man of faith and power! How can he even suggest that I could be under stress?*

The truth was, I was handling many issues in our rapidly growing church while learning to be a good father to Jessica, who was a preschooler at that time. So much was going on, and I wasn't even aware that I was under stress and that it was beginning to affect my physical body. That experience really caused me to pay attention to stress levels in my life and to learn what it means to live the let-go life.

Stress Spares No One

We live in a high-speed, instant-gratification world today with everything quite literally on demand. Even the seemingly carefree, hipster, pour-over-coffee millennial generation is a pretty stressed-out generation. In fact, research has shown that stress among college-age students has been on a steady rise. A recent American College Health Association Survey[1] of about 100,000 students showed that:

- 86% felt overwhelmed by all they had to do, compared to 64.5% in 2000.
- 82% felt exhausted (not by physical activity), compared to 63.8% in 2000.
- 66% felt very sad, compared to 60.7% in 2010.
- 60% felt lonely, compared to 56.4% in 2010.
- 59% felt overwhelming anxiety, compared to 48.4% in 2010.
- 54% felt they had been under more than average and tremendous stress in the past twelve months, compared to 50.7% in 2010.

According to another study of over 3,000 adults aged eighteen to over sixty-nine across America by the American Psychological Association,[2] 75 percent of Americans reported experiencing at least one symptom of stress in the past month, and this included feeling irritable or angry, anxious, fatigued, depressed, over-whelmed, or having a lack of interest in life. It showed that those who tended to struggle consistently with stress included women, millennials, and Gen Xers, as well as parents with children under eighteen. The study also highlighted the top four sources of stress: money, work, family responsibilities, and health concerns.

The point is, stress is cross-generational—young or old, it spares no one. Stress can cause you to have more gray hairs than you should have and more wrinkles than you want to have. It can cause you to lose sleep and eat excessively. It can lead you into dark, depressive, and even suicidal thoughts. Stress can wreak havoc in your physical body and on your mental health. Stress is a serious issue.

But do you know that our Lord Jesus has already addressed the problems we've just talked about? I had always thought that Matthew 6:25–34 was about food, drink, and clothing. But when the Lord opened up the whole passage to me that day, I started to see that it was about so much more and that He actually emphasized health. I really believe that He unpacked Matthew 6:25–34 for *our* benefit—because He loves us. Even if you don't feel like you are under much stress, I hope you will pay attention to the truths I am about to share. Don't wait until it's too late and the stress in your life has reached destructive levels. The time to overcome stress, anxiety, depression, and fear is *now*.

> The time to overcome stress, anxiety, depression, and fear is now.

Some of you may have a constant fear of being laid off and you are always on alert for signs that might confirm your fears. Some of you might be struggling to manage two jobs and you hardly ever take time to relax. Some of you might be gripped by the fear of failure in school and that has driven you to hit the books incessantly, not allowing yourself to have sufficient rest. Such sustained fears and other factors that keep you feeling stressed put you at an increased risk of numerous health problems, including mental illnesses, eating disorders, infertility, memory and concentration impairment, heart attacks, and arrhythmias. Chronic stress also makes you more prone to frequent and severe viral infections.

Now, is there a way out?

The answer is *yes*, and that is what the Lord wants me to show you! Let's go straight to the Word:

Therefore I say to you, do not worry about your life, what you will eat or what you will drink; nor about your body, what you will put on. Is not life more than food and the body more than clothing?

—*Matthew 6:25*

Here, the Lord revealed to me that I should read this Scripture in the context of having a quality life and a quality body. Remember, Jesus came to give us life and life more abundantly! The abundant life speaks of the quality of our life and the quality of our bodies.

This is what the Lord opened my eyes to see:

Therefore I say to you, do not worry about your life, what you will eat or what you will drink; nor about your body, what you will put on. Is not [a quality] life more than food and [a quality] body more than clothing?

—*Matthew 6:25 (boldface words mine)*

What our Lord Jesus was speaking to us about was beyond just food and drink. He was talking to us about experiencing a quality life and having quality health for our bodies. What is the point of wearing branded three-piece suits and impeccably tailored shirts if your body is decaying and riddled with disease? What the Lord is saying is, a quality body is more important than the clothes you wear, and a quality life is more important than the food you eat. Our Lord Jesus goes on to give us two vivid illustrations, and I was simply amazed.

To illustrate how a *quality life* is more than just food, He talked about how God feeds the birds of the air. When God gives us a quality life, there *will* be food! We can have a quality life because, as I mentioned in the previous chapter, we have a heavenly Father who values us and will take care of all our practical needs. When you love someone, you want to see them free from worries. Even as an earthly father, one of my greatest joys is watching my children rolling on the floor with great big belly laughs, playing and having fun without a care in the world. Can you imagine how much more our Abba wants to see us completely without worry? Our part is not to be stressed. My friend, even as we manage our jobs and various responsibilities, we can live freely and without cares because *He* is our provider!

> We have a heavenly Father who values us and will take care of all our practical needs.

The Key to Divine Health

To teach us about having a *quality body*, our Lord Jesus tells us how God clothes the lilies and the grass of the field. This was the other revelation that the Lord opened my eyes to, and I want to camp on this here. Let's look at the verses again:

> *Which of you by worrying can add one cubit to his stature? So why do you worry about clothing? Consider the lilies of the field, how they grow: they neither toil nor spin; and yet I say to you that even Solomon in all his glory was not arrayed like one of these. Now if God so clothes the grass of the field,*

> *which today is, and tomorrow is thrown into the oven,* will
> He *not much more* clothe *you, O you of little faith?*
> —*Matthew 6:27–30*

Can you just imagine our Lord Jesus on the Mount of Beatitudes, running His fingers over the grass or bending over to touch one of the flowers around Him, as He taught the people with great tenderness and a smile? Oh, how I love my Jesus. He always comes down to our level. He is so gentle and yet so majestic. He is altogether lovely.

In Matthew 6, Jesus spoke about how the beauty, glory, and splendor with which God clothed the flowers and the grass surpassed how Solomon—the wealthiest man who ever lived—dressed himself. But don't make the mistake that I used to make—thinking that our Lord was talking only about physical clothing. Let me ask you this: What kind of clothing do flowers have? The Lord showed me that flowers don't change their clothing like we do; their clothing *is* their body. So the clothing that the Lord was talking about was actually their *health*! He was talking about the health of the lilies!

Now, what did our Lord want us to consider about the lilies of the field? He said, "Consider the lilies of the field, **how they grow**: they neither toil nor spin" (boldface mine). Did the flowers grow physically healthy and strong by toiling and spinning? No, *your* heavenly Father clothed them! With all his wealth, Solomon could buy the most exquisite clothing, but he could not buy what the lilies had—health. Money can buy you access to the best doctors and medical facilities, but it can't buy you health. Divine health comes only from the Lord! He clothes you with the best clothing—divine and supernatural health—that one could have. And you don't even have to toil or spin, because it is a *gift* that you can simply receive because of what Christ has done! Hallelujah!

> *Money can't buy you health. Divine health comes only from the Lord.*

Divine health doesn't come from spending hours on the treadmill, in a CrossFit box, or by going through the latest exercise or dieting fad. If that were so, even nonbelievers would be able to walk in divine health. You can get fit naturally, but divine health—the quality of health that clothed the lilies—comes from the Lord. So by all means, hit the gym, lift, run, brisk walk, and eat wisely—just do it without being stressed out over the condition of your body. Let go of the fears about your physical body and let the Lord supply to you His abundant and quality life, as well as His divine health and resurrection power.

Lose Your Fears When You Know God Loves You

You know, I used to rush through reading about the grass of the field, but during my conversation with the Lord, He told me to stop here and to meditate on what He said. Many of us think that God is only interested in big, important things—things of eternal value. But consider this: The Bible tells us that the grass of the field is alive today, but will be cut and thrown into the furnace as fuel tomorrow. And yet, God clothes them and cares for them. If God even takes care of temporary things that have such a transient existence, how much more will He take care of you and clothe you with good health, you who are His cherished and beloved child!

Are you fearful about your future because doctors have told you there is no hope and no cure for the condition you are battling? Or are you dreading the possibility that you might develop a particular disease because it is "supposed" to be hereditary? Perhaps you have begun to experience symptoms in your body and you are terrified of what they could be pointing to. I say to you, *do not fear.* Consider the lilies and the grass of the field. Your heavenly Father clothes them with divine health and robust life springing forth from within them. Are you not of more value than they? How much more will He clothe you with health!

Do you know why our Lord Jesus could talk about divine health? Because He knew that He would be paying for it for us. He knew what He was going to go through at the cross for you and me. He knew that He would be purchasing for us health, wholeness, and strength with His own body. Today, we live on the other side of the cross. He has already paid the price so that right now, you can declare that by His stripes, you *are healed* (see Isa. 53:5). You are not *going to be* healed; you are *already* healed in Christ!

Jesus has already paid the price so you can declare that by His stripes, you are healed.

It doesn't matter what the diagnosis is or where the tumor is. It doesn't matter how advanced the disease is or how many years you have suffered. The Bible says our Lord Jesus is "**far above all principality and power and might and dominion, and every** name that is named, not only in this age but also in that which is to come" (Eph. 1:21, boldface mine). Whether the condition you have is called cancer, tuberculosis, or depression, the name of Jesus is far above it!

Doctors may think that some conditions are not possible to be treated, but the Bible says that with God, *nothing*—no thing—is impossible (see Luke 1:37). Doctors may tell you that you have a high chance of developing a certain condition, but the Bible declares this: "A thousand may fall at your side, and ten thousand at your right hand; *but* it shall **not** come near you" (Ps. 91:7, boldface mine). Whose report will you believe today?

Healed of Thirty-Eight Years of Chronic Skin Disease

I want to end this chapter by sharing with you a precious testimony sent in by Benson from California. He was told over and over again that his skin condition could not be cured. But let's see what happened when he simply believed that God blesses those whom He loves:

> *I suffered from folliculitis (an inflammation of the hair follicles) for over thirty-eight years (since I was fifteen years old). I saw over a hundred doctors and every single one of them told me that this condition could not be cured. I did everything. I bought every kind of cream and medicine available and most of them made my condition worse. There were thousands of red dots all over my back, chest, and arms. I could never take my shirt off in public and avoided going out because people would think that I had an infectious disease. They cringed when they saw my skin.*
>
> *The condition was itchy and it would worsen when I perspired. If it got cold and dry suddenly, the skin on my back would tear and bleed when I reached for something quickly. I*

lost track of the number of times someone told me that blood on my back was seeping through my shirt. While that was horrible, the real damage was emotional. Throughout my school days, I rejected pool or beach party invites. When I did go to the beach, I would visit a remote one at an unpopular time to avoid people.

I have also been a Christian since 1982 but stopped attending church in the last five years because every sermon seemed to say that I had to try harder. After thirty years of trying to work my way to heaven, I was exhausted.

*Then, two years ago, I started listening to Pastor Prince's sermons during long morning walks. This went on for months and things began to change. I started to believe that God blesses those whom He loves, and started to **rest in what He has done for me** and not trust in what I was trying to do for Him.*

Today, my skin is miraculously healed! It is perfectly clear and soft like a baby's bottom! Even my wife is completely amazed. For the first time in thirty-eight years, I can take off my shirt when I play tennis with friends.

*Pastor Prince shared about the Lord's restoration in some of his messages, and I have been restored. My new skin is the least of the blessings. God has also restored to me His perfect peace. **I no longer worry, but I just cast my cares on Him and receive His favor. Fear and oppression are far from me.** Thank You, Jesus, for going to the cross for me.*

I can only imagine what Benson went through during those thirty-eight years. But all praise to our Lord and Savior, Jesus, who did what over a hundred doctors could not do—heal Benson's skin condition! There was no striving and no toiling on Benson's part. He simply rested in God's love for him, stopped worrying, and enjoyed the Lord. And just like that, he received healing for a condition that had plagued him for almost four decades. By the way, I noticed that Benson was listening to sermons and spending time with the Lord while taking long walks. (We are in the flow, Benson. I love taking walks with the Lord too!)

My friend, whatever you might be going through today, I pray that like Benson, you too will receive the miracle that you need as you cast your cares and worries into the hands of your loving Savior. You are deeply loved!

4.
THE WAY TO LIVING
WORRY-FREE

———

When I began my journey of learning to live the let-go life, one of the areas that really got me was my daughter. I had always thought I was very restful. But when my daughter was born, *oh boy*. She was so beautiful. So adorable. I could not take my eyes off her. And every little sneeze or cough from her would get me sitting upright and wondering, *What happened? Is she too cold? Too hot?* And I didn't stop there. I started telling Wendy not to expose her to crowds or bring her to dusty areas. When she started eating solid foods, I insisted that she eat only organic.

If you had asked me why I made those decisions at that time, I would have told you that it was "wisdom." I did not think I was "worried" about her. I mean, come on, I was God's "lean, mean, preaching machine," so how could I be worried? But in reality, I was hiding a heart full of laboring over my little girl's health. And the problem was, the more I was worried about her, the more she seemed to fall ill! She would recover from one viral attack only to get another a short while later. And after she finally got better, she would fall ill in some other way.

Finally, I went to the Lord and said, "Lord, I really don't understand. Jessica is eating the best. We're protecting her, keeping her surroundings spotless; we're doing all the right things, and yet she keeps falling sick. Help, Lord!" (I found that even my prayers for her had become "desperate" prayers.)

The Lord said to me, "Son, each time you worry over her health, you actually endanger her. You are putting a big button over her for the devil to push. The devil sees that he can push this button and your preaching for that Sunday is affected. He can push this button and your relationship with your wife is affected. He can push this button and you are no more the same Joseph. Your very worrying over your daughter is hindering My supply of health to her."

I asked, "So what do I do, Lord?" And the Lord showed me what to do. "Cast your daughter into My hands and I will take care of her," He said. "I love her more than you can. And the best attitude you can have toward your daughter is to be carefree. Don't worry about her anymore."

I wish I could tell you that the sweet revelation that the Lord loved Jessica more than I ever could helped me to stop worrying about her immediately. The reality is, it took me a while. But once I started letting go of my worries about Jessica, she got healthier, stronger, and fell ill less. The less I worried about her, the more I saw God's blessings over her life.

Whatever *you* tend to worry about—whether it's your health, your business, or your marriage—it will probably take you some time to learn to let it go to the Lord. But let's start somewhere, all right? The Lord's hands are so much bigger than ours. He can surely take care of any area of our lives we are worried about! I just know for sure that our worrying does not help. In fact, did you know the word *worry* comes from the Old English word *wyrgan*, which means "to strangle"?[1] And sometimes it feels like that. When you worry, it feels like you're being strangled of the very life, of the very breath you're breathing.

What worries you? Perhaps it's your weight, and you have

put upon yourself the burden to scrutinize every calorie and every bite you take. Maybe you are so fearful of falling behind in your career that you are working overtime every day and checking your emails incessantly. Perhaps you dread the thought of aging, and that has driven you to spend thousands of dollars on any treatment that claims it can keep wrinkles at bay. Or perhaps you made a terrible mistake some time ago and you cannot stop obsessing about when and how it will come back to haunt you.

Let me ask you this question: Has your worrying given you your ideal weight, led you to excel at work, stopped new wrinkles from developing, or turned back the clock to undo that mistake you committed? I submit to you that you are not seeing much fruit or supply in the area you're worried about precisely because you have been worrying instead of putting the problem in the Lord's hands and allowing His grace to flow.

Grace Flows in Worry-Free Areas of Our Lives

Remember the picture of golden pipes from heaven that I shared about earlier in this book? The ones that minister God's manifold graces to us? In the areas we worry about, we strangle and constrict God's supply in those areas. His grace toward us *never* stops flowing. But when we worry about a certain area, it's like we've caught hold of the pipe that brings His supply to that area and we are squeezing it so tightly that the supply cannot flow through to us. Conversely, the Lord showed me that *grace flows in the worry-free areas of our lives*! He asked me to check my life and showed me that I was still struggling in the very areas I was worried about. But in the areas that did not worry me, His supply was flowing. I don't know about you, but I want to see His supply flow in *every* area of my life. I don't want my worrying to hinder *any* of His supply!

Because of our Lord's finished work on the cross, grace is flowing for our health, for the soundness of our minds, and for our intimacy with the Lord. Grace is flowing for us to walk holy, for us to have revelation of His Word, and for us to have the wisdom to parent our children. His grace is flowing and as long as you *refuse to let your heart be troubled*, that grace of God flows unhindered to you in every area. I know it is not easy, especially when the enemy gives you lying symptoms to get you worried. For instance, he might give you a lying symptom in the area of your physical health. The more you are troubled about your health, the more you fret about it all the time, the more problems seem to pop up in your body. On the other hand, when you choose to let go of your worries to Him and to trust Him *even* when you see some challenges, His grace—His healing supply—flows.

> *As you refuse to let your heart be troubled, the grace of God flows unhindered to you in every area.*

All These Things Shall Be Added to You

This brings me back to Matthew 6 because our Lord Jesus teaches us something very powerful in the following passage:

> *Therefore I say to you, **do not worry** about your life.... Therefore **do not worry**, saying, "What shall we eat?" or "What shall we drink?" or "What shall we wear?" For after all these things the Gentiles seek. For your heavenly Father knows that you need all these things. But seek first the kingdom of God and His righteousness, and all these things shall be added to you. Therefore **do not worry** about tomorrow,*

*for tomorrow will worry about its own things. Sufficient for
the day is its own trouble.*

—Matthew 6:25, 31–34 (boldface mine)

Did you notice that our Lord Jesus said the words "Do not
worry" three times? He seldom repeats His words, but when He
does, it's clear He wants to bring home the point. So don't go
around thinking that "stop worrying" is *my* advice to you; it's
from the Lord!

Think of all the needs you are worried about. Do you believe
that your heavenly Father already knows you need those things?
He knows you have practical needs like food, drink, and clothing. And He tells you that *all* these things shall be added to you.
Not just "given"—one can give only the bare minimum—but
"added," which speaks of ever increasing. In other words, *all* these
things shall be added to you in greater quantity and quality (see
Eph. 3:20)! And He cares for you even beyond basic concerns.
In the last chapter, we saw how our Lord Jesus wants us to enjoy
quality lives and have quality bodies. *All* these things shall be
added to you!

Seek First the Kingdom of God and His Righteousness

But He also tells us what is of *first* importance before all these
things can be added to us—seeking the kingdom of God and His
righteousness (see Matt. 6:33). There are people who claim that
to seek God's kingdom is to go out into the mission fields and
serve the Lord full-time. We know how important missions are
and we believe we are blessed to be a blessing. But this is not what

the Lord was saying. To understand what He meant, we have to first define what the "kingdom of God" is. The book of Romans defines it as such:

The kingdom of God is not eating and drinking, but righteousness and peace and joy in the Holy Spirit.
—Romans 14:17

So what is the kingdom of God? It is righteousness, peace, and joy in the Holy Spirit. This means your first priority each day is to seek *His* righteousness—not your own righteousness. And when you focus on His righteousness, the Bible tells us, "all these things"—whether it is food, clothing, or other necessities in life—will be added to you. They will not just be given to you, but *added* to you as your inheritance in Christ. You know, you don't need to use your faith for every single need in life. You just need to use your faith for one thing—to believe that as a child of God, you are the righteousness of God in Christ (see 2 Cor. 5:21)—and it will cause all the blessings you seek to come after you and overtake you!

Righteousness Is a Gift

Some of you might be thinking, *But why must I prioritize His righteousness?*

My friend, I have been encouraging you to let go of your worries to the Lord. But unless you are *first* established on the foundational truth that you are righteous because of what Jesus has done, you will not be able to let go and let His supply flow into your life. Knowing that you are righteous in Christ is what gives you the confident assurance to let go of your cares, worries, and anxieties to the Lord.

> *Knowing that you are righteous in Christ gives you the assurance to let go of your cares and anxieties to the Lord.*

Perhaps you are struggling to let go today, and you think that you have to "get right" with God before you can receive His help in your area of need. Maybe you think you are not righteous enough and have no right to ask God for wisdom, healing, and provision. If that describes you, then it is time for you to go back to the first thing that God wants you to do—be established in *His* righteousness. Many people believe that they have to get righteous by "doing" right, and being perfect in all their actions before they can let go of their worries and believe in God for their healing and provision. That is why the Lord reminds us to "seek **first** the kingdom of God and **His** righteousness" (boldface mine); only then will "all these things" be added to you.

When you received Jesus Christ as your Lord and Savior, you received the gift of righteousness. Righteousness is a *gift* that we as believers have received. And because we have the gift of righteousness, all the good things that Jesus deserves, we get (see Eph. 1:3). I want you to read this verse for yourself:

> *For if by the one man's offense death reigned through the one, much more those who receive abundance of grace and of the **gift of righteousness** will reign in life through the One, Jesus Christ.*
>
> *—Romans 5:17 (boldface mine)*

We did not become righteous by *doing good*; we received righteousness as a *gift*. This means that as believers in Christ we *cannot* lose our righteousness *even when we fail*. In fact, it is His righteousness that can help us up when we fail! This is so important for you to know because like it or not, you *will* fail. You *will* fall short. And if you are not established in your righteousness in Christ, the devil will accuse you and make you think that you don't deserve to be healed, that you are not qualified to receive His supply, and that you should be condemned to live a defeated life filled with stress, worries, and anxieties.

At the cross, the divine exchange took place. As our Lord Jesus became sin with our sin, we became righteous with His righteousness. The Bible declares this:

> *For He made Him who knew no sin* to be *sin for us, that we might become the righteousness of God in Him.*
> —*2 Corinthians 5:21*

At the cross, our Lord Jesus became sin by receiving our sin so that we can become righteous by receiving His righteousness. When He became sin, He was cursed; when we become righteous, we are blessed. He was cursed not because He deserved it; we are blessed not because we deserve it!

The Word of God tells us that when you receive the abundance of grace and gift of righteousness, you will *reign in life*! To reign in life means you have the power to win over every sin and addiction! To reign in life means you can break free from the bondage of the enemy and walk in greater measures of victory and holiness! The good news is, you can trust God for healing and provision not because everything in your life is perfect, but because of His righteousness in your life. God does not move for you because you are perfect in every way. He moves on your behalf because of what our Lord Jesus has accomplished at the cross. The more you understand His righteousness, the less you will struggle to let go of your cares to Him.

> *The more you understand His righteousness, the less you will struggle to let go of your cares to Him.*

How the Ungodly Could Be Made Righteous

But, Pastor Prince, how can God make the ungodly righteous?

At the cross, a holy God took all your sins and my sins and laid it on Jesus. His inflexible righteousness and unbending holiness caused Him to unleash all His righteous wrath and holy vengeance against all our sins in the body of His Son. He sent His Son so that His Son could bear all our sins. And because all our sins have been punished in Jesus' body at the cross, God sees us righteous based on what Christ has done when we believe (see Rom. 4:5). When God looks at us today, He sees only the loveliness and perfection of His beloved Son. Hallelujah!

Beloved, I pray that from this day forward, you will be so established in His righteousness that it will be so easy for you to let go and receive every blessing promised to the righteous. They are yours because your Savior has paid the price! You don't have to depend purely on your own smarts and unceasing toiling to do well in your career—the Bible declares that the Lord surrounds you with favor like a shield (see Ps. 5:12). Yes, by all means be diligent in your place of work, but do it with a spirit of rest, not stress. My friend, you can let go of all your worries and burdens to the Lord because His Word says that when you cast your burdens upon Him, He will sustain you. He will take care of you. He will never allow the righteous to be moved (see Ps. 55:22)!

Every blessing promised to the righteous is yours because your Savior has paid the price.

How to Know You Are Established in Righteousness

Pastor Prince, how will I know that I'm established in righteousness? Look at what this Scripture says:

In righteousness you shall be established; you shall be far from oppression, for you shall not fear; and from terror, for it shall not come near you.

—*Isaiah 54:14*

This is how you know you are established in righteousness: You are far from oppression because you are not fearful and you are far from terror because it will not come near you. "Oppression" is Old Testament language for what we call "stress" today. When you are established in His righteousness, you are far from stress because you are not fearful. If you are regularly struggling with stress and fear and if you still find it extremely challenging to let go of your worries and anxieties to the Lord, then perhaps you are not truly established in His gift of righteousness and you are still depending on your own righteousness. I would encourage you to keep listening to the gospel of grace until this truth is cemented in your heart and you know beyond the shadow of a doubt that all the blessings of the righteous belong to you. May you be so assured that because you are righteous, your prayers avail much (see James 5:16) and you can cast all your cares to the Lord!

> Keep listening to the gospel of grace until you know all the blessings of the righteous belong to you.

Listen to this praise report that Cali, who lives in Switzerland, sent to us:

Pastor Prince, my family and I have been listening to you through your podcasts, television broadcast, and YouTube channel. We are so grateful for your life-transforming and empowering messages on God's grace. **They have given us the freedom to rest in the liberty that Jesus paid for with His life and the assurance of salvation that depends not on our self-efforts but His finished work on the cross.**

Before coming across your broadcasts, I had been a Christian for many years but wondered if I had done enough to be pleasing to God. However, your messages opened my eyes of understanding. I learned it was not about what I must do but what Jesus has already done on the cross.

I also realized you have been consistent and accurate in your teachings through the years. I would cross-check whatever you taught with the Bible and have been amazed by how much I had not seen or understood before. On many occasions, while listening to you, I also received answers to questions concerning the grace gospel.

I have shared the gospel with others, such as my niece and sister. My sister is now trusting God without fear of condemnation and my niece even called her friends imme-diately to share the gospel! Today, she keeps declaring that she is the righteousness of God in Christ Jesus!

Your teachings have helped to anchor our belief that we are righteous by faith in Jesus' finished work. *They continually help us to grow in grace and in the knowledge of our Lord Jesus Christ. My family also regularly partakes of the Holy Communion together, and on top of that I often partake of it on my own.*

*Today, our youth is being renewed—people often tell my husband and me that we always look young. God has also healed me of a four-year high blood pressure condition. I am no longer under medication and **I know I received my healing because of Jesus' finished work!***

Last but not least, God has blessed our family financially beyond our wildest imagination. We recently bought a car debt-free, and God put a desire in our hearts to bless a family in church with our previous car. Indeed, as God has been gracious to us, He enables us to be gracious to others!

Thank you so much, Pastor Prince! Truly, the grace revolution has begun and is spreading! Praise God!

I rejoice to hear the wonderful blessings that Cali and her family have received in the areas of healing and provision, as well as in so many other areas! What I love is how she referred to her belief that she and her family are righteous by faith in Jesus' finished work and how they credit their blessings to that. Beloved, as you are established in His righteousness and His finished work, may you also experience His manifold blessings flowing toward you! As His Word promises, all these things the world seeks shall be added to you. The world is running ragged after health and wealth. Our Lord says to us, "Don't stress yourself out pursuing these things. I know you have need of these things. Pursue My righteousness and all these things the world seeks will pursue you."

Do Not Worry about Tomorrow

I want to bring you back to the last verse of Matthew 6. It says:

Therefore do not worry about tomorrow, for tomorrow will worry about its own things.
—*Matthew 6:34*

Do you know why God doesn't want you to worry about tomorrow? It's because He wants you to enjoy *today*. There is nothing wrong with planning for events, making preparations, and taking the necessary steps to budget and to save for your future. By all means, be led by the Lord to plan ahead. But you can do it without being worried about your future.

When He gave *manna* to the children of Israel, He gave it to them *daily* (see Ex. 16:4). He doesn't give you tomorrow's bread today. He only gives you sufficient supply for *today*. Don't try to live next week today. There is no supply and grace for next week today. There is only grace for today. When tomorrow comes, He wants you to look to Him again for the supply. In other words, the Lord wants you to live one day at a time. Don't wait for only special occasions, like birthdays, to celebrate your love for your family—celebrate and love them *today*. Don't worry about the future and ask, "What if?" or live in the past by regretting and saying, "If only." Neither one is living in the present. God supplies you with abundance today and I promise you this: When tomorrow comes, tomorrow will become *today*. Enjoy to the fullest the grace that He has for you today!

5.
THE RHYTHM OF REST

What is the rhythm of your life today? Does it feel like a furious drumbeat that jolts you out of bed and keeps pounding faster and faster every day? Or is it a nice, steady groove that gives you room to savor the important things in life? Are you keeping a tempo that is healthy and sustainable? Or is it one that runs you ragged and leaves you completely drained?

I ask these questions because I believe that God has called us to run a marathon and not a sprint. Our heavenly Father desires for us to live a long, good life marked by blessings and health. That is why the closing portion of Psalm 91 says, "With long life I will satisfy him, and show him My salvation" (Ps. 91:16). Long life that satisfies you is your portion in Christ!

> Our heavenly Father desires for us to live a long, good life marked by blessings and health.

Even if doctors have told you that you will not live long, let's choose to stand right now on the authority of God's Word, which declares that you will live long and live strong. No matter what symptoms you might have in your body, I declare over you that no weapon, no sickness, and no disease formed against you shall prosper. May the supply of God's healing power flow unabated as you let go of all your cares to Him!

Beloved, your heavenly Father loves you. You are the apple of His eye and He is *for* you (see Zech. 2:8, Rom. 8:31). Just as earthly fathers guide their children because they want the best for them, your Abba wants to guide you on how to live life because He loves *you*. In the book of Isaiah, it says:

> *Thus says the* LORD, *your Redeemer, the Holy One of Israel:* "I am *the* LORD *your God, who teaches you to profit, who leads you by the way you should go.*"
> —*Isaiah 48:17*

He wants you to profit in your marriage and family life, your financial life, your social life, and your health. He wants to see you succeed in every area of your life, and He wants to lead you by the way you should go. Will you be still and listen to His voice today? I know a never-ending stream of emails and notifications from your mobile devices are screaming for your immediate attention all the time, but I ask that you take a few moments each day to pay attention to what the Lord is speaking to your heart through His Word.

Has Stress Become Your Lifestyle?

For some of you, being worried, stressed, and anxious may be the only way you know how to live. This frantic rhythm of rushing through life may be all you know and all you are familiar with. Stress may have inadvertently become a lifestyle, a habit, and maybe even an addiction. You know what they say about a bad habit? You take away the *h* and you still have "a bit." You remove the *a* and the "bit" lingers. You remove the *b* and you are still left with "it." Only when we take away the *i* (self-effort) leaving the *t* (the cross) can all our negative habits be removed!

By the power of the cross, let's believe for the habit of worrying to be broken in Jesus' name. Whether you are an occasional worrier or a serial "worryholic" (someone addicted to worry), may you be filled with the truth of God's Word, be freed from this oppression of stress, and step into His river of rest. Let God reset your heart, your focus, and your mind-set through the washing of His Word. Trust Him. His desire is not for your life to be cut short with stress, but for you to walk in accordance with His rhythm of rest.

Listen to this invitation that the Lord has extended to you:

> *Come to Me, all you who labor and are heavy laden, and I will give you rest. Take My yoke upon you and learn from Me, for I am gentle and lowly in heart, and you will find rest for your souls. For My yoke is easy and My burden is light.*
> —*Matthew 11:28–30*

The Lord wants you to come to Him, and when you do, He will give you *rest*. Not rules to follow or requirements to live up to. Rest. That is His heart for you. He wants to give you rest.

When you come to Jesus, He will give you rest.

Let me show you another translation of the same passage:

> *Are you tired? Worn out? Burned out on religion? Come to me. Get away with me and you'll recover your life. I'll*

show you how to take a real rest. Walk with me and work with me—watch how I do it. Learn the unforced rhythms of grace. I won't lay anything heavy or ill-fitting on you. Keep company with me and you'll learn to live freely and lightly.

—*Matthew 11:28–30* MSG

Isn't that beautiful? I love how our Lord Jesus invites us to "learn the unforced rhythms of grace." I love how our Lord Jesus has a rhythm. Grace has a rhythm. And that is why I started this chapter by asking you to think about the rhythm of *your* life.

Unforced. Gentle. Easy. Light.

These are the words that describe what it is like to keep company with our Lord Jesus.

His invitation is extended to anyone who is tired or worn out. Anyone who is burned out on Christian religion. Anyone. There is nothing that you need to do to qualify for this invitation. Your very area of weakness qualifies you. If you labor and are heavy laden, you qualify. If you are weary, you qualify.

All you need to do is to simply…come.

Come to Him. Look away from your challenges and keep your eyes on the One who loves you to the uttermost. Walk with Him. Keep company with Him and He will show you how to take a *real* rest. His rest is not just a physical rest even though that is important. The rest that He gives you will refresh you and strengthen you. As you learn how you can flow with His rest and His unforced rhythm of grace, you will find rest for your *soul*. This means that in Christ, there is rest for your worried *mind*, for your turbulent *emotions*, and for your troubled *heart* and *conscience*—a rest that goes down deep into your spirit.

Do Not Follow the Tempo of the World

We live in a society where people sometimes seem to almost boast about the number of hours they have to clock in at work. It's almost as if someone who works seventy hours a week must be so important with so many demands on them that they have no time to simply smell the flowers, relax, or even kiss their wives. Now, I am not saying you should not work hard. The book of Proverbs tells us that "a slack hand causes poverty, but the hand of the diligent makes rich" (Prov. 10:4 ESV). But if you have fallen for the lie that you need to work nonstop all the time *in order to* succeed in life, I want to share with you this story:

> *There was once a man who worked at a frantic pace. He worked every day and hardly had time for his children. He did not get to see them grow up because all his days were spent at his workplace. He boasted that he would retire a rich man and told himself that when he was a rich man, he would rest.*
>
> *Over time, he did achieve financial success. He was planning to hand over his business to someone else to run while he took the money and finally enjoyed his life.*
>
> *Unfortunately, he never did get to enjoy his life or his family, because he died suddenly from a heart attack. He had literally worked himself to death. Within half a year, the only ones who seemed to remember him were the few friends he had and his own family.*

If you know someone who passed on young, please accept my condolences and know that I do not mean any disrespect by sharing this story. I just want to highlight the sad truth that if we keep doing things at a frenetic pace, we will lose out in the end. So often, people use all their health to get wealth, only to find that they end up having to use all their wealth to get their health back.

Instead of trying to keep pace with the world, let's trust that when we do things God's way and follow Him as He leads us in the way we should go, He will cause all things to work together for our good (see Rom. 8:28). Instead of trusting in our toiling and spinning, let's trust that He can prosper the work of our hands as we rest in Him. Let's trust that He can open doors of opportunity for us to have positions at our workplace where we can be a blessing even as we are blessed. Let's trust that truly, the Lord *Himself* will build our houses, our careers, our marriages, and our finances.

> *He will cause all things to work together for our good as we rest in Him.*

The Key to Strength and Long Life

I would also like to share this portion of Scripture with you:

> *For thus says the Lord GOD, the Holy One of Israel: "In returning and rest you shall be saved; in quietness and confidence shall be your strength."*
> —*Isaiah 30:15*

Take some time to meditate on these truths: In returning to God and resting in Him, you will be saved. In quietness and confidence (in God) shall be your strength.

There are a number of Hebrew words for *strength*, but the word here is *gabuwrah*,[1] which is the same word used in Psalm

90:10 when it talks about the strength to live a long life. What does this tell us? It tells us that the more at rest you are, the more it will *prolong your life!*

Don't Join the Frantic Race

There is a beautiful verse in the Bible that I want you to see:

For the Scripture says, "Whoever believes on Him will not be put to shame."
                                                            —Romans 10:11

I don't know about you, but I want to be someone who will not be put to shame! Do you know that the Bible is actually quoting itself? Romans 10:11 is quoting from Isaiah 28. Look at what this Scripture is really about:

Therefore thus says the Lord GOD: "Behold, I lay in Zion a stone for a foundation, a tried stone, a precious cornerstone, a sure foundation; whoever believes will not act hastily."
                                                            —Isaiah 28:16

In the King James Version, it says, "he that believeth shall not make haste." Whoever believes in God can be cool; he does not have to make haste. I believe the Lord is telling us, "Slow down." Maybe the people of the world have to be hasty because they can only rely on themselves to watch their backs. But you have a heavenly Father. Don't keep striving, rushing, and pushing to get ahead. Don't live like you are competing in a Formula One championship. Those cars can go at eye-popping speeds, but their engines are put through such high stress that they have to be replaced after being driven for less than 6,000 miles.[2]

> Because you have a heavenly Father, you don't have to keep striving, rushing, and pushing to get ahead.

In contrast, diesel engine trucks may not be known for their speeds, but they are designed for the long haul and can last up to 600,000 miles.[3] Are you looking to last just a few hundred miles? Or do you want to live the long, satisfying life that is your portion in Christ? My friends, we are in this world but not *of* this world. The rhythm of the world is forceful, aggressive, and hurried. But we are called to walk in the unforced rhythms of grace!

Rest Finds Grace

I found some fascinating truths when studying the word *rest*. In Hebrew, one of the words for *rest* is *nuwach*. You find this word appearing in Genesis 8:4, where it says "the ark **rested** in the seventh month," and in Exodus 20:11, where it says God "**rested** the seventh day" (boldface all mine).

Nuwach is also where Noah's name comes from, so Noah's name also means "rest."[4] The first time you find *grace* mentioned in the Bible is in Genesis 6:8, where it says "Noah found grace in the eyes of the Lord." Every time the Bible mentions something for the first time, in this case grace, there is a divine significance. What is the divine significance here? *Rest finds grace with the Lord.* When you are in rest, you will find grace with the Lord. Grace means you are not working; God is working. When we rest in Him, we find Him working on our behalf!

The Hebrew word *nuwach* (rest) originates from the idea of "respiring" or "drawing breath."[5] In a while, I will tell you why I was so excited when I first learned this. But first, I want to share with you some information that I found while studying stress.

Our bodies have a "stress response" or "fight-or-flight response," which is what our bodies do in response to danger. While it is unlikely that we will have to fight off physical predators or aggressors in our modern world, our stress response is constantly activated as we face multiple demands, from taking care of our families to shouldering huge workloads to managing relationship problems and even more day-to-day stressors such as traffic jams. A Mayo Clinic study found that our bodies treat these events and pressures as threats, and our adrenal glands respond by releasing a surge of hormones, including adrenaline and cortisol.[6]

Once a perceived threat has passed, our hormone levels as well as other affected systems such as our heart rate and blood pressure are supposed to return to normal. But when the fight-or-flight mechanism is constantly activated, it leads to an over-release of cortisol and other stress hormones. This puts us at risk of many health problems, including anxiety, depression, digestive problems, headaches, heart disease, sleep problems, weight gain, and memory and concentration impairment. The stress response also suppresses the immune system, increasing our susceptibility to colds and other illnesses.

The Benefits of Deep Breathing

While we can't avoid all sources of stress in our lives, there are healthy ways we can respond to them to counter the negative effects triggered by them. According to a study published by Harvard Medical School, deep breathing is one of the techniques

that can quell our bodies' stress response.⁷ An article published
by the Michigan State University Extension also mentions deep
breathing as one of the ways by which we can lower cortisol levels
in our bodies.⁸

Now you know why I got excited when I discovered that
the original idea for *nuwach* (rest) lies in drawing breath. I had
been practicing deep breathing for some time. I found it so help-
ful especially when I was tired or when I got into stressful situations like near accidents on the road that caused my heart to beat
really fast. In such situations, I would take a deep breath, release
it slowly, and pray, looking to the Lord. But I never taught on that
because I thought it was so natural. It was only after the Lord led
me to the root word for *rest* that I felt the release to share on the
beneficial effects of deep breathing. One of the natural means to
being at rest was hidden in the Hebrew word *rest* for us! Let everything that has breath praise the Lord!

Live Like the Tortoise, Not Like the Lion

I want to draw your attention to two animals, the tortoise and the
lion. The book of Proverbs tells sluggards to go to the ants and
learn from them (see Prov. 6:6). God uses insects and animals to
teach us. I believe God designed us to live like the tortoise, not the
lion.

In the wild, lions are predators. They are aggressive and highly
territorial. Living like the lion means you are always hunting for
survival against competitors, fighting to defend your territory at
work, and perhaps roaring at your children or subordinates. Is
that the rhythm you want to constantly live with? Just know this:
Lions are known to have short life spans, especially in the wild.

Researchers found that the adrenal glands of lions in the wild are swollen and tend to be about 25 percent heavier than lions in captivity with similar body weights.[9] You can imagine the adrenal overdrive that lions in the wild are subject to.

In contrast, look at tortoises. They do everything slowly, moving one stubby leg at a time, taking their time to chew leisurely and refusing to be hurried. They were probably the last animals to arrive at Noah's ark, and perhaps Noah even had to pick them up and carry them into the ark because they plodded so slowly and it had already started drizzling! But at the end of the day, tortoises live long. Giant tortoises, for example, have an average life span of over a hundred years.[10] Whose rhythm would you rather follow?

Beloved, you don't have to run the rat race like the rest of the world only to become the number one rat, or focus all your energy to frantically climb the ladder only to realize too late that it was leaning on the wrong building. The world we live in is one that desperately needs rest, and of all the blessings that our Lord Jesus could give us, He said, "Come to Me . . . and I will give you **rest**" (Matt. 11:28, boldface mine). The Bible tells us that the race is not always to the swift or the battle to the strong, "but time and chance happen to them all" (Eccl. 9:11). The world may depend on toiling to get ahead, but only God can put you at the right place at the right time. You can rest in Him and put your trust in Him. You can let Him take your hand and lead you to walk in accordance with His rhythm—the unforced rhythm of grace . . . and the rhythm of rest!

6.
WALKING IN THE
RHYTHM OF GRACE

I n the previous chapter, we saw how Jesus extended an invitation for us to get away with Him and to learn from Him (see Matt. 11:28–30 MSG).

Have you done that?

Have you taken the time to walk with Him and watch how He walks in the rhythm of grace? Let's start by taking a peek at what a day in His life looked like.

The Gospel of Mark records how our Lord Jesus spent a whole day teaching the multitudes. When evening had come, He instructed His disciples to bring Him over to the country of the Gadarenes on the other side of the Sea of Galilee. I believe He had heard the cry of one man and had traversed the lake just to deliver him. This man was roaming the tombs and mountains, constantly screaming and cutting himself with sharp stones. He was the most demon-possessed man in the entire Bible. But with one command from our Lord Jesus, the demons were cast out and the man was delivered (see Mark 4:33–5:15).

If you have been cutting or hurting yourself, if you have been isolating yourself, indulging in self-sabotaging behavior, and having thoughts of death and suicide, would you allow me to speak to you for a moment? Because the devil hates you, he has been feeding you lies. He has been feeding you lies of condemnation, making you believe that you need to punish yourself, deceiving you about your worth, and causing you to detest and despise yourself. But I want you to know that our Lord Jesus loves *you*. He cares for you. He crossed the lake for just one person who was hurting, and now He is reaching out to *you*.

I pray that your heart will be opened to our Savior, who is full of tenderness toward you. Psychiatrists can prescribe tranquilizers and other medications, but the effects of those drugs don't last, and when they wear off, you are left in deeper depression than ever before. Only our Lord Jesus can save you. He wants to give *you* rest. He wants to give you a peace that surpasses understanding. I am praying for you, my friend. May you experience His sweet love for you and find freedom from the oppression that binds you.

> *Our Lord Jesus wants to give you rest and a peace that surpasses understanding.*

I believe the devil knew that our Lord Jesus wanted to deliver the Gadarene demoniac from his oppression, and that was why he raised up a great windstorm as Jesus crossed the lake. Our Lord, who was asleep in the stern, was woken up by His terrified disciples. He rebuked the wind and the waves and a great calm ensued.

After He had delivered the demon-oppressed man, He crossed over the lake again by boat to the other side.

As soon as He reached Capernaum, a large crowd gathered around Him, and Jairus, one of the rulers of the synagogue, anxiously begged our Lord Jesus to go to his house, as his young daughter was dying. As Jesus followed Jairus, the multitude followed Him and pressed in around Him. Yet, He stopped when a woman with an issue of blood touched Him and obtained her healing. He could have just moved on, but He took the time to look for her and to minister to her face-to-face. While Jesus was still speaking to her, someone from Jairus's house turned up to announce that Jairus's daughter had died. Jesus immediately reassured Jairus, saying, "Do not be afraid; only believe" (Mark 5:36). He then went to Jairus's home, raised his daughter back to life, and even ensured that she was given some food to eat.

All that in *one* day.

He accomplished so much, yet He was always restful, never hurried. He was not frazzled by the multitude that thronged Him or burdened by the incessant demands placed on Him. Whether it was for the lowly woman whom others considered unclean or for the stately ruler of the synagogue, our Lord Jesus always had time.

That, my friend, is what the rhythm of grace looks like in action.

> *Jesus was always restful, never hurried. This is what the rhythm of grace looks like.*

How to Walk in the Rhythm of Grace

You might be wondering, *What about me? How can I walk with the same rhythm that Jesus walked in?* Our Lord Jesus answers this question for you in John 15:

> *Abide in Me, and I in you. As the branch cannot bear fruit of itself, unless it abides in the vine, neither can you, unless you abide in Me. I am the vine, you are the branches. He*

*who abides in Me, and I in him, bears much fruit; for with-
out Me you can do nothing.*

—*John 15:4–5*

As believers, we are all connected to the Lord Jesus. He is the true Vine and we are its branches. The Vine and the branches are one. So what do the branches need to do? Abide. Simply stay and remain as branches. We are already there—there isn't any place we are trying to get to. That's how easy the Lord made it for us.

In the same way, the Lord Jesus uses the word *abide* over and over again. And that's the only criteria given to the branches—you and me. Our part is to abide in Christ. Our part is to rest! As we abide in Him and put our trust in Him, we *will* bear fruit because of the supply of sap, life, and fatness that flows to us from the Vine. In fact, the supply is constantly flowing (remember my vision of the golden oil flowing through the golden pipes?) and the branches simply have to remain as branches and not restrict the supply.

Abide in Him and Let His Supply Flow

Would you like to know what your life as a "branch" would look like when you are abiding in the Vine? Picture this: When you are faced with a stressful situation, your Vine—our Lord Jesus—supplies you with His peace. When you need to make a key decision and you don't know what to do, your Vine supplies His wisdom. When you have to tackle many tasks but feel so tired, His strength flows through you. What a life of rest that is! You are putting your dependence on Him and Him alone, and if you truly believe that He is the Vine and you are but the branches, you can't help but be restful.

Labor to Enter His Rest

Unfortunately, while it sounds so easy to simply abide and rest in Him, it's often the hardest thing for us to do. And that is why the Lord has to tell us to "labour therefore to enter into that rest" (Heb. 4:11 KJV). It is so hard for us to rest because we want to have a part to play. We want to do something. We want to get some of the glory. Other times, it's because of unbelief—we find it so hard to believe that God has done it all. That is why the only labor that God tells us to pay attention to is the labor to enter His rest.

> The only labor that God tells us to pay attention to is the labor to enter His rest.

Stop laboring by your own efforts to be healthy or to get rich. Stop laboring by your own strength to watch your back or make sure you don't get retrenched. The more you struggle to achieve all that, the more you are hindering His supply because you are putting your trust in your own efforts instead of His promises. There is only one labor that God asks of you, and that is the labor to enter His rest. And as you rest in Him, you will bear *much* fruit in every area of your life!

Now, I'm not talking about sitting on your hands and doing absolutely nothing at all. You can be outwardly working, but inwardly, you are at rest. The more you rest and abide in Him, the more His supply flows. Your task as a believer is to enter into restfulness. But abiding in Him and living the life of rest is not about living a passive, lazy life. When you are connected with Him, there will be a divine supply of life and rhythm that is not frantic. You will be doing, yet not expiring. You will be like the burning bush, burning strong but not burning out. Just look at our Lord Jesus Christ. No one was more active yet restful than He was. He did everything with a restful rhythm, and He accomplished much more than any human being could ever accomplish in the three and a half years of His ministry.

As new covenant believers, we live by grace, which is about *resting* in the power of the Holy Spirit, who works in us to give us both the willingness and the ability to do what pleases God (see Phil. 2:13). God gives us the desire to do what He wants us to do, and then He gives us the power to perform it. That is how God works in us and through us when we rest!

When we abide in Him, we can have restful increase. When we try to produce results and fruits by our own efforts, there might be increase, but it is likely to be *stressful* increase. Which would you rather have? The world thinks, *Unless I do something, nothing will be done.* But our Lord clearly says, "Without Me you can do nothing." I think I will choose to put my trust in His unlimited supply and not in my puny strength! That's what the let-go life is all about—letting go of whatever constricts His supply and simply allowing His vine life to flow in and through us!

> When we abide in Him, we can have restful increase, not stressful increase.

Saved by Grace, Not by Works

Let me share with you a testimony from a lady who lives in Texas:

> *When I was nineteen years old, I went down the wrong path and began to smoke marijuana and cigarettes, which ultimately led to fornication, heavy drinking, and severely abusive relationships because I was trying to find friends and blend in with others.*

When I was twenty-seven, my voice failed me because of my smoking and my dreams of becoming a great singer were smashed. After that, I fell into great depression for eight years. This was until Father God sent me the wonderful message of grace. I have since quit smoking altogether and I have found my true love, Jesus Christ. I'm no more in abusive relationships.

*I am also pleased to report that the Lord has restored my voice and it is now even better than before. I have also been blessed with a new opportunity to work with a well-known talent manager. So even though I am about ten years older than when I first started, the Lord has restored my soul and my youth, and given me a fresh start. Pastor Prince's message of grace really transformed my whole way of life and my entire way of thinking. I now understand that **it is not by my own works but by His grace that I have been saved.** Thank You, Lord Jesus.*

As she learned that it was not her own works but by His grace that she had been saved, this lady experienced His vine life flowing through her. That healed her, restored her, and saved her from abusive relationships. It gave her a fresh start despite her rocky past and renewed her youth. And if He can do it all for this lady, He can also do it for you.

As He Is, So Are We in This World

Do you want to know another way of saying that Jesus is the Vine and we are the branches? I want you to memorize this simple truth and keep it in your heart:

As He is, so are we in this world.

—*1 John 4:17*

As He is healthy, strong, and whole today, so are we right now, in this world!

I've received so many testimonies from precious people around the world who had received healing miracles after listening to my preaching on 1 John 4:17. A lady in our church discovered a lump in her breast during a medical checkup. She was scheduled to go for further tests but before she went for the second test, she wrote this on her medical report: "Does Jesus have lumps in His breast? No! As He is, so am I in this world." To cut a long story short, when she went back for her checkup, doctors could no longer find the lump—it had disappeared! This testimony has sparked off many other similar testimonies.

For instance, another lady from Minnesota wrote to share how some time after she had recovered from throat and neck cancer, doctors found a mass in her throat again. At that time, she had been watching my broadcast on television and had heard me share the testimony of that lady from my church who had stood on 1 John 4:17 and received her healing. She decided to lay hold of that Scripture for herself as well, declaring that as Jesus was free from cancer, so was she. Fear tried to enter her thoughts over the next few days, but she hung on to those words even when doctors told her she might have cancer again and scheduled her for surgery. Finally, when she was being prepped for surgery, her doctor informed her that her tonsillectomy had been cancelled, as her biopsy showed she had no cancer. Hallelujah!

Now, I am not asking you to throw away all your medicines— please take your medication. But let your faith be centered on our Lord Jesus! I am asking you to start declaring, "As He is, so am I in this world." Thank God for doctors, but don't put your trust in doctors or in medicine alone; put your trust in the Lord. He is your living Vine, and the same health that flows in Him flows in you. I believe people are being healed right now as they read this. As you abide in Him, the same resurrection life that flows in the Vine flows in your body, creating health, creating new parts, removing obstacles, removing growths, removing hindrances, and removing obstructions in your arteries. New cells are being created, and your DNA is being readjusted and programmed for health, wholeness, and longevity. Right now, the same vine life that flows in the Vine flows in you, the branch. You don't have to struggle—simply receive it in Jesus' name!

Lifted Up by Jesus

There is so much more for us to learn about what it means for Jesus to be the Vine, and we the branches. Let's go back to John 15:

I am the true vine, and My Father is the vinedresser. Every branch in Me that does not bear fruit He takes away; and every branch *that bears fruit He prunes, that it may bear more fruit. You are already clean because of the word which I have spoken to you. Abide in Me, and I in you. As the branch cannot bear fruit of itself, unless it abides in the vine, neither can you, unless you abide in Me.*

—John 15:1–4

Look at verse 2: "Every branch in Me that does not bear fruit He takes away." In the past, I used to be very concerned about this verse. I read a commentary by a well-respected Bible scholar of the nineteenth century on this passage, and he interpreted this verse to mean that if a believer did not bear fruit, God would take the believer home to heaven. This sounds quite frightening, doesn't it? Unfortunately, he wasn't the only Bible scholar who interpreted the verse in this way. But more people are realizing the truth, which is that the phrase "takes away" is actually the Greek word *airo*, which in this context means to "lift up."[1]

Why "lift up"? Because the branch of the vine must be lifted up in order for it to bear fruit. If the branch is lying in the dust on the ground instead of being lifted up on a trellis, it cannot bear fruit. In the same way, the reason many believers cannot bear fruit is that the devil has cast them down and they are depressed—they are wallowing in the dust.

Incidentally, when you study the etymology of the Hebrew word for *Philistines*—Israel's greatest enemies, including Goliath in the Old Testament—you will come to the word *palash*, which means to roll or wallow in the dust.[2] The serpent's food is the dust (see Gen. 3:14). And when a believer is wallowing in the dust and not bearing fruit, the Lord helps by *lifting* the believer up.

Throughout the gospels, we see our Lord Jesus lifting people up. When a demon-possessed boy was brought to our Lord Jesus, He cast out the demon, took the boy by the hand, and lifted him up (see Mark 9:27). When Jairus's daughter was dead, Jesus took her hand and raised her back to life, and she arose and walked (see Mark 5:41–42). At the Pool of Bethesda, He told a man who had been sick for thirty-eight years to rise, take up (*airo*) his bed, and walk (see John 5:8). Another time, He healed a paralytic by telling him to rise, take up (*airo*) his bed, and return to his house (see Mark 2:11). Jesus was always lifting up, raising to life, restoring. Don't you just love Him?

A sermon from God should always lift you up, not grind you into the dust and make you feel sin-conscious. We've seen how He lifts up. John 15:2 goes on to tell us, "every *branch* that bears fruit He prunes, that it may bear more fruit." I've heard preachers teaching that the pruning here refers to how God chastises us with painful afflictions. But the Greek word used for "prune" here is *kathairo*, which means "to cleanse."[3] The vinedressers in Jesus' time used to pour water on the branches to cleanse them of the deposits made by pests so that the deposits would not hinder the branches from bearing fruit. In the next verse in John 15:3, the root word *katharos* is used when our Lord went on to say, "You are already clean [*katharos*] because of the word which I have spoken to you."

Do you know where and when Jesus spoke these words? It was in the Upper Room, on the same day that He had washed His disciples' feet. Do you remember how Peter asked Jesus to wash not just his feet but his head as well? Jesus responded by saying, "He who is bathed needs only to wash *his* feet, but is completely clean" (John 13:10). Once you have been washed from all your sins by the blood of Jesus, you have been "bathed" all over and are clean. From then on, you only need to "wash your feet with water" each day.

That means you must get into the Word daily and allow it to wash you (see Eph. 5:26). You can read the Word, use a Jesus-centered devotional, or listen to sermons. Just make sure you let the Word wash you! How Jesus cleanses us, whether it's from depression, bitterness, or lying symptoms, is through the washing of the water of His Word. We are cleansed through the Word that He speaks to us. The more you sit under anointed teaching that lifts you up and washes you, the more fruit you'll bear!

The more you sit under anointed teaching that lifts you up and washes you, the more fruit you'll bear.

Do the One Thing

Now I would like you to read this passage for yourself:

Now it happened as they went that He entered a certain village; and a certain woman named Martha welcomed Him into her house. And she had a sister called Mary, who also **sat at Jesus' feet and heard His word.** *But Martha was distracted with much serving, and she approached Him and said, "Lord, do You not care that my sister has left me to serve alone? Therefore tell her to help me." And Jesus answered and said to her, "Martha, Martha,* **you are worried and troubled about many things. But one thing is needed,** *and Mary has chosen that good part, which will not be taken away from her."*

—*Luke 10:38–42 (boldface mine)*

Many things, like helping the poor, healing the sick, and sharing the gospel, are important. But our Lord Jesus said that only "one thing is needed." Let's not be like Martha, who was "distracted with much serving" and forgot to listen to her Savior. People who are always worried about many things don't do that *one* thing. But the people who do that one thing are not worried about anything.

You and I are probably the same. Like me, you probably have a hundred and one things calling for your attention from the moment you wake up. But I always remind myself, *Joseph Prince, one thing is needful.* And I find that if I do that one thing, God takes care of every other area of my life. The enemy may try to start many fires to distract you. My friend, forget about all the fires. Turn your back on what the devil is doing. Pay attention to what your Savior has done and is saying! I know there are areas to take care of. I know there are challenges to focus on. But turn your back on them and do the *one* thing. Sit at Jesus' feet and listen to His Word. Open up your Bible and say, "Lord, speak to me." Do that one thing, and you know what? God will take care of all the fires, and the many things that you are worried and troubled about will be no more!

Our Lord Jesus Himself prioritized the one thing. Throughout the gospels, we find Him pulling away from the crowd and going into the wilderness to be with His Father (see Matt. 14:23; Mark 1:35; Luke 5:16, 6:12). Is your rhythm out of control? Are things moving so fast in your life that you are left breathless and unable to keep up? If you are tired of that and want to walk in the restful, unhurried rhythm that our Lord Jesus walked in, I am here to tell you the good news: You can. You can reset your tempo daily simply by pulling away from the multitude of demands and going into the "wilderness" to be with your heavenly Father. Let him remind you how loved and how valued you are—if He takes care of the birds and clothes the lilies, how much more will He take care of you!

7.
REST BRINGS GOD'S COMMANDED BLESSINGS

If you had joined us at the start of this book, I want to thank you for choosing to read on. I pray that as you read these pages, you are already beginning to live freely and lightly. Don't wait till the end of the book to start living the let-go life—release your biggest cares to Him right *now*!

You would already have read enough pages of this book to see the word *rest* mentioned several times. If you think that rest would be a nice thing to have when you finally have time, or that rest is only for lazy people, this chapter is for you. I hope to show you more clearly what "rest" is about and what better chapter to deal with rest than chapter 7, since 7 in Bible numerics is the number of rest, completion, and perfection![1]

The Bible tells us that God "rested on the seventh day from all His work which He had done" (Gen. 2:2). Much of this chapter will be about the Sabbath rest that God ordained for the seventh day. I believe that the Lord is about to reveal truths to you both from the natural and the spiritual applications of the Sabbath that will set you free to enjoy the rest that He purchased for you on the cross. I pray that the Lord will open your eyes to just

how important rest is. May you learn to get away with our Lord
Jesus and allow Him to show you how to "take a real rest" (Matt.
11:28 MSG).

Rest Is Holy

In the fast-paced world we live in, where too many people are
connected every moment to demands placed on them by work,
friends, and family through unrelenting notifications from their
smartphones, the concept of "rest" might be foreign and perhaps even absurd. But we cannot let the world tell us how to live
our lives, and we should want to know what our Creator has
to say!

The first time the Hebrew word for holiness (*qadash*) appears
in the Bible is in the second chapter of Genesis:

> *And on the seventh day God ended His work which He had
> done, and He rested on the seventh day from all His work
> which He had done. Then God blessed the seventh day and
> sanctified it, because in it He rested from all His work which
> God had created and made.*
>
> *—Genesis 2:2–3*

The Hebrew word used for "sanctified" here is *qadash*, which
means "to be set apart" and "to be consecrated."[2] It is the same
word used for "holy," hence the New Living Translation renders
verse 3 as "And God blessed the seventh day and declared it holy."
So we see that the first mention of holiness is tied up with *rest*,
which is also mentioned for the first time here. God set apart the
seventh day as a day of rest and made it holy. My friend, this is
what I want you to see: Rest is *holy*. The Creator of the heavens

and the earth Himself rested. So who are we to think that we do not need to rest or that we cannot afford to rest?

> *The Creator of the heavens and the earth Himself rested. Who are we to think that we cannot afford to rest?*

The Sabbath rest was so important to God that He included it in the Ten Commandments:

Remember the Sabbath day, to keep it holy. Six days you shall labor and do all your work, but the seventh day is the Sabbath of the LORD your God. In it you shall do no work: you, nor your son, nor your daughter, nor your male servant, nor your female servant, nor your cattle, nor your stranger who is within your gates. For in six days the LORD made the heavens and the earth, the sea, and all that is in them, and rested the seventh day. Therefore the LORD blessed the Sabbath day and hallowed it.
—Exodus 20:8–11

I want you to read another passage just so you can see how serious God is about the Sabbath and about rest:

Speak also to the children of Israel, saying: "Surely My Sabbaths you shall keep, for it is a sign between Me and you throughout your generations, that you may know that I am the LORD who sanctifies you. You shall keep the Sabbath, therefore, for it is holy to you. Everyone who profanes it shall surely be put to death; for whoever does any work on it, that person shall be cut off from among his people. Work shall be

done for six days, but the seventh is the Sabbath of rest, holy
to the LORD. Whoever does any work on the Sabbath day, he
shall surely be put to death."

—*Exodus 31:13–15*

Thank God we are no longer under the law of Moses; otherwise many of us would have to be "put to death"! Nevertheless,
there is value in studying and understanding the principles of the
Sabbath and what it means in the New Covenant because the Sabbath was already divinely inspired way before the Ten Commandments were given.

Rest the Rest of Redemption

The principles behind the observance of the Sabbath are beautiful, and there is so much we can learn. Let me ask you, why did
God rest (see Gen. 2:2–3)? According to the prophet Isaiah, God
"neither faints nor is weary" (Isa. 40:28). So God did not rest
because He was tired. He rested because He had finished the
work (see Ex. 31:17). That was the Rest of Creation.

Israel observes the Sabbath on Saturdays, but as believers, our
day of rest is on Sunday. Why? Because while Israel rests the Rest
of Creation, we rest the Rest of Redemption. Our Lord Jesus rose on
a Sunday, bringing forth a new order. That's why the early church
worshiped on Sunday[3]—the first day of the week (see Acts 20:7).

Begin Your Day with Rest

An interesting fact about the Jewish Sabbath (or the Shabbat) is
that it begins on Friday evening and ends on Saturday evening. Do

you know why? It's because the Jewish day *begins* in the evening.[4] If you think they've gotten it the wrong way round, let me tell you that it's the rest of the world that has gotten it wrong. Starting the day in the evening is actually God's way. Look at what it says in Genesis:

> *So the evening and the morning were the first day.*
> —*Genesis 1:5*

Did you notice that the evening came before the morning? I believe this shows us how God wants our day to begin with rest. Beginning the day in the evening also means the day begins with sleep. This means that when the Jews wake up in the morning, it's not the beginning of the day for them—it's already midway through the day, and they start off rested and empowered, having spent time with God and with their family and loved ones.

God wants our day to begin with rest.

Rest Is Prioritizing Your Relationship with God

The Jews set apart the Sabbath as a time for physical rest, relationships, worship, thanksgiving, and celebration. There are three key priorities in the Jewish observance of the Shabbat, beginning with their relationship with God. By resting and setting apart the seventh day, the Jews are acknowledging and remembering that God is the Creator. They are also emulating the example that God set when He rested on the seventh day.[5]

For us as believers, our Sabbath is a day where we spend time with our Savior, gather as a church to worship Him and hear His

Word, and celebrate the intimacy we have with God because our sins have all been taken away at the cross of Jesus. It is a day of rest, and rest is not about doing nothing—it is about making Him everything, celebrating Him, worshiping Him, and honoring Him with our tithes and offerings.

Rest Is about Relationships

The second priority during Shabbat is relationships with family, loved ones, and friends. At the start of Shabbat, many Jews have an evening meal together with their family and loved ones. I love how they purposefully set aside time each week to gather as a family. I personally find spending time with my family so therapeutic. Shabbat is also a time where parents (usually the fathers) would declare blessings over their children.

Growing up with the blessing of their fathers, it's no wonder the Jewish people are often achievers, movers, and shakers in every realm of society, with the *chutzpah* and audacity to conquer different fields and industries in the marketplace. Just look at how a disproportionate number of Jews have been awarded Nobel Prizes. Although Jews comprise less than 0.2 percent of the world's population, over 20 percent of Nobel laureates are Jewish.[6] I find this amazing and I believe that their observance of Shabbat has contributed toward this remarkable statistic.

I want to take this opportunity to tell you that God did not design man to journey alone—it is so important for you to have kingdom friendships that are replenishing. Just as the Jewish people prioritize their family and community, it is important for you to build deep friendships so that when you encounter difficulties in life, your friends can be there to pray for and with you. Likewise, you want to be part of a community where you can step up to believe with your friends for breakthroughs when *they* go through trials.

> God did not design man to journey alone. We need kingdom friendships that are replenishing.

If you are not already a part of a local church, I encourage you to join one. And if you are already attending a local church, praise the Lord! But I challenge you to find a way to get involved. Don't simply drift into church on Sunday, not make any connections, and leave. Instead, start serving somewhere and start putting your roots down, for Psalm 92:13 tells us, "Those who are planted in the house of the LORD shall flourish in the courts of our God." Do you want to flourish? Then start getting planted in His house today!

A study was conducted by Harvard University over seventy-five years to track the psychosocial predictors of physical and emotional well-being as one ages. Researchers used medical reports, self-reported surveys, as well as interactions with the participants to arrive at their conclusions, which basically showed that it was good relationships, not the amount of money one earned or the accolades collected, that keep us happier and healthier.[7] Don't spend all your time climbing the corporate ladder and trying to earn more money. At the end of the day, happiness really isn't about what car you drive or how many followers you have on social media—it's your family, loved ones, and close friends that really matter and bring you the greatest happiness and fulfillment.

Importance of Physical Rest

Another principle that we can learn from the Jewish practice of the Sabbath is the importance of sleep and physical rest. In the verses that we looked at earlier, God made it so clear that no work should be done on the Sabbath.

God made man last so that man could enjoy everything that He had created. Man was created on the sixth day and God rested on the seventh. Can you see? Man's first full day was God's day of rest. God wanted man to live a life of rest. I would definitely encourage you to observe one day of rest out of seven because your body requires adequate rest. That's how God designed our bodies. For me personally, as I preach in church on Sundays, I take Mondays as my day of rest. Since it is a day of rest, Wendy and I have an agreement not to deal with heavy subjects on Mondays.

Christ Is the True Sabbath

By Jesus' time on earth, religious leaders had made a whole set of rules and regulations to govern the Sabbath. The Scribes and Pharisees made it all about a list of dos and don'ts and were so zealous about the laws governing the Sabbath that they forgot why God had instructed that His people observe the Sabbath in the first place: He wanted them to rest.

Our Lord Jesus Himself said, "The Sabbath was made for man, and not man for the Sabbath" (Mark 2:27). In other words, God had made the Sabbath for the good of man, not the other way round, where man has to keep all the rules and laws surrounding the observance of Sabbath. In fact, the Sabbath was instituted to point people to Christ. The book of Colossians puts it this way:

> *So let no one judge you in food or in drink, or regarding a festival or a new moon or sabbaths, which are a shadow of things to come, but the substance is of Christ.*
> —*Colossians 2:16–17*

The true Sabbath is not a day; it is the lovely person of our Lord Jesus. He is the true substance of the Sabbath!

The religious leaders of Jesus' time missed this completely. Instead of rejoicing when people were healed, they were furious that Jesus performed such miracles on the Sabbath, because they believed He had violated the Sabbath law by "working." For example, the Bible tells us, "For this reason the Jews persecuted Jesus, and sought to kill Him, because He had done these things on the Sabbath" (John 5:16). The Jews wanted to kill our Lord Jesus simply because He had, on the Sabbath, healed a man at the Pool of Bethesda who had had an infirmity for thirty-eight years.

Jesus Shows Us What True Rest Is

The man at the Pool of Bethesda had lain on his bed for thirty-eight years. There was no activity on his part because he could not move. But was that *true* rest for him? No! Rest for him was when the Lord Jesus told him, "Rise, take up your bed and walk" (John 5:8), and he was able to do so after almost four decades. That was the greatest Sabbath of his life! Yet, the Jews told the man, "It is not lawful for you to carry your bed" (John 5:10), because it was the Sabbath. The book of Mark also records how Jesus healed a man with a withered hand on the Sabbath and how the Pharisees "went out and immediately plotted with the Herodians against Him, how they might destroy Him" (Mark 3:6).

In another incident, our Lord Jesus healed a woman who had been bowed down for eighteen years when He was teaching in a synagogue on the Sabbath. The ruler of the synagogue was upset and said, "There are six days on which men ought to work; therefore come and be healed on them, and not on the Sabbath day" (Luke 13:14). To the ruler, healing was work, and it broke the law of the Sabbath. But our Lord Jesus replied, "Ought not this woman, being a daughter of Abraham, whom Satan has bound... for eighteen years, be loosed from this bond on the Sabbath?" (see Luke 13:16).

Our Lord Jesus showed us that the true substance of the Sabbath rest is not about doing nothing. It is not *inactivity*; it is *activity directed by the Spirit of God*, the way our Lord Jesus was led to heal and restore. He came to give us true rest—rest from our infirmities, rest from the cares that cause us to be bowed down, rest from the bondages of sin!

> Rest is not doing nothing. It is not inactivity; it is activity directed by the Spirit of God.

Look at how Jesus responded to the Pharisees who sought to kill Him because He healed the man at the Pool of Bethesda on the Sabbath. He said, "My Father has been working until now, and I have been working" (John 5:17). Ever since Adam fell, God has been working for man's redemption, man's wholeness, and man's blessings. You can rest because He is at work for you!

Whether you have been paralyzed by your fears and anxieties, or depression has robbed you of all your strength, whether you have been bound to an addiction for years, whether you have been bent over by the weight of hopelessness, I want you to know that you can find rest and victory in our Lord Jesus. No matter how long you have been suffering in your condition, there is hope in Him. *He does not want you to remain in your condition. Come to our Lord Jesus—one touch from Him can set you free.* Ought not you, child of the Most High God, be loosed from every shame, every stress, and every infirmity that binds you?

No matter how long you have been suffering, there is hope in Jesus.

Rest Is for Our Benefit

There is a law in the Old Testament in which the children of Israel were to let the land rest every seventh year. In the seventh year, they were not to sow, nor reap, nor gather. In His wisdom, God knew that even the land needed to rest. There are examples throughout the world of how overintensive farming and unrelenting grazing have destroyed lands, but the most infamous example would have to be the Dust Bowl that occurred in America in the 1930s.[8] For years, farmers refused to listen to the advice given by soil conservation scientists to allow the land to rest. Finally, the unsustainable farming practices largely led to weakened soil that was easily blown away by the prairie winds.

He who has ears, let him hear—when God tells us to rest, it is for our good. Our physical bodies are made from the dust of the ground. We must allow our bodies to rest. Otherwise, one way or another, our bodies will find a way to rest, and we might end up in a place where there are many beds to rest on and where people have to come visit us!

> When God tells us to rest, it is for our good.

The children of Israel learned this lesson the hard way. They failed to observe the Sabbath and let the land rest. But because one way or another the land had to rest, it got its rest when the children of Israel were brought into captivity in Babylon for seventy years. The Bible clearly tells us this happened "to fulfill the word of the LORD by the mouth of Jeremiah, until the land had enjoyed her Sabbaths. As long as she lay desolate she kept Sabbath, to fulfill seventy years" (2 Chron. 36:21).

Rest Brings Commanded Blessings

Some people are afraid to set aside time for rest because they are concerned that they will not have enough time to finish their work, or they will not earn enough money. But, beloved, you don't have to be afraid of being shortchanged or falling behind. The world's way is to work nonstop with little rest because people are depending on their own efforts to bring increase to their lives. God's way is this: Begin in rest, work out of rest, and continue in His rest. Out of that rest, you will experience increase on every front. That's what restful increase is all about! Can I assure you that you will never go wrong when you do things God's way? Look at what God promises when you obey Him and rest:

> *And if you say, "What shall we eat in the seventh year, since we shall not sow nor gather in our produce?"* **Then I will**

command My blessing on you *in the sixth year, and it will bring forth produce enough for three years. And you shall sow in the eighth year, and eat old produce until the ninth year; until its produce comes in, you shall eat* of *the old* harvest.
—*Leviticus 25:20–22 (boldface mine)*

> God's way is this: Begin in rest, work out of rest, and continue in His rest.

Do you know what this means? It means that rest brings God's commanded blessings! When you choose to obey Him and rest, He will command His blessings upon you and on your career. He will command His blessings on your bank account, on your ministry, on your family, on your business, on everything you touch! When you rest and live under God's commanded blessings, you will always have more than enough, like the children of Israel.

They could rest on the seventh day because God provided a double portion of manna on the sixth day (see Ex. 16:29–30)! Would you rather depend on your toiling and laboring? Or would you rather let go and let His commanded blessings and double-portion supply flow unabated in your life?

Resting in God Brings Timely Provisions

I want to encourage you today by sharing with you a testimony from Jaine, who lives in Maryland and who learned to rest in Christ and trust God for His supply to flow:

My husband and I are self-employed and paychecks can be few and far between. I often find myself fretting over our lack of money and dwindling resources.

Recently, I found myself troubled over our lack. I then remembered something I'd heard in one of Pastor Joseph Prince's messages about thriving in areas of our lives where we do not worry. So I told myself to stop worrying and instead have faith in God and believe in Him for His provision.

That very morning, I was looking through some unopened bills on my desk and a handwritten envelope caught my attention. We were about to leave our house but I decided to open it anyway. Much to my amazement, it was a refund check for $1,500 from a title company we'd used for a refinance on our house years ago! We had no idea it was coming and they had apparently been trying to track us down as we'd moved.

I can't tell you how many times this has happened to us. Whenever I start to worry, I tell myself to stop and rest in God's provision and amazingly, I get some freelance work, or an unexpected check arrives, or an old client calls up unexpectedly. I love it! God's grace is perfect.

In the same way that God provided for Jaine whenever she chose to rest in His promises, I pray that the Lord will *command* His blessings upon you as you choose to rest in His finished work. May the Lord grant you a new anointing of rest in Jesus' name!

8.
HAVE A THRONE
ATTITUDE

There is a very powerful truth about rest that I pray you will catch today, and that's the truth that we can rest *in the midst* of our challenges. The Word of God tells us that our Lord prepares a table for us *in the presence* of our enemies—not *in the absence* of our enemies (see Ps. 23:5). What enemies are you surrounded by today?

Is there a loved one you are deeply troubled about? Is your blood pressure out of control, or are you in desperate need of a financial breakthrough? My friend, our Lord wants you to be able to sit at His table of provision, healing, and supply *in the presence* of your enemies. You don't have to wait for all the issues to be resolved before you rest. Even now, you can sit back and partake of the feast that He has prepared for you! To be at rest while facing a crisis goes against human logic. That is why our Lord told us that the peace and rest He gives us is *not* as the world gives. The world can never understand nor provide the supernatural rest that He gives to His beloved. Do you want to know how you can rest in the midst of your challenges?

Once, while I was preparing for a message, the Lord said to me, "Son, tell my people to have a throne attitude." Let me explain what this means. I want to show you Psalm 110, a Messianic psalm. David was speaking prophetically by the Holy Spirit as he said this:

> The LORD said to my Lord, "Sit at My right hand, till I make Your enemies Your footstool."
>
> —*Psalm 110:1*

We are eavesdropping on a divine conversation between the Father and the Son that took place after Jesus conquered sin and death and rose from the dead. We know this because in the book of Ephesians it says:

> *He raised Him from the dead and seated Him at His right hand in the heavenly places, far above all principality and power and might and dominion, and every name that is named, not only in this age but also in that which is to come. And He put all things under His feet, and gave Him to be head over all things to the church, which is His body, the fullness of Him who fills all in all.*
>
> —*Ephesians 1:20–23*

Our Lord Jesus returned to the Father and the Father said, "Sit at My right hand, till I make Your enemies Your footstool." What is the attitude our Lord Jesus has at the Father's right hand right now? In biblical times, defeated enemies were brought back in chains and the victorious king would sit on his throne and put his feet up on their backs as a sign of victory. In the same way, Jesus' throne attitude is to sit, as His Father brings all His defeated enemies under His feet. We, the church, are the body of Christ. This means God Himself is making our enemies our footstool. We can rest in Christ because with each passing day, the defeated enemies of disease, poverty, depression, and all kinds of curses are being put under our feet!

Jesus Is Seated Because the Work Is Finished

Do you know why Jesus can be seated? Hebrews 10 tells us the answer:

> *And every priest stands ministering daily and offering repeatedly the same sacrifices, which can never take away sins. But this Man, after He had offered one sacrifice for sins forever, sat down at the right hand of God, from that time waiting till His enemies are made His footstool.*
> *—Hebrews 10:11–13*

In the Old Testament, the priests had to stand ministering daily because their work was never finished. The sacrifices they offered could never take away sins. But our Lord Jesus *sat down* at the Father's right hand because His work was finished through His one sacrifice on the cross. At the cross, Jesus Christ conquered the enemies of sin, depression, poverty, and premature death. Hallelujah! Hebrews tells us that after He sat down, He is "from that time waiting till His enemies are made His footstool." The enemies have *already* been conquered at the cross and since then, God has been putting those enemies under Jesus' feet.

We Are Seated with Christ

This is so exciting because the Bible tells us that God "raised **us** up together, and made **us** sit together in the heavenly *places* in

Christ Jesus" (Eph. 2:6, boldface mine). You and I are *in* Christ, seated with Him at the right hand of the Father. And as He is, so are we in this world (see 1 John 4:17)! To sit is to rest. Our Lord Jesus is resting as poverty, depression, curses, lack, fear, anxiety attacks, eating disorders, and obsessive-compulsive disorders are put under His feet. We are in Him—so all these enemies are also coming under the feet of the church!

We Can Rest in the Presence of Our Enemies

Now listen carefully: This is what I really want to communicate to you by the power of the Holy Spirit. God did *not* say, "You can rest when all your enemies have been destroyed and every problem in your life has been resolved." That's not what He said. He wants us to sit down and rest *first.*

Those symptoms might still be in your body. Those challenges might still be besetting you. Those adversities might still be screaming in your face. But I want you to hear the Father saying to you, *"Sit at My right hand, **until** I make all these enemies your footstool. In the midst of those symptoms, rest in the finished work of Jesus Christ. Remain in rest and let not your heart be troubled! I'll make those physical symptoms in your body your footstool. I'll make your child's behavioral problems and educational challenges your footstool. I'll make that financial debt your footstool. I'll cause that negative medical report to become your footstool. I, not you, will make your enemies your footstool. Your enemies have already been defeated—there is no battle for you to fight—your part is to rest!"*

Whatever you are going through in your life right now, you can have the attitude that every enemy that comes against your family is already defeated. You don't have to fight your enemies. The Lord has already won the victory. And one by one, they are becoming

His footstool until the last enemy—physical death—is also put under His feet. He is simply waiting while God makes them His footstool, and you are *in* Him, "far above all principality and power and might and dominion, and every name that is named, not only in this age but also in that which is to come" (Eph. 1:21).

> You don't have to fight your enemies. The Lord has
> already won the victory.

A Land Flowing with Abundance

Do you see how God's way is different from ours? God's way is for us to rest before He brings forth the results. We, on the other hand, want to see the results *before* we will allow ourselves to rest. Trust me, I know firsthand that it is a real struggle to rest because it is so contrary to our human nature. We always want to do something about the challenges we see and we think we are being "responsible" when we worry. No wonder the Bible tells us to "labor" to enter rest (see Heb. 4:11 KJV). As you read this book, I believe that the Lord is showing you just how to labor to enter His rest and to be diligent in living the let-go life. The children of Israel struggled to rest and to believe God's promises because they focused on the obstacles, and today we want to learn from their story.

God delivered them out of slavery in Egypt and told them He would bring them into "a land flowing with milk and honey" (Ex. 3:8). It was a sure promise, a statement of what God would definitely do. It would have been good enough if God promised them a land *with* milk and honey. But the land didn't only *have* milk and honey; it was also *flowing* with milk and honey. What a beautiful picture of God's abundant supply and provision, and doesn't it remind you of the golden pipes of supply that we spoke about in earlier chapters?

Now let me point you to something interesting about the fruits of the land. The fruits in Egypt were cucumbers, melons, leeks, onions, and garlic (see Num. 11:5), which all grew on the ground. But the fruits in the promised land were pomegranates, grapes, and figs, which hung from vines and trees (see Num. 13:23). Harvesting fruits from Egypt was backbreaking work, but in the promised land, you just needed to reach out and pluck them—a picture of how the promises of God are so easy and simple to partake of.

God also told the Israelites that the land would have large and beautiful cities that they did not build, houses full of all good things that they did not fill, hewn-out wells that they did not dig, and vineyards and olive trees that they did not plant (see Deut. 6:10–11). All that is a picture of what God wanted for them—to step into a *finished* work.

God Is Bigger than Our Giants

Sadly, something happened when the Israelites were at Kadesh Barnea, just at the brink of the promised land. They sent twelve spies to evaluate the land and while they saw that the land was indeed flowing with milk and honey, they also saw that the cities were fortified and very large and that the inhabitants of the land were giants (see Num. 13:27–29).

Two of the spies, Joshua and Caleb, were ready to take possession of the land. They told the people that the Lord would bring them into the land and give it to them. They saw the giants and told the Israelites not to fear them, for "they *are* our bread" (Num. 14:9). They urged the people not to fear the giants, as they believed the Lord was with them. They declared, "Let us go up at once and take possession, for we are well able to overcome it" (Num. 13:30). Joshua and Caleb had a different spirit. They had a spirit of rest and they rested in God's promise that He had given them the land. Even in the presence of their enemies and adversities, they were able to stay in rest. Why? Because their faith was not established on the giants that they saw, but on God's promises!

But the remaining ten spies gave a bad report because they focused on the formidable walls and the giants of the land:

> We are not able to go up against the people, for they are stronger than we.... The land through which we have gone as spies is a land that devours its inhabitants, and all the people whom we saw in it are men of great stature. There we saw the giants (the descendants of Anak came from the giants); and we were like grasshoppers in our own sight, and so we were in their sight.
>
> —Numbers 13:31–33

Instead of putting their trust in God, who had already promised them the land, the children of Israel chose to believe the report of the ten spies who said that the Israelites could not take the land because it was inhabited by giants from the tribe of Anak. In Hebrew, the word *Anak* means "a collar" or "neck chain."[1] A chain around the neck is a yoke that weighs you down. Although God had delivered the children of Israel from their taskmasters in Egypt and they were no longer slaves, they still had a slave mentality. Instead of focusing on God's goodness and promise, they focused on their giant problem—the Anakim—and were weighed down with anxiety and fear. As a result, the whole generation apart from Joshua and Caleb could not enter the land (see Num. 14:29–31) and wandered in the wilderness for forty long years.

Rest Is Our Promised Land

Hebrews 3 describes how the children of Israel were not allowed to enter the promised land because they doubted God's Word. However, instead of saying, "They shall not enter My promised land," God said:

"They shall not enter My rest."

—*Hebrews 3:11*

God called the promised land "My rest." This means that what the physical land was to the children of Israel in the Old Testament, God's grace and rest are to the believer under the new covenant. Our promised land today is God's rest! God did not deliver the children of Israel out of Egypt to leave them wandering in the wilderness. He brought them out to bring them in! In the same way, God wants to bring you out of lack and into the land of promise and abundance. He wants to bring you out of sickness into robust health. The promised land He wants to bring you into is the place of His rest.

The promised land He wants to bring you into is the place of His rest.

Be Rest-Conscious, Not Giant-Conscious

Unfortunately, some of us still have a slave mentality. We are so focused on our "Anakim"—our problems and symptoms—instead of Jesus' finished work on the cross that we cannot enter our promised land of rest. If that describes you, know this: God doesn't want you to fear the "giants" that you are faced with. God's

Word always tells us to "fear not" (see Isa. 41:10, Luke 12:32). But do you know that there is one thing the Bible tells us to fear?

> *Therefore, since a promise remains of entering His rest, let us fear lest any of you seem to have come short of it.*
>
> *—Hebrews 4:1*

God tells us to fear that we fail to enter His rest. So don't focus on your giants and be stressed out. Place your confidence not in what you see, but in what God has promised in His Word.

> *Place your confidence not in what you see, but in what God has promised in His Word.*

Will you side with Joshua and Caleb, or will you side with the ten spies? In other words, will you give more weight to your problems or to God's promises? Before your body is healed, before the debt is cleared, before the problem in your life is resolved, will you believe that God will deliver you according to His Word and walk in rest?

God wants you to have the revelation that whatever you need Him to do for you has already been done because Jesus has accomplished all for you. In spite of the giants you see, you can choose to go up and enter the promised land of His rest. When your confidence is in Christ and His finished work, you will be rest-conscious and not giant-conscious!

Let me share with you a testimony from Kimberly, who lives in Texas. Kimberly chose to rest in Christ even before she saw her breakthrough:

> *I am a thirty-five-year-old mother with three wonderful chil-*
> *dren. Two of them are from a previous marriage. Following*

my divorce, my ex-husband wanted my daughter to live with him and I could not refuse, as not agreeing to his request would involve a drawn-out court battle that was beyond my means.

Over the years, my daughter became very unhappy because her father had remarried and his household had become a toxic environment for her. Whenever she visited me, she would cry terribly when she had to leave.

*Then I heard Pastor Prince's sermon about turning my children over to the Lord because He loves them better than I can. **I rested in the fact that she was taken care of by Jesus and prayed that she would be restored back to me.***

Shortly after I heard the message, my ex-husband called and told me that my daughter wanted to move in with me. She did so and has lived with me ever since.

Today, there is such a light and joy in her heart. The Lord has blessed me with all my children under one roof and I couldn't be happier. Praise Jesus!

Notice that Kimberly *rested* in our Lord Jesus even before her daughter moved back in with her. As Kimberly rested, the Lord brought her daughter, who had been living with her ex-husband for years, back to her home!

Sing, O Barren!

There is a beautiful passage of Scripture in Isaiah 54 that I want to show you. Isaiah 54 comes after Isaiah 53, which is a Messianic chapter that talks about our Lord Jesus' sufferings on the cross for us. Do you know how we can partake of all that Jesus has done? Look at how Isaiah 54 opens up:

"Sing, O barren, you who have not borne! Break forth into singing, and cry aloud, you who have not labored with child! For more are the children of the desolate than the children of the married woman," says the LORD. "Enlarge the place of your tent, and let them stretch out the curtains of your dwellings; do not spare; lengthen your cords, and strengthen your stakes. For you shall expand to the right and to the left, and your descendants will inherit the nations, and make the desolate cities inhabited."

—Isaiah 54:1–3

You might be in the same place as the barren woman today. Perhaps you are barren of a physical baby, or perhaps you are barren of finances or health. But this is what God says to you: "Sing, O barren, you *who* have not borne! Break forth into singing, and cry aloud!"

You might not have borne any fruit yet, but because of what Jesus has done, you can sing out loud and proclaim His praises. Don't wait until you see the manifestation of His promises. Stop postponing your praise and your joy. Stop telling yourself that you will rest only when you have paid off the mortgage on your house. Stop waiting until you find a spouse before you rejoice. Sing *now*! And as you sing, you can start preparing for growth. You can start lengthening the cords of your place of work and strengthening the stakes of your bank account because you *shall* expand to the right and to the left!

Even in the midst of your adversity, you can sing, you can rest, you can rejoice! Your Shepherd prepares a table before you *in the presence* of your enemies. Even when the enemies are still around, you can feed by the green pastures and rest by the still waters because your Shepherd watches over you. The Lord loves you so much. He wants to bring you into a land where you will dwell in cities you did not build and eat from vineyards and olive trees you did not plant. It's all based on the work of Jesus Christ. Your part is just to believe and to rest as He makes your enemies your footstool!

9.
TUNE IN TO PEACE

A great multitude surges around one Man. With their faces a blur, their voices raised in curiosity and demand, the crowd press in on Him. They clamor for His attention, everybody straining to get a closer look. They've heard of how He has the power to heal sicknesses and cast out demons, and now it's their chance to see Him. Occasionally, shouts of "There He is!" rise above the cacophony and the sound of voices shouting His name punctuate the chaotic scene. Now and again they catch a glimpse of Him and then He's swallowed up again by sweat-streaked bodies jostling against each other for a chance to get just that bit nearer.

Then the fragile hand of a woman reaches out. Closes in on His person. Touches the hem of His garment.

Suddenly, there is silence. The horde is still pressing—pressing in, pressing forward, pressing against. But for a moment, all other sound is suspended as He turns around and asks, "Who touched My clothes?"

Just like that, sound returns once again, the myriad voices rise in impatience and excitement, until one of His disciples finally says to Him with undisguised incredulity, "You see the multitude thronging You, and You say, 'Who touched Me?'"

You know what happens next. The woman realizes that she has been miraculously healed the *instant* she touched His clothes.

She had had a flow of blood for twelve years and had suffered many things from many physicians. Nothing she had tried to do to cure herself had worked and she had bankrupted herself trying again and again. But when she heard about Jesus, she said to herself, "If only I may touch His clothes, I shall be made well." And so, even though she knew she was regarded as "unclean" because of her flow of blood and would be stoned if the people knew about it, she still pushed her way through the mob and reached out to Jesus.

When Jesus stopped and looked around the crowd to see who had touched Him, she knew He was looking for her. She fell down before Him in worship and gratitude and told Him the whole truth.

I have no doubt you would have heard many wonderful messages preached based on this amazing story of healing in the Bible (see Mark 5:25–34). How this woman's touch of faith stood out from that of the masses who were pressing against our Lord Jesus, tugging, pulling, and doing all that they could to get His attention.

But I want you to focus on what Jesus said to the woman. Our Lord Jesus told her, "Daughter, your faith has made you well. Go in peace, and be healed of your affliction" (Mark 5:34). One day, the Lord said to me, "Son, look up this phrase, 'go in peace' in the original Greek." (Our New Testament was not written in English— it was originally written in Greek.) I had never thought of looking up this phrase because I had always assumed that "go in peace" was simply a farewell phrase, like "see you again" or "have a good day."

Go into Peace

Do you know what I found when I studied the phrase? I discovered that our Lord Jesus did not say "go *in* peace" as it says in our English translation, but "go *into* peace." In the original Greek text, the word used is *eis*, meaning "into."[1] If "in" had been the intended meaning, the Greek word *en* would have been used. So what our Lord really said was "go *eis eirene*" or "go *into* peace." He wasn't simply bidding her farewell; He was telling her to step *into* the realm of peace, the way you might step *into* a house.

My friend, you might be going through a prolonged season of challenges in which nothing you have done seems to work. The woman with the issue of blood had been hemorrhaging for twelve years. She had spent all her money on doctors and had only gotten worse. Perhaps you might be dealing with a chronic condition and every cure and method recommended to you has failed. Maybe you are a single parent struggling to make ends meet and it seems like you have exhausted all your energy and resources and have nothing else to give. Or perhaps you have done all that you can to mend that broken relationship with your child, but all your efforts have come to naught and it seems like things have only gotten worse. As you reach out to the Lord by faith, allowing Him to work a miracle in your situation, He is inviting you to step out of your place of fear, worry, and anxiety, and to step into a realm of peace. He is asking you to go *into* peace.

He is inviting you to step out of your place of fear and anxiety and into a realm of peace.

Do you want to know more about this "peace" that the Lord wants us to go into? It is not an ordinary peace, but a peace that He Himself has given us. I want you to read this for yourself:

Peace I leave with you, My peace I give to you; not as the world gives do I give to you.

—John 14:27

Do you know when our Lord Jesus spoke these words?

During the Last Supper.

He knew His death was imminent. And in His last moments, the inheritance that Jesus chose to leave with us—the precious gift that He bequeathed to us—was peace. And not just any peace, but *His* peace. An inheritance is not put into effect until there is a death, and that is why our Lord Jesus laid down His life upon the cross—so that today, we can receive His peace as our inheritance. Whatever you might be going through in your life, I pray that you will walk in His peace today and not allow your blood-bought inheritance to go to waste!

He Gave Us His Peace

The world has its version of "peace" that it tries to achieve through different means. Some people take tranquilizers and medication to calm their anxieties. Some people visit spas, use aromatherapy, or practice yoga. Some people turn to alcohol to numb the stress they feel, or even resort to shock treatments in psychiatric hospitals when they can't seem to break free from oppressive and depressive thoughts that bind them.

But what happens when the medication or treatment wears off? What happens when we are caught in a traffic jam with the blare of car horns constantly assaulting our senses? My friend, our peace cannot be dependent on soft music nor on the physical posture that we are in. That is why Jesus said that the peace He gives is "not as the world gives." Aromatherapy, relaxation techniques, and all that might have their place, but the peace that He has given us is not affected by external factors. His peace is a peace that is robust and stable, a peace that surpasses human understanding, a peace that guards our hearts and minds (see Phil. 4:7).

> *The peace that Jesus gives us is a peace that surpasses human understanding, a peace that guards our hearts and minds.*

Feeling Overwhelmed? You Have a Helper

Take a look at the context in which Jesus said He has given us His peace:

> *These things I have spoken to you while being present with you. But the Helper, the Holy Spirit, whom the Father will send in My name, He will teach you all things, and bring to your remembrance all things that I said to you. Peace I leave with you, My peace I give to you; not as the world gives do I give to you. Let not your heart be troubled, neither let it be afraid.*
>
> —*John 14:25–27*

If you are feeling overwhelmed by the demands that are placed on you, I want you to know that our Lord Jesus did not leave us to fend for ourselves in this world. He gave us a "Helper"—the Holy Spirit. A helper is someone who helps us. In fact, the Greek word for "helper" here is *parakletos*, meaning someone who is "called to one's side" to help.[2] You have a Helper who will teach you all things. This means that instead of being stressed or anxious, you can ask the Holy Spirit to teach you how to handle that situation.

Do you know what "all things" means? It means *all* things. The Holy Spirit doesn't only teach us spiritual things. If He did only that, then where would we learn about having a successful marriage? Where would we learn how to raise our kids? We would turn to the world for answers, and while there are good principles we can glean, as believers in Christ, we have something better. God has given us His Holy Spirit, who will teach us *all* things.

You can ask Him to teach you how to handle the situation in your marriage. You can ask Him to teach you how to handle your finances or how to meet those sales targets. You can ask Him to teach you how to handle your rebellious teenager. He will teach you *all* things. As long as you have received Jesus as your Lord and Savior, you have the Holy Spirit and He will teach you *all* things.

The Wavelength of Peace

Do you want to know how you can learn to be led by the Holy Spirit? Look at Isaiah 55, which tells us how we can partake of all that our Lord Jesus did on the cross as prophesied in Isaiah 53.

We are told to "listen carefully," to "incline your ear," and to "hear" (see Isa. 55:2–3). As we listen to our Lord through reading the Word, praying and hearing sermons about His finished work, the Bible tells us, "You shall go out with joy, and be led out with peace" (Isa. 55:12). As we listen to His Word on the way to work, while we are doing housework, or as we take a walk in the park, joy and peace will lead us. We will be led out of trouble and worry. We will go out with joy and be led forth by His peace in every area of our lives.

Many times, the Holy Spirit, who teaches us all things and brings to remembrance all things the Lord has spoken to us, teaches us through the presence or absence of peace. I have been in situations where the options presented to me appeared very reasonable, but I held back because there was no peace to go ahead with them. Conversely, I have also been faced with opportunities that did not seem to make sense, but I took them up because I felt the peace to do so.

> *The Holy Spirit teaches us through the presence or absence of peace.*

I thank God that good has come out of those times when I followed the leading of His peace. Miracles have even resulted. So it's not hard to follow God. You don't have to be a rocket scientist or genius to follow the Holy Spirit. You just have to follow the presence or absence of peace, like what Kenneth, a brother from my church, did:

I would like to give glory and praise to my Lord Jesus. His unmerited goodness and faithfulness saw me through a tough season in my career. As a result of several retrenchment exercises and new business strategies being implemented, I had to work with four different line managers within a year, and feared for my job security.

*During this period, I was given an opportunity to change jobs when I was given a referral for a new position in a start-up company. At the first interview, I was immediately given a "soft offer" and was invited to a follow-up meeting. I was very attracted by the offer, as it meant an immediate pay bump and a change of environment. I gave myself about two weeks to consider the offer. **However, no matter how*** *much I tried to convince myself and my wife, there was an absence of peace to proceed deep down in my spirit.*

I asked the Lord to give me an answer through the Bible, and He showed me that the main reason I found myself wanting to pursue that opportunity was largely because of the monetary benefit. Shortly after, my wife and I met our church leaders for dinner and what they shared further confirmed my lack of peace to proceed with the new job offer.

When I finally settled in my heart to stay put in my job, I started experiencing favor with my clients and doors of opportunities rapidly opened to me. God truly blessed me in a year of drought. Through His supply, I became the top performer in my team. In a year when the number of staff promoted was reduced significantly by 60 percent, and when most received no increments and experienced cuts of 20 percent or more in their bonuses, I received a double-digit increment for my monthly wage and a bonus payout that was better than that of my previous year. All the glory goes to our Lord Jesus!

Even though Kenneth was given an offer that was very attractive in the natural, he chose not to take it up because of the lack of peace. Soon after his decision to stay on in his current company, he experienced supernatural favor and breakthroughs and was truly blessed in spite of the drought that other staff in the company were experiencing. In addition, who knows what the Lord could have protected him from when he chose to listen to the leading of the Holy Spirit not to join the start-up company? May we always be sensitive to His leading and be found at the right place at the right time!

Tune In to His Wavelength

Maybe you might be wondering, *Why is it the Holy Spirit doesn't seem to be teaching some Christians, who are defeated in some areas of their lives?* I submit to you that it's because the Holy Spirit teaches on the wavelength of peace. Just as you can't listen to a particular radio channel if you are not on the correct wavelength, the Holy Spirit can't teach you if you are not tuned in to His peace.

Why do I say that? Because right after our Lord tells us that the Holy Spirit will teach us all things, He says, "Peace I leave with you, My peace I give to you; not as the world gives do I give to you. Let not your heart be troubled, neither let it be afraid" (John 14:27). Verses 26 and 27 are tied together in the same context and should be studied together. The Holy Spirit teaches on the wavelength of peace. He teaches you all things when you step into the peace that the Prince of Peace has left you with, and the way to step into that peace is to guard your heart from being troubled and afraid.

Another Bible verse states it like this: "And **let the peace of God rule in your hearts**, to which also you were called in one body; and be thankful" (Col. 3:15, boldface mine). The Greek word for "rule" here is *brabeuo*, which means "to arbitrate, decide" or "to act as an umpire."[3] In other words, we are to let the peace of God govern our hearts. We are to let the peace of Christ rule or decide as an umpire. In a tennis match, an umpire decides when the ball is "in" or "out." If the umpire decides that the ball is "out," there is no point in arguing or throwing down our rackets in protest. The umpire has the final say. In the same way, let us allow the peace of Christ to rule or have the final say in our hearts and in all our decision making. Amen!

Unfortunately, instead of allowing the peace of God to rule their hearts, too many believers are letting the news headlines or their bank statements rule their hearts. They are letting their doctors' reports or rumors of retrenchment rule their hearts. In short, they are letting stress, fear, worries, and anxieties rule their hearts.

Beloved, if that describes you, I pray that as you go through the pages of this book, you will learn to tune in to His peace and break free from every worry and anxiety. I want you to know this: If you are a child of God, you do not have to try to get His peace—it is a gift that the Lord has already given you. His peace is our portion and our inheritance. The same peace that our Lord Jesus possesses *has* been given to you. I pray that as you let the peace of God rule and umpire your heart, you will experience such freedom and joy as your heart is no longer troubled and you learn to lean on the leading of the Holy Spirit to make wise decisions restfully.

The same peace that our Lord Jesus possesses has been given to you.

Step into Complete Wholeness

Let's go back to the story of the woman with the issue of blood, because there is another powerful revelation that I want to share with you. Remember the last words that Jesus spoke to the woman?

Daughter, your faith has made you well. Go in peace, and be healed of your affliction.

—Mark 5:34

Remember what I showed you earlier? Jesus was telling the woman to go *into* peace and be healed. Now, don't forget she was already healed—"your faith has made you well." So what does it mean when Jesus tells her again, "Go in peace, and be healed of your affliction"?

If you study the Greek tenses for this passage, you will see that the action "has made you well" carries the Greek perfect tense. This means that the woman's healing was already completed at a specific time in the past—when she touched Jesus' garment. But the following phrases "go in peace" and "be healed" both carry the Greek present tense—continuous action.[4] So Jesus was actually saying, "You are already healed. Go into peace and remain in peace, and your healing will be permanent."

I was so excited when the Lord opened my eyes to this powerful truth. I felt like jumping up in my study. He gave her the secret of not only receiving healing, but also of staying healed and walking in divine health! You can trust the Lord for divine healing when you or your loved ones are unwell, but do you know what is better than divine *healing*? It is to live in divine *health*! God's best for us is to walk in His divine health and He showed us how to do it—by going into His peace and remaining there!

> God's best for us is to walk in His divine health by going into His peace and remaining there.

I believe the woman's issue of blood was caused by a lack of peace. In our modern vernacular, doctors will not tell you that your condition is caused by "a lack of peace." They will tell you that it is caused by stress, as severe stress can lead to many psychosomatic conditions, such as high blood pressure, irritable bowel syndrome, depression, and heart problems. If a lack of peace had caused the woman's condition, the condition would return. So our Lord was showing her how to *keep her healing* and walk continually in divine health. In the same way, I pray that as you tune in to His peace, you too will experience a supernatural healing miracle and continue to walk in divine health.

10.
ALL-ENCOMPASSING
SHALOM

A s you meditate on the scriptural teachings in this book, my prayer for you is that you will begin to take ownership of the peace that our Lord Jesus has given to you as your inheritance. Our Lord Jesus stated that He has *given* us His peace. We are not trying to *get* His peace—His peace is *already* our portion. Let us step into His peace and enjoy all that He has given us!

> We are not trying to get *His peace—His peace is* already *our portion.*

The Power of *Shalom*

When our Lord Jesus spoke to His disciples about leaving them His peace at the Last Supper, being a Jew, He would have spoken in Hebrew. The New Testament was, however, written in Greek, so the word used for "peace" in John 14:27 is *eirene*. But since Jesus spoke in Hebrew, the actual word He would have used is the Hebrew word for "peace"—*shalom*. This means He would have told His disciples, "*Shalom*, I leave with you, My *shalom* I give to you." And He would have said to the woman with the issue of blood, "Go into *shalom*."

Why is this important?

Because *shalom* is a Hebrew word that is so rich in meaning. It doesn't just mean "peace of mind"—it is an all-encompassing word that includes so much more. According to James Strong, a Hebrew scholar, *shalom* means "welfare," "health, prosperity, peace."[1] It also means "a state of untroubled, undisturbed well-being."[2] This means that what the Lord bequeathed to us as our inheritance was His very own health, His very own provision, and His very own peace.

> The Lord bequeathed to us as our inheritance His very own health, provision, and peace.

Peace Can Be Multiplied

Did you know that you can walk in a greater measure of *shalom*? The Bible tells us:

Grace and peace be multiplied to you in the knowledge of God and of Jesus our Lord.
—2 Peter 1:2

The New Living Translation puts it like this:

May God give you more and more grace and peace as you grow in your knowledge of God and Jesus our Lord.

This means that the favor and *shalom* of God can be multiplied in our lives! But His *shalom* is not multiplied in our lives by us doing more or trying to achieve more. It is multiplied in our lives through the *knowledge* of God and Jesus our Lord, or as Kenneth Wuest, a noted Greek scholar, puts it, "by the full knowledge of our God, even Jesus, the Lord."[3] The more we know Jesus, the more we will experience His *shalom* being multiplied to us. The Word of God tells us that our Lord Jesus is the Prince of Peace (see Isa. 9:6). As you partake of the beautiful person of Jesus by spending time in His presence and in His Word, His peace will be infused into every fiber of your being. Even when you are confronted with a crisis, His peace will garrison and fortify your heart.

> The favor and shalom of God are multiplied in our lives through the knowledge of God and Jesus our Lord.

Why Aren't We Experiencing More Peace?

Once we have peace *with* God through the precious blood of our Lord Jesus Christ, we have the peace *of* God in our hearts. All the inherent benefits of His *shalom*—health, provision, and peace—have already been released to us. So the question to ask is not, "Do we have it?" It is already ours! The question to ask is, "Why are we not experiencing more of His *shalom*?"

To understand this, let's go back to what Jesus said:

> *Peace I leave with you, My peace I give to you; not as the world gives do I give to you. Let not your heart be troubled, neither let it be afraid.*
>
> *—John 14:27*

Pay close attention to the end of the verse. Our Lord tells us, "Let not your heart be troubled, neither let it be afraid." In the original Greek text, this is said as an imperative, which means it is a command or an injunction.[4] As I mentioned earlier, the whole verse has to be read in its context. I believe that our part is to honor that injunction to "let not" our hearts be troubled. Because the Lord loves us so much, He does not want our hearts to be troubled. He loves us so much that even His injunctions are injunctions of love, urging us not to let our hearts be troubled. But this is something that we have to do ourselves. Pastors and leaders cannot "let not" for us. You cannot "let not" for your spouse. You cannot "let not" for me. Even our Lord could not "let not" for His disciples.

Our part is to believe and to walk by faith by not allowing our hearts to be troubled or afraid. When we do that, the all-encompassing *shalom*-peace of God can flow in increasing measures in our lives. When we choose to not let our hearts be troubled, the peace that is in our spirits will go from our hearts to our souls and into our bodies, and we will experience the fullness of the health, provision, and peace that He paid for us to enjoy!

The Heart Is a Gateway

Why is it so important for us to not let our hearts be troubled?

Our heart is the gateway of our spirit. All the *shalom* in our spirits will do us no good if our hearts are clogged with worries, cares, and anxieties. We have to remove those cares. In the Parable of the Sower, our Lord Jesus talked about how the "cares of this world" and the "deceitfulness of riches" are the thorns that choke the Word and cause the hearer to be unfruitful (see Matt. 13:22).

Seeds cannot germinate and bear fruit when they are crowded and choked by thorns. In the same way, when our hearts are full of cares, we cannot bear fruit. When our hearts are filled with concerns about our children's education or nagging symptoms in our bodies, we choke the peace and it cannot flow out into our lives. Our hearts are the valves by which peace flows out—if our hearts are troubled, His peace cannot flow out.

If our hearts are troubled, His peace cannot flow out.

My friend, I know that we are confronted with real struggles. Demands are always pressing down on us. Your clients could be chasing you as deadlines close in on you. You might have had yet another quarrel with your spouse over the bills that seem to be mounting faster than you can pay them off. The new school year might be starting, but perhaps you don't have the money to pay for your kids' school supplies. Perhaps you are feeling anything but peaceful. But whether you *feel* His peace or not, by faith in His Word believe that He has already given it to you, and I pray you will possess your inheritance.

Peace Keeps What Grace Gives

I know it isn't easy. There was a time I considered myself a worry-holic, but the Lord led me to a place where I began to take the *shalom* that He left me seriously. I told myself this: "It doesn't matter whether I feel it or not right now. Since my Lord Jesus paid the price to bequeath His *shalom* to me, I am going to possess it by faith and not by what I feel."

During that time, the Lord opened my eyes to see that in the Bible, grace and peace always go together. So many of Paul's epistles begin with a salutation of grace and peace (see 1 Cor. 1:3; Phil. 1:2; Rom. 1:7). We need both grace and peace. The Lord also told me, "Son, My grace gives you all things freely because the blood of Jesus has paid for them. But," He continued, "My peace will keep everything that I have given." *The peace of God will retain and keep everything that grace has given.* Don't you think that is just so powerful? Remember what our Lord Jesus said to the woman with the issue of blood? He told her to go into peace and keep her healing. Peace keeps what grace gives!

How to Be "Undevourable"

It should come as no surprise then that our enemy—the devil—seeks to steal our peace, because before he can steal anything from us, he must cause us to have troubled hearts. How do I know this? Look at these verses with me:

> *Therefore humble yourselves under the mighty hand of God, that He may exalt you in due time, casting all your care upon Him, for He cares for you. Be sober, be vigilant; because your adversary the devil walks about like a roaring lion, **seeking whom he may devour.***
> —*1 Peter 5:6–8 (boldface mine)*

The devil goes about seeking whom he *may* devour, which means he cannot devour just anyone. There are people whom he can devour and people whom he can't. So he has to go about *seeking* whom he *may* devour. Let's keep him seeking.

But would you like to know whom the enemy *can* devour? The answer lies in the preceding verse, which tells you to cast all your cares upon the Lord. In other words, if you are full of care and worry, and your mind is always troubled, the enemy can devour you. But if you refuse to allow your heart to be troubled by casting your cares to the Lord, the enemy cannot touch you. In fact, the Bible tells us that "the God of peace will crush Satan under your feet" (Rom. 16:20). When you walk in peace and in the power of *Jehovah Shalom*, you can walk all over the enemy and not be afraid!

> *If you refuse to allow your heart to be troubled by casting your cares to the Lord, the enemy cannot touch you.*

When the Lord was teaching me how to walk in His *shalom*, He told me this: "Son, make it a game every day to cast your cares to Me." This is how the "game" works: Each time the devil throws you a care, you throw it to Jesus as quickly as possible. You can't hold on to it because it's like poison. The moment a worrisome thought comes, you cast it to the Lord. Whatever cares and worries come toward you, cast them to the One who cares for you with deepest affection, the One who laid down His life on the cross for you, and leave those cares and worries in His hands! According to the Oxford Dictionary, *cast* means to "throw (something) forcefully in a specified direction."[5] Don't take your time and allow that care to linger on your heart. Cast it to the Lord immediately. Quickly let it go to Him because He cares for you and you will become "undevourable"!

The Lord also told me to quote this portion from John 14:27 whenever I felt troubled: "Let not your heart be troubled." So that's what I did. I found it so hard at first because there were so many issues that I felt were *my responsibility* to be troubled about.

But the Lord told me, "Your only responsibility is to *take care of your heart on the inside*. Don't let your heart be troubled. And *I will take care of your outside*."

> *Your only responsibility is to take care of your heart on the inside and He will take care of your outside.*

Try it for yourself. Every time you catch your heart being troubled, say, "Let not your heart be troubled," and I believe you'll find yourself walking in increasing health, provision, and peace. I believe there is such power when we memorize, meditate on, and quote the words of our Lord. So learn to speak those words to yourself each time your heart feels troubled. Your heart will obey the voice of our Lord Jesus as you declare His words: "Let not your heart be troubled"!

Healed of Chronic Conditions

Rosabel, an occupational therapist from Texas, wrote to share what happened when she taught one of her patients about staying in peace and confessing verses such as John 14:27, the same Scripture that the Lord told me to quote. Read this amazing testimony for yourself:

> *I am an occupational therapist who treats patients in their homes. One of my patients had been severely debilitated for five years due to chronic obstructive pulmonary disease, obesity, and severe arthritic pain. I got her to watch Pastor Prince's program on television and her perspective changed after that. Things that used to bother her no longer had a hold on her for she knew that the Lord would handle them.*

I brought Holy Communion sets to her home and taught her to focus on Jesus' finished work and not the confession of sins when she partook of the Lord's Supper. **I shared with her what I had learned about staying in peace from Pastor Prince's sermon, Live the Let-Go Life.** *I also wrote her some verses to confess, such as,* **"Let not your heart be troubled, neither let it be afraid"** *(John 14:27). She followed through with these daily confessions when worry attempted to creep into her mind and continued watching Pastor Prince teach on TV.*

Within a few months, she was miraculously healed. She had no more knee pain, the doctor could not find evidence of lung disease, her shortness of breath improved drastically, she lost thirty-seven pounds, and she could independently carry out daily activities.

I have been a therapist for over twenty-three years and I can state from experience that no one, in the natural, regains their independence after being debilitated by chronic diseases for five years. Only Jesus can restore so completely and effortlessly!

What a powerful testimony of right believing in Jesus and our Daddy God. Praise the name of our Lord and Savior, Jesus Christ!

All glory to our Lord and Savior!

The Price for Our Peace Has Been Paid

I want to show you something else about the Hebrew word *sha-lom*. If you study its etymology, you will discover that it is related to the Hebrew word *shalem*.[6] Having been to Israel many times, I have learned the Hebrew phrase *Ani mi shalem*. So after a meal with my pastors, I would often go to the cashier and say, "*Ani mi shalem*," which means, "I will pay." I pay the bill so that none of the other pastors have to pay. Now do you see how *shalom* is tied to *shalem*? We cannot have *shalom*—well-being, health, provision, and peace—without a payment.

Do you know who paid the price for your *shalom*?

When our Lord Jesus was taken to the house of Caiaphas, the high priest, those who were gathered there threw questions at Him, falsely accused Him, "spat in His face and beat Him" (Matt. 26:67). He was then bound and brought to the residence of Pontius Pilate, where He was stripped and savagely scourged by Roman soldiers. The soldiers would have used a whip made of leather strips knotted with many bits of sharp bone and jagged metal.[7] Each stroke would have wrapped the whip around our Lord's body and torn off skin and flesh when it was yanked away, leaving His back torn to shreds and exposing His bones (see Ps. 22:17).

But His ordeal did not stop there. He was taken to the praetorium, where the whole garrison gathered around Him. He was then stripped in front of the garrison and further humiliated and mocked before He was led away to be crucified (see Matt. 27:27–31). I have only skimmed the surface of the horrifying things that were done to our Lord Jesus…to our King. Why did our Lord allow all that to happen to Him, when we know that He could have called down more than twelve legions of angels to fight His captors (see Matt. 26:53)?

The prophet Isaiah tells us why:

But He was wounded for our transgressions, He was bruised for our iniquities; the chastisement for our peace was upon Him, and by His stripes we are healed.

—*Isaiah 53:5*

Beloved, the chastisement for our *shalom*-peace fell upon Him. In the Hebrew, it says the demand and requirement for the payment of our sins was *exacted* from Christ, so that peace might come on us (see Isa. 53:7 YLT). He bore blow after blow, scourging after scourging, because He was saying, *"Ani mi shalem"*—"I am paying the price for your *shalom*. I am paying the price for your well-being, your wholeness, your completeness, and your health."

> The demand and requirement for the payment of our sins was exacted from Christ, so that peace might come on us.

Our sins were punished in the body of our Messiah and today, we are completely forgiven because on the cross, He was saying, *"Ani mi shalem"*—"I am paying the price for your forgiveness." He allowed Himself to be spat upon and stripped of all dignity because when man sinned against God, man realized he was naked and started hiding in shame from God. Our Lord Jesus took our place and He was saying, *"Ani mi shalem"*—"I'm paying the price for you to receive double honor" (see Isa. 61:7).

Maybe you are thinking, *Pastor Prince, you don't know the things I have done. You don't know the thoughts that I think. I don't deserve peace or health or forgiveness!*

My friend, you are right. You don't deserve any of it, and neither do I. In fact, you and I are supposed to be punished for our sins. We are supposed to be cursed. We are supposed to find ourselves at the wrong place at the wrong time. And that is why we need to know the foundation of the *shalom* that Jesus bequeathed to us. We did not earn it—Jesus Christ paid for it. When He rose from the dead, His first words to the disciples were "Peace *be*

with you," and then He showed them His nail-pierced hands—
the receipts of the payment He had made (see John 20:19–20).
Because the price has been paid, we have every right to the
peace, completeness, welfare, provision, and health that He has
bequeathed to us!

11.
ABOVE ALL THINGS, GUARD YOUR HEART

A precious brother who attends our church suffered from various problems for nine years. It all started when he was laid off. Unable to provide for his family, he came under great stress. Struggling to get just two hours of sleep a night, he became addicted to sleeping pills. To compound the problem, he developed such severe sinusitis that he had to undergo multiple operations and take expensive rounds of antibiotics. The heavy doses of antibiotics in turn led to gastritis. He then started having panic attacks that were so debilitating he seldom left his house. Every day, he was taking up to thirty tablets to keep his conditions under control and ended up struggling with severe depression and suicidal thoughts.

His turnaround came when he started attending our church. One day, he felt God prompting him to pray in the Spirit as often as he could. He obeyed. The moment he started to pray in the Spirit, he felt a rest and a peace. The more he prayed in the Spirit, the more rest and peace he felt.

His sinuses began to clear up and he was healed of gastritis. Slowly, the fears and panic attacks left him, and he started to have quality sleep without the need for sleeping pills. The Lord also

turned his financial situation around. This man is now a counselor in our church and has helped many people break free from
their worries, fears, and anxieties. Praise the Lord!

Find Rest and Refreshing

To counter stress, many people resort to things like tobacco, alcohol, or tranquilizers. These things, besides having harmful side
effects, are costly and often lead to addictions and other com-
plications. In the case of the brother from our church, one problem led to another, and he remained bound to his conditions for
years. God had something better for him and it is something that
we can tap into as well. It is powerful, costs us nothing, and has
no harmful side effects. It is called the rest and the refreshing:

> *For with stammering lips and another tongue He will speak
> to this people, to whom He said, "This is the rest with which
> you may cause the weary to rest," and, "This is the refreshing."*
> —*Isaiah 28:11–12*

This is one of the few Old Testament verses that refer to praying in the Spirit. As that brother prayed in the Spirit regularly,
God gave him a powerful rest and refreshing that delivered him
from years of insomnia, panic attacks, and other ailments. My
friend, you can enjoy this rest and refreshing from the Lord too.

Can I encourage you to start praying in the Spirit regularly?
You can pray in the Spirit even when you are in the midst of your
problems and even when you don't know what to pray. In fact,
the Bible tells us that when we don't know what to pray, the Holy
Spirit helps us in our weaknesses and makes intercession for us as

we pray in the Spirit (see Rom. 8:26). I don't know about you, but I want the Holy Spirit to make intercession for me!

> When we don't know what to pray, the Holy Spirit helps us in our weaknesses and makes intercession for us as we pray in the Spirit.

Be Anxious for Nothing

I want to share this beautiful passage of Scripture with you:

> *Be anxious for nothing, but in everything by **prayer** and **supplication**, with thanksgiving, let your requests be made known to God; and **the peace of God, which surpasses all understanding, will guard your hearts and minds through Christ Jesus.***
>   *—Philippians 4:6–7 (boldface mine)*

I believe this passage refers to praying in the Spirit because the Greek words used for "prayer" and "supplication"—*proseuche* and *deesis*—are the same words used in Ephesians 6:18, where it talks about "praying always with all **prayer** and **supplication in the Spirit**" (boldface mine).

You don't have to live with anxiety or stress. As you pray in the Spirit, as you bring your requests to Him and thank Him in faith for the answers, the *peace of God* will guard your heart as well as your mind through Christ Jesus. You may not understand how God's peace works—how it can guard your emotions and reasoning despite the negative circumstances—but that is why it is a true peace that the world cannot give!

Not as the World Gives

The world tries to sell you peace in various forms. It tells you that you can get peace by having music playing gently in the background as you turn down the lights and allow calming scents of lavender and bergamot to waft over you. It tells you that you can get peace when your body is in the right posture and you practice breathing in the right way. The world tells you that you can get peace when you are tucked away at a mountain resort, far from civilization. I have nothing against all that.

But the truth is, if having "peace" depends on external circumstances, then it's not true, lasting peace, as circumstances can easily change. Peace has to come from inside your heart, and only the Lord Jesus can give you this true peace—a peace that is rugged, strong, abiding, and unaffected by outward circumstances. Do you want to know what it is like to have the peace that our Lord Jesus gives?

Only the Lord Jesus can give you true peace that is rugged, strong, abiding, and unaffected by outward circumstances.

Let's take a look at Peter. The Bible tells of how King Herod had ordered the apostle James killed, and when he saw how much this pleased the Jews, he had Peter arrested and thrown into prison. He planned to bring Peter out before the people in a public trial and possibly have him executed (see Acts 12:1–11 NLT).

Just imagine the conditions that Peter would have been in. The "aroma" that surrounded him would have been the stench you would expect from a squalid prison crammed with filthy inmates who probably had to defecate in their own cells. The "music" that must have been playing in the background would have been the groans and cries of other prisoners being beaten up by hardened guards. As for being in the right "posture," the Bible tells us that Peter was trussed up in two sets of chains and bound to two soldiers, who flanked him at all times, scrutinizing his every move. There was no way he could escape, and he knew what awaited him in the morning—he would be dragged before the rabble, unjustly tried, and probably executed. I can only imagine the fear and desperation that would have gripped anyone in Peter's position.

But I want you to see for yourself the state that Peter was in when he had an unexpected visitor:

> *Suddenly, there was a bright light in the cell, and an angel of the Lord stood before Peter. The angel **struck him on the side to awaken him** and said, "Quick! Get up!" And the chains fell off his wrists.*
>
> *—Acts 12:7 NLT (boldface mine)*

Peter was so full of peace that he could go to sleep in spite of all that was happening to him and around him. Some of us might not even be able to sleep when we have a presentation to deliver or when we're expecting a doctor's report the next day! Peter was in such a deep sleep that he did not even stir when an angel appeared in his cell in a blinding flash of light. In fact, the angel had to strike him on his side to awaken him.

Peace Inside Affects the Situation Outside

Doesn't Peter remind you of another Man, who stayed fast asleep even though there was chaos all around Him (see Matt. 8:24)? A great tempest arose as this Man was crossing the Sea of Galilee, the howling winds whipping the waves into a frenzy. Over and over again, the hapless boat He was in pitched toward the thundering skies, came violently crashing down, only to be heaved upward again as it was tossed about by the swollen waters. Many of the other men in the boat were seasoned fishermen who spent most of their lives navigating the sea. And yet, they feared for their lives as it began to fill with water despite their best efforts at bailing.

In the midst of all this, the Prince of Peace was sleeping, oblivious to the screaming winds and tumultuous waves. Finally, His disciples woke Him up, crying, "Teacher, do You not care that we are perishing?" (Did you notice that it wasn't the storm that woke Him? It was the cry of His disciples.) Our Lord Jesus got up, rebuked the wind, and said to the sea, "Peace, be still!" And just like that, the wind ceased and there was a *great* calm (see Mark 4:38–39).

Here's what I want you to see: Our Lord Jesus was not affected by the storm that was all around Him. Instead, He could affect the storm and bring peace to His outside circumstances, because He was full of peace on the inside. In the same way, long before our external situations can change, we need His peace, which surpasses all understanding, to guard our hearts and minds. Thank God He has bequeathed this peace to us—a peace that is not as the world gives, but a peace that can prevent our hearts from being troubled or afraid. As we are filled with His peace, I believe that what begins on the inside will start affecting our circumstances on the outside!

When You Need a Miracle

Years ago, the Lord told me something that grew into one of the cornerstone messages of my ministry: *If it's a miracle you need, a miracle you will get—if you remain in peace.* I know you will be greatly blessed by this message, so I would like to share it with you. All you need to do is to download my free app to access it. You can get more information by heading to the resource section at JosephPrince.com/LetGo.

> *If it's a miracle you need, a miracle you will get—if you remain in peace.*

When the Lord first told me, "Son, if you let not your heart be troubled, you'll even get a miracle if that's what you need," I found it very hard to believe. I thought, *You mean to tell me that all I need to do is to not let my heart be troubled? But that wouldn't change anything about my challenge, would it?* But what God was saying was that my part was to guard my own heart and not guard all the situations around me. And as I guarded my heart and did not allow it to be troubled, He would take care of the situations and every other area of my life. In fact, He would even bring about a miracle if I needed one. Do you know what else happens when you do not allow your heart to be troubled? The peace of God will reign in your heart (see Col. 3:15)!

Guard Your Heart above All Things

The Lord also led me to study this portion from Proverbs 4:

My son, give attention to my words; incline your ear to my sayings. Do not let them depart from your eyes; **keep them in the midst of your heart;** *for they are life to those*

who find them; and health to all their flesh. **Keep your**
heart with all diligence, for out of it spring the issues
of life.

—*Proverbs 4:20–23 (boldface mine)*

Proverbs 4:20 tells us to pay attention to the words that will
follow because they are *life* to those who find them and *health* to
all their flesh. Immediately following this instruction, the Bible
tells us to *keep our hearts with all diligence.* This means that when
we keep our hearts with all diligence, it will bring life to us and
health to *all* our flesh.

What does it mean to *keep* our hearts? The Hebrew word used
here is *natsar*, which means "to watch, to guard" or "to preserve,
to guard from dangers."[1]

God makes it so clear why it is important for us to guard
our hearts—because out of our hearts spring the issues of life. Is
health an issue of life? Is provision an issue of life? Is the well-being
of your family an issue of life? Instead of trying to guard all these
areas, let's just do what the Word of God tells us to do—"Guard
your heart above all else, for it determines the course of your life"
(Prov. 4:23 NLT)!

Some guard their children, some guard their money, some
guard their shares and investments, and some guard their competitors. But God didn't tell us to guard all these things. The only
thing He told us to guard was our *hearts.* And as we guard our
hearts, trust Him to guard everything else. Let God handle that
situation. When He does it, it's so perfect we cannot add to it!

No matter what challenge you might be faced with, decide
right now by faith not to allow it to trouble your heart! Instead,
guard your heart with His peace on the inside of you—and
God will guard everything else, and even change your outward

circumstances, causing all things to work together for your good and to His glory!

> Guard your heart with His peace on the inside of you and God will guard everything else.

How to Guard Your Heart When Things Go Wrong

Perhaps you really want to be able to remain in peace, but you don't know how to because a huge debt is threatening to crush you, or you are faced with a storm of problems crashing down on you all at the same time. Let me share with you how you can practically guard your heart and apply His *shalom* to your life no matter what you might be going through.

Second Kings tells the powerful story of a Shunammite woman who, knowing that Elisha was a man of God, built a room for him to rest in whenever he passed by. One day, her young son died. She placed the body of her son on Elisha's bed. Then she shut the door, went out, and told her husband she was going to look for the man of God. She did not tell her husband what had happened to their son, and when he asked why she was going to look for Elisha, she simply answered, "*It is* well" (2 Kings 4:23).

If you study the phrase "*It is* well" with a Hebrew lexicon, you will see that it is made up of only one Hebrew word—*shalom*. When you don't know what to say, say "*shalom*." Say "*shalom*" to whatever situation you might be battling!

The woman got on her donkey and went to look for Elisha at Mount Carmel. When Elisha saw her some distance away, he got his servant to run to meet her and ask, "*Is it* well with you? *Is it* well with your husband? *Is it* well with the child?" And again, she answered, "*It is* well" (2 Kings 4:25–26). *Shalom.*

Even though her beloved son had died in her arms, she kept confessing and declaring, "*It is* well." She kept declaring *shalom.* When she finally met Elisha, she caught him by his feet, her soul "in deep distress" (2 Kings 4:27). But still, she did not say anything about her child's death. It was Elisha who figured it out. To cut a long story short, he went back with her, prayed for her son, and her child was raised back to life.

Unleash His *Shalom* by Speaking

This is what I pray that you will catch today: Do not underestimate the power of the Lord's *shalom.* I believe that the Shunammite woman had a robust understanding of *shalom* and that was why she kept speaking forth "*shalom*" even though her emotions would undoubtedly have been in great turmoil. She did not say what she felt—she spoke forth *shalom.* She was able to guard her heart in the midst of a great trial and adversity by guarding her mouth. There is a correlation between our hearts and our mouths—the Bible tells us that out of the abundance of the heart, the mouth speaks (see Luke 6:45). One of the ways you can guard your heart is by guarding your mouth and changing the words you speak.

Whatever situation you might be in, unlock the power of Jesus' *shalom.* When things in your life might not be going as planned, speak forth His *shalom.* When fears and anxieties might be overwhelming you, speak forth His *shalom.* Pray in the Spirit, bring your requests to God, and allow His peace to guard your heart. Keep holding on to His promises and hiding them in the midst of your heart. And as you remain in His *shalom*-peace, get ready for good things to happen. Get ready for your miracle. Get ready for dead dreams to be raised to life, dead cells to be resurrected, and dead relationships to be infused with new life!

Fear Shuts You Up

Read this passage with me to see what happened when Jesus rose from the dead:

> *Then, the same day at evening, being the first day of the week, **when the doors were shut** where the disciples were assembled, **for fear** of the Jews, Jesus came and stood in the midst, and said to them, "Peace be with you." When He had said this, He showed them His hands and His side. Then the disciples were glad when they saw the Lord.*
> *—John 20:19–20 (boldface mine)*

Why were the doors shut? It was "for fear." But then something happened. Jesus came and stood in the midst of their fear. And what was the very first word of the resurrected Jesus to His frightened disciples? In our English Bibles, He said, "Peace *be* with you," but our Lord would have spoken in Hebrew, so He would have used the word *shalom*. Then He showed them His nail-pierced hands and His side where the centurion had pierced Him with a spear—the receipts of His payment for their *shalom* and the tokens of their guaranteed peace.

Beloved, our Lord Jesus has paid the price for your *shalom*. Because of that, you don't have to be full of cares and worries. Even when things are not perfect, you can declare, "It is well!" Do you think for one moment that the Shunammite woman's heart was not full of grief or that she did not have fearful thoughts? The fears were there. But you know what? Her mouth was not shut by the devil. Fear happens when the door that is your mouth is shut. Your mouth is the door to your salvation. The Bible tells us that if you confess with your *mouth* that Jesus Christ is Lord, you shall be saved (see Rom. 10:9). Your mouth is the door the devil wants to shut. Let's not allow the enemy to shut our mouths. Let's speak out the promises of God in faith.

> Jesus has paid the price for your shalom. Because of that, you don't have to be full of cares and worries.

If doctors have given you a negative prognosis, proclaim, "But He *was* wounded for our transgressions, *He was* bruised for our iniquities; the chastisement for our peace *was* upon Him, and by His stripes we are healed" (Isa. 53:5)!

If you are fearful of growing old, declare that the Lord redeems your life from destruction, crowns you with lovingkindness and tender mercies, and satisfies your mouth with good things, so that your youth is renewed like the eagle's (see Ps.103:4–5).

If you are struggling in your finances, pronounce by faith that the Lord will command the blessing on you in your storehouses and in all to which you set your hand (see Deut. 28:8).

Do not allow the enemy to shut your mouth from speaking forth *shalom* and declaring God's promises. The situation might appear bleak. The negative report may be staring at you. But you do not have to speak what you see in the natural. Guard your mouth and fill it with unshakable and eternal truths from the Word of God. And the peace of God that surpasses understanding shall guard your heart!

12.
PEACE IN YOUR CONSCIENCE

W̲e have seen how powerful the peace of God is—how peace on the inside can even change our situations outside, how His *shalom* is all-encompassing and affects every area of our lives, and how our Lord Jesus bequeathed to us His own peace. But until you have a settled peace in your conscience, you cannot freely receive what the Lord Jesus has purchased for you. I pray that as you read this chapter, you will be so established in the knowledge that as a believer in Christ, you are forever saved, your sins have been forgiven, and heaven is your home!

> *Until you have a settled peace in your conscience, you cannot freely receive what the Lord Jesus has purchased for you.*

When I was a teenager, I read a book that convinced me it was possible for a believer to commit an unpardonable sin. Today, I know that the *only* sin that is unpardonable is the rejection of the person of Jesus. Hence, it is not possible for someone who has received Jesus to *ever* commit the unpardonable sin. (In case you want to find out more, I've written about the unpardonable sin in greater detail in my earlier book *Destined to Reign*[1].) But at that time, reading that erroneous teaching opened a can of worms in my mind.

As a young and naïve believer, I concluded that I had committed the unpardonable sin by blaspheming the Holy Spirit. The moment I no longer had peace in my conscience and no assurance that all my sins were forgiven by the blood of Jesus, my heart began to trouble me and I fell into depression. Day and night, my conscience relentlessly accused me of committing this sin that could *never* be forgiven. I believed that I was condemned to go to hell and that I would never be able to regain my salvation.

I went all out to serve the Lord in my church and would walk around the main shopping district in Singapore to share the gospel with strangers and get them saved, all the while believing that I had already lost my own salvation. With all sincerity, I hoped that they would make it to heaven and when God saw them, He would remember me in hell. Can you believe that? Needless to say, I didn't have peace in my heart. My mind also became unsound, and I began to be tormented by dark and destructive thoughts. My thought life was oppressed daily, and it came to a point where I felt like I was on the brink of collapsing mentally.

His Blessings Are Legally Ours

During that period in my life, I cried out to the Lord and one of the things He showed me was that I could never have *settled peace*—real peace in my conscience—until I understood that we receive all that Jesus purchased for us on the cross *judicially*.

He heals us, provides for us, and gives us peace in our hearts and minds *not* because of His mercy, but because these blessings are *legally* and *righteously* ours.

Why is it so important to understand that we can receive from Jesus judicially? Let me give you a simple illustration. Imagine if you looked at your bank balance one day and realized that your statement shows you have $100,050 in your account. But the last time you checked, you only had $50 left. Somehow, $100,000 had been added to your account. Perhaps you might be really excited for a moment, but can you really enjoy the money, not knowing how it got into your account? Now, suppose you found out that one of your closest friends had received an inheritance and decided to bless you with $100,000. How would you feel, knowing that every dollar in your account is legally yours and that you are free to use it? In the same way, until you know what Jesus has done for you, you can never have settled peace in your conscience!

Our Lord Jesus, who is altogether perfect and without sin, has finished the work on the cross and answered every accusation that can ever arise, be it from our conscience, the devil, or the claims of divine justice. He took *all* our sins upon His own body. He bore stripe after stripe and punishment after punishment for our sins on *our* behalf. He died in *our* place, conquered death, rose from the dead, and is now seated at the Father's right hand. Today, because of all that He has done, nothing can separate us from the love of God. *Nothing.*

My friend, God loves us. He is *for* us and not against us. He doesn't want us to live under constant condemnation and sin-consciousness, with no confidence that we have been forgiven. There is no peace in such insecurity! He paid the ultimate price to purchase our justification, to give us the gift of no condemnation, to tear down every wall that keeps us from His love. Do you think for one moment that there is something we, as His children, can do that is so great it can negate all that our Lord Jesus has done for us?

Hebrews 10:10 tells us that we have been sanctified through the offering of the body of Jesus Christ "once for all." Our Lord Jesus was the perfect offering. He has sanctified and cleansed us once for all. Today, we should have no more consciousness of sins because to be full of sin-consciousness would be an insult to the finished work of Christ. Hebrews 10:2 puts it this way: "For the worshipers, once purified, would have had no more consciousness of sins."

Nothing Can Separate Us from the Love of Christ

No one says it better than the apostle Paul, so I would like to invite you to take a few moments to meditate on what he wrote. Don't rush through this passage. Read it word by word. Let its truths soak into your spirit and silence every bit of insecurity, fear, and doubt you might have in your heart that you can be separated from God's love for you:

If God is for us, who can be against us? He who did not spare His own Son, but delivered Him up for us all, how shall He not with Him also freely give us all things? Who shall bring a charge against God's elect? It is God who justifies. Who is he who condemns? It is Christ who died, and furthermore is also risen, who is even at the right hand of God, who also makes intercession for us. Who shall separate us from the love of Christ? Shall tribulation, or distress, or persecution, or famine, or nakedness, or peril, or sword? As it is written: "For Your sake we are killed all day long; we are accounted as sheep for the slaughter." Yet in all these things we are more

than conquerors through Him who loved us. For I am per-
suaded that neither death nor life, nor angels nor principali-
ties nor powers, nor things present nor things to come, nor
height nor depth, nor any other created thing, shall be able
to separate us from the love of God which is in Christ Jesus
our Lord.

—Romans 8:31–39

My friends, nothing—and no one—can separate you from the love of Christ. Not even yourself! No one can bring a charge against you to condemn you before God—our Lord Jesus is your defender! It saddens me that the Bible is so clear on this but so many precious believers have heard a mixed message. As a result, they have not experienced peace in their conscience. Instead, they have been weighed down by a constant sense of guilt and condemnation for not doing enough to qualify for God's approval, healing, and blessing in their lives. They have believed the *lie* that God is disappointed with them and that they are not good enough to deserve His love.

Nothing—and no one—can separate you from the love of Christ.

We Are Justified by Faith

The truth I want to declare to you today is this: God wants us to live with full security and assurance of His love and forgiveness. The moment you receive Christ as your Lord and Savior, look what happens:

Therefore, having been justified by faith, we have peace with
God through our Lord Jesus Christ, through whom also we

have access by faith into this grace in which we stand, and
rejoice in hope of the glory of God.

—*Romans 5:1–2*

Let's study these verses closely. As believers in Christ, we have been justified—made righteous, acquitted of sin, and declared blameless before God (see Rom. 5:1 AMP). How? By faith. By *believing* that on the cross, Jesus took away all our sins. Aren't you glad we are not justified by our works or by our obedience? We are justified by our *believing* and not by our *doing*! Even our best good works cannot make us righteous; only His perfect work can do that.

Does that mean we don't bother with doing good works? Not at all! In fact, when we receive His righteousness as a gift, we will produce good works in our lives that are the *fruits* of His righteousness. Right believing always produces right living. Many people want to see right living but are not having lasting results. Do you want to know why? I believe it's because they are trying to change the fruits instead of addressing the roots. But unless our believing is first changed, outward behavior modifications won't last. Conversely, when we believe right about our Lord Jesus, right living that is permanent will follow!

Set Free from Drug Addiction

Stephie, a lady from my church, wrote to me to share the amazing turnaround she experienced after she became established in the knowledge that she was justified by *believing* in our Lord Jesus as her righteousness:

I left school at the age of thirteen and began taking drugs.
I was even making a comfortable living selling them in

nightclubs. From the time I was sixteen, I started going in and out of prison because of my drug problem. I often felt angry with myself for what was happening. I tried a few times to stop taking drugs but would give in within half a day.

Then, a friend brought me to New Creation Church and it changed my life forever. After attending church for a few weeks, I woke up one morning with clarity of mind. I finally realized that every curse had already been taken away from me, and I did not have to live the cursed life that I thought I was doomed to live. I had found grace.

With this fresh revelation, I prayed to God to help me overcome my addiction. **Whenever I felt the urge to take drugs, I declared, "I am the righteousness of God in Christ." I also told myself that I shouldn't rely on my own willpower and to tell God, "I cannot, but You can." Initially, my drug addiction actually got worse. Still, I continued praying and I kept telling God, "I really don't know how, but I know I'm relying on You."**

One day, the drug that I was addicted to ran out of stock. I was desperate and worried about the effects of withdrawal on my body but even after two weeks, I did not have any withdrawal symptoms. I was miraculously set free from my drug addiction!

Today, I am happily married with two kids and blessed with a growing business. Thank you, Pastor Prince, for preaching the word of no condemnation. That was exactly what I needed to hear during my struggle with drug addiction. I am so grateful and humbled by the fact that God did not spare His own Son for my sake. I can't imagine where I would be without my Savior, the Lord Jesus Christ. Thank You, Abba Father!

Praise the Lord. What a wonderful testimony. I am so glad Stephie continued to see herself as the righteousness of God in Christ even in the midst of her drug addiction. As she kept putting her trust in God and not in her own willpower, which had failed her time and again, the power of God flowed into her situation and broke the addiction that had bound her for years!

Freed from Fear, Anxiety, and Obsessive-Compulsive Disorder

There is another praise report I want to share with you. Jason from South Africa wrote to share how he suffered from fear, anxiety, and obsessive-compulsive disorder but was set free as he began to put his trust in the grace of God:

> *I was a believer at an early age. However, I was misled into thinking I had committed the unpardonable sin. When I was thirty, I went into a downward spiral of fear and anxiety, and suffered from obsessive-compulsive disorder. My mind was flooded with blasphemies and swearing directed at God and the Holy Spirit. For three years, I was a nervous wreck and had to take medication for my anxiety and to sleep. I consulted church leaders and even though they meant well, their advice made me feel condemned. I was in a desperate place.*
>
> *One morning, when I turned on the television, I saw Pastor Joseph Prince preaching on grace. I started listening to his grace messages and something deep inside me resonated with what he was preaching. I later found out*

that Pastor Prince went through what I was experiencing. Just knowing that he had the same experience gave me hope.

It was scary at first to trust a grace preacher when all I was familiar with was legalism and self-effort. However, I made the decision to be bold and to put my trust in God's grace. It was not long before I found that my blasphemous thoughts were starting to clear up.

I stopped being muddled and confused and started developing the ability to think clearly. Fears began to leave. Through God's grace working inside me, I was able to take myself off the medication for obsessive-compulsive disorder and depression. **The more I let go of my own efforts and trusted Him, the more my mind became sound. Where I was worried about my eternal salvation, I started having a confident expectation of good for my life** and for what will happen when I finally meet my loving Savior face-to-face. I thank God for people brave enough to boldly preach the message of God's grace.

Although I still have days where doubts creep in, thankfully, I am able to resist them by being established in grace through good teaching and revelation from God's Spirit inside me. I am gaining new ground every day and I am fully confident that I will be fully restored in the very near future! What the enemy has stolen from me will be returned sevenfold! Thank you, Pastor Prince, for being so bold in preaching the gospel of grace.

Hallelujah! I love that Jason highlighted how he had been worried about his eternal salvation but started to hope (which is defined in the Bible as having the confident expectation of good) and break free from his fears when he understood more about how good God is and what grace had done for him.

We Have Peace with God through Christ

Going back to Romans 5:1, let me ask you this: What happens now that we have been justified by faith? This is so crucial and I pray the Lord brands this truth into your spirit today (boldface mine):

> *Therefore, having been justified by faith, **we have peace with God through our Lord Jesus Christ.***

We have *peace with God* through our Lord Jesus Christ. Jesus *is* our peace. He broke down the wall that separated God from man, and today we can have full assurance that God is not angry with us! We have peace with *God*—the One who loves us. The One who knows all our secret thoughts and concealed failures and still loves us. The One with whom nothing is impossible. The One who is our hiding place during these perilous times. The One who is greater than any disease. The One who is more powerful than any financial trouble. *He* is the One with whom we have peace. Hallelujah!

What a wonderful gift it is to have peace with the One who spoke the earth into existence and who hung the stars in the sky. And all we have to do to receive this peace is to believe by *faith* in Him who made it possible. There is no list of requirements for us to fulfill, no standard of perfection that we have to meet. We cannot earn or deserve this peace. We only have access to peace with God because we have been justified by *faith* and faith alone. There is no part for us to boast in, for all glory goes to Jesus Christ. It cost us nothing, but it cost Jesus His life, for the chastisement for our peace fell upon Him (see Isa. 53:5).

> *All we have to do to receive peace with God is to believe by faith in Him who made it possible.*

Have a Good Opinion of God

Beloved, as we rejoice in knowing we have peace with God, I want you to see that there is no true peace without the blood of our Lord Jesus. The Lord hid a shadow of this truth in the Old Testament. On the night of the Passover when God was preparing to deliver the children of Israel out of Egypt, He told them to put the blood of a lamb on their doorposts, for the angel of death was going to pass through the land of Egypt to strike all the firstborn. And God said, "When I **see the blood**, I will pass over you" (Ex. 12:13, boldface mine).

Imagine if one of the Israelites had decided not to apply the blood to his doorposts—he would be weeping for his first-born in the morning even though God *had* prepared a way out. On the other hand, imagine if another one of the Israelites had applied the blood to his doorposts but did not fully trust that the angel of death would pass over his household and spent the night full of fear and trembling. When the morning came, nothing would have happened to his firstborn *because of the blood*—and he would have spent the night in needless apprehension and anxiety.

That is a picture of many Christians today. Many believers are not enjoying and *possessing* their peace with God even though they *already have* peace with God. The blood is on their door-posts, but they are still fearful because they cannot believe that God is truly that good. We have to have a good opinion of God, because He is kinder than you can ever dream of and He's more loving than you can imagine! Because of all the mixed teachings that people hear about God, many believers can't believe God is really *for* them. They seem to expect the worst to happen in any situation they are in.

But faith can be defined as having a good opinion of God. The Bible says that Abraham was "strong in faith, giving glory to God" (Rom. 4:20 KJV). The Greek word for "glory" here is *doxa* and one of its meanings is "good opinion."[2] Do you see? Abraham could be strong in faith because he had a good opinion of God and was fully convinced that what God had promised, He was also able to perform. Let's have greater faith in God's promises to heal, protect, and provide for us than in the negative reports about the economy, terrorism, and our health!

> *Let's have greater faith in God's promises to protect and provide for us than in negative reports.*

No True Peace without the Blood

When we look at how the Lord delivered His people from Egypt, we see that all the riches, nobility, and accolades of the Egyptian masters could not save them from the angel of death. Neither could any amount of sincere hope or charitable works. Only *the blood* could save. But for the blood to be applied, the lamb had to die.

You see, God is love, but He also has inflexible righteousness and unbending holiness. Sin must be punished, and the Bible tells us that the wages of sin is death (see Rom. 6:23). That's why our Lord Jesus had to lay down His life on the cross. He did no sin, in Him was no sin, and He knew no sin. But He was punished because He was carrying *our* sins. For God so loved you and me, He sent His only begotten Son to be the Lamb who takes away our sins and to bear every punishment and every judgment that *we* deserved. At the cross, God's love blended with God's justice. Righteousness and mercy met. Mercy and truth kissed. At the cross, the divine exchange took place—Jesus was punished so that we could go free. He was cursed so that we could be blessed. He was rejected so that we would be accepted!

> At the cross, the divine exchange took place—Jesus was punished and cursed so that we can be blessed.

He Paid the Price for Our Peace of Mind

Do you know what else our Savior did for us? As the King of kings and the Lord of lords, He deserved a royal diadem, a crown of jewels and precious stones. Instead, after He had been severely scourged, a garrison of Roman soldiers stripped Him and put a scarlet robe on Him. They twisted a crown of thorns and rammed it on His head. They put a staff in His right hand like it was a scepter and kneeled before Him to ridicule Him, saying, "Hail, king of the Jews!" Then they spat on Him and took the staff and struck Him repeatedly on the head (see Matt. 27:27–31 niv), each blow driving the thorns deeper into His head and drawing blood afresh.

Why?

Why did our Lord allow Himself to go through all that?

Thorns represent the curse. Our Lord Jesus took our curse of depression. He took our curse of stress and anxiety. He took our filthy imaginations. He took our dark and evil thoughts. He took it all and He paid it all so that He could crown us with His peace that surpasses understanding.

Beloved, you don't have to live under that cloud of despair anymore. You don't have to allow those thoughts of hatred toward yourself to define you. You don't have to live in perpetual shame and condemnation. He did not deserve any of the spit, the nakedness, the shame, the crown of thorns—we did. But He took it all for us. He paid the price for our peace of mind. Right now, receive that peace in Jesus' name. *It has been paid for.*

Fix Your Mind on Jesus

Let me share this powerful passage with you:

> *You will keep* him *in perfect peace,* whose *mind* is *stayed* on You, *because he trusts in You. Trust in the* LORD *forever, for in* YAH, *the* LORD, *is everlasting strength.*
>
> —Isaiah 26:3–4

When we keep our minds *stayed* and fixed on our Lord Jesus, the Word of God tells us that He will keep us in perfect peace. Today, let's keep our minds fixed on His sacrifice. Let's keep our minds stayed on the price that He paid. Let's keep our minds focused on His finished work. We can never do enough to merit any of His blessings. But praise be to God, He has done it all—we can rest. We can let go. We can depend wholly on our Savior!

Peace with God Gives You Access to His Grace

When we possess our peace with God, we also have access by faith into His grace (see Rom. 5:2), His wonderful, unearned, undeserved favor, and His gift of no condemnation. Grace and peace go together. The Bible also says this in the book of Job:

> *Now acquaint yourself with Him, and be at peace; thereby good will come to you.*
>
> *—Job 22:21*

You don't even have to look for good when you are at peace—good will come to you! As a believer, you don't have to be restless and worried all the time. You can be at peace and at rest—you can live the let-go life—because you know that God is for you and not against you! The Bible also tells us that when we "seek peace and pursue it," we will "love life and see good days" (1 Pet. 3:10–11)! What does it mean to "pursue peace"? Pursuing God's peace is simply pursuing our Lord Jesus, the Prince of Peace. He is the Lord of peace and He will "give you peace always in every way" (2 Thes. 3:16). Praise the Lord!

13.
STAND STILL

The twelfth chapter of Exodus tells the story of how, after more than four hundred years in Egypt, the children of Israel were finally delivered on the night of the Passover. Pharaoh had stubbornly refused to free God's people from slavery despite repeated warnings. But in the tenth and final plague, every firstborn son in the land of Egypt was struck dead, and on that very same night, Pharaoh ordered Moses to leave Egypt with the Israelites.

But when word came back to Pharaoh that all the Israelites had really left Egypt, his heart was hardened and he regretted releasing the Israelites from slavery. He mobilized all his chariots, horsemen, and troops, and charged after the fleeing Israelites, bent on showing them who their masters were.

Can you imagine how the children of Israel must have felt? They had barely tasted freedom and now their former slave masters were hunting them down with the full force of Pharaoh's army. They probably remembered the vicious whippings and brutal punishments they had suffered for years as they saw the war chariots and troops thundering nearer and nearer, closing in for the kill. Where they were at this point in their journey, there was no escape. Behind them, the ruthless army was poised to attack, and stretched out in front of them like a watery grave was the Red Sea. It looked like they were doomed.

Terrified, they cried out to the Lord and complained to Moses, "Because *there were* no graves in Egypt, have you taken us away to die in the wilderness? Why have you so dealt with us, to bring us up out of Egypt? *Is* this not the word that we told you in Egypt, saying, 'Let us alone that we may serve the Egyptians'? For *it would have been* better for us to serve the Egyptians than that we should die in the wilderness" (Ex. 14:11–12).

When he was confronted by enemy troops intent on wreaking vengeance on the Israelites, you would have expected Moses to lead the people in taking up whatever weapons they had so that they could defend their families. Instead, look what happened:

> *And Moses said to the people,* **"Do not be afraid. Stand still, and see the salvation of the Lord,** *which He will accomplish for you today. For the Egyptians whom you see today, you shall see again no more forever.* **The Lord will fight for you, and you shall hold your peace."**
> —*Exodus 14:13–14 (boldface mine)*

The children of Israel stood still. And the pillar of cloud that had led them in the wilderness moved behind them and stood between them and the Egyptian army. As such, the enemies of Israel could not come near them at all that night. But God did not just hold back Israel's enemies. The foreboding sea that had blocked their path was rent in two as God opened up the Red Sea for His people.

What a sight that must have been to see the waters of the sea being divided and held back like walls on each side for the Israelites to walk "into the midst of the sea on dry *ground*" (Ex. 14:22). However, once the pillar of cloud lifted, Israel's enemies' resolve to go after the Israelites returned and they continued their ferocious pursuit. All of Pharaoh's horses, chariots, and horsemen went after the Israelites onto the dry path that had opened up in the Red Sea. Some of the Israelites could have looked back at the formidable army following close behind and despaired. But they did not need to, for God was firmly in control.

The Bible tells us how God put the Egyptian army in a state of confusion and made their chariots hard to drive. The Egyptians themselves recognized that the Lord was fighting for the Israelites (see Ex. 14:24–25). Finally, when every single one of the Israelites had crossed over to the other side of the sea, the same sea that had parted for them covered the great army of Egypt that followed them and destroyed it. Not even one of the enemies that the Israelites had been so fearful of just hours before survived.

Your God Fights for You

My friend, perhaps the Lord had rescued you from one situation but you now find yourself caught in another conundrum that makes your previous predicament look easy. Perhaps you are in a situation where it seems like you have been trapped and there is no way out. Maybe you made some bad choices and now you can't seem to extricate yourself from them. It could be that you are in a financial bind, and the options you have explored all seem to lead to dead ends. Or perhaps you have been pushed into a corner, and any decision you make in one area will likely have a detrimental effect on another area. If so, I want you to know that it is not over. God can *still* turn things around for you, just like He did for the children of Israel.

You don't have to be afraid of problems in your tomorrows because you have a God who goes before you to lead you and clear the way for you. You don't have to be afraid of attacks coming from behind because the God of Israel is also your rear guard (see Isa. 52:12). Even if it looks like there are enemies and challenges coming at you from every direction, you do not have to fear. The Lord can prepare a table before you *in the presence* of your enemies (see Ps. 23:5). The Red Sea did not disappear, just as your problems will not simply vanish. But even if you are faced with a sea of problems, the Lord can split it apart for you. Your part is to stand still and see the salvation of the Lord!

You don't have to be afraid of problems in your tomorrows because you have a God who goes before you to lead you and clear the way for you.

The Hebrew word for salvation is *Yeshua.* So in Exodus 14:13, the Bible is saying *stand still and see Jesus!* Fix your eyes on Him and not on your challenges. Let your mind be stayed on His goodness and faithfulness. Get hold of sermons that unveil Jesus. Listen to them day and night, for just by beholding Jesus, the waters will part before you. Just by beholding Jesus, you will come out of your Egypt.

The people of the world cry out, "Don't just stand there, do something!" When *they* stand still, nothing happens. But you are not of the world. You are a believer in our Lord Jesus, who has laid down His life for you. When you stand still *in Him,* putting your trust in Him, He fights your battles for you! Even when there seems to be no way to a breakthrough in your business, your finances, your health, your marriage, or your parenting, let not your heart be troubled.

The children of Israel went *into the midst of the sea* on dry ground. I am believing with you for dry ground to open up for you in the midst of whatever seemingly impossible situation you might be in. I am believing with you for the Lord Himself to fight for you. I am believing with you for that army of problems that you think will destroy you to be completely and irrevocably obliterated in the mighty name of our Lord Jesus!

This is what the let-go life is about. Standing still and allowing Him to fight your battles. It's about letting go and allowing His abundant supply to flow. Our worrying cannot add even one cubit to our stature, but our *trusting* in Him can result in miracles. I'm not saying you should curl up in bed all day and do nothing. In the midst of your trial, stand still *inwardly* and look to the Lord to fight for you.

> *Worrying cannot add even one cubit to our stature, but trusting in Him can result in miracles.*

I know this goes against everything that is in our human nature, but that's precisely why I am writing this book—the let-go life goes against the grain of human nature! Our human nature is to respond, fight back, argue, and be in a state of stress, turmoil, and unrest. But God's ways are better. His ways are ways of *shalom*-peace and quietness and I pray that you will begin to walk in that *shalom* today!

God's Blessings Are Practical

The Lord is so practical in the way He provides for us. Look at how He provided for the children of Israel in the midst of the barren wilderness. When they were hungry, He sent so much quail that they covered the camp. He also sent manna from heaven to feed them (see Ex. 16:13–15). Another time, when they were thirsty, He told Moses to strike a rock with his rod, and water came out of it for the people to drink (see Ex. 17:6).

God didn't send gold or precious stones when the Israelites hungered and thirsted. He met them at their point of need, so you can trust Him today to provide practically for your needs. If you are trusting Him for better clientele or more business leads, He can supernaturally cause doors of opportunity to open for you. If a particular revenue stream has dried up, or perhaps you need creativity and ideas to flow for that upcoming project or business campaign, the Lord can cause what you need to gush forth from unexpected sources. Put your trust in Him and He will provide exceedingly abundantly above all that you ask or think (see Eph. 3:20)!

> Put your trust in Him and He will provide exceedingly abundantly above all that you ask or think.

Trust in the Lord, Not in Your Efforts

But there's another truth I want to highlight to you here. Just imagine if the Israelites had tried to hunt for their own food. How many quails do you think they would have caught out there in the desert? In the same way, how much water do you think Moses could have brought forth if he had gone around trying to get water out of rocks all day?

What I want you to see is this: While it is important that we do our best and be excellent in all that we set our hands to, our trust and dependence have to be on the Lord, and not on our hard work and efforts. Our blessings are not dependent on the economy, on the state of the property market, or on the stock market. God can bless us in the midst of our wilderness and He can bless us in the presence of our enemies. But if our dependence is on ourselves and not on Him, we can hit or squeeze rocks all we want and the only thing that will flow out is our own blood!

> *While it is important to do our best and be excellent in all that we do, our trust has to be in the Lord.*

Thou Shalt Not Sweat

Let me show you something interesting about God's instructions to His priests in the Old Testament:

> *And it shall be, whenever they enter the gates of the inner court, that they shall put on linen garments; no wool shall come upon them while they minister within the gates of the inner court or within the house. They shall have linen turbans on their heads and linen trousers on their bodies; they shall not clothe themselves with* anything that causes *sweat.*
> —Ezekiel 44:17–18

The priests were not allowed to gird themselves with *anything that causes sweat.* Right now, let me declare to you, thou shall not sweat! If there is an area in your life where you don't see the manifestation of God's promises, can I submit to you that it's because you are "sweating it" and worrying in that area? God wants His priests to wear *linen* turbans because He does not want our heads to sweat with worries and cares. Stop worrying. He feeds even the birds of the air and He clothes the lilies of the field. He will take care of you. You can have rest in your mind and stop allowing anxiety to dictate how you live your life. Stop holding on to all your cares so tightly and let them go into the loving hands of your Savior!

Every time the enemy comes to you and demands, "What are you going to do about it?" do you know how you should respond? When the accuser of the brethren demands to know what you are going to do about that situation in church, or that conflict at work, or your child's behavioral problems, say this: "I'm not going to worry about this! My Lord Jesus is going to handle it." Amen?

Once again, let me clarify that I'm talking about an *inward* rest. I preach multiple services every week. Sometimes when I speak at conferences, I have to preach several sessions at different locations on the same day. If I placed the demand on myself, I would be completely depleted in no time. But I have learned to rest and to allow the Teacher to take over. Sometimes, as I drive to church before I'm about to preach, I say to the Lord, "Lord Jesus, You are my guest speaker today. I can't wait to hear what *You* have to say to the people!" Honestly (and please know that I am not saying this with pride), there are times when I feel like taking notes on what I'm preaching because I know that there's no way I could have come up with those revelations—He had taken over as I rested! That makes ministry so fun—it's not dependent on me. It's all on Jesus!

Redeemed from Sweat

Do you know what the very first area our Lord Jesus redeemed us from is? Before He redeemed us from sin at the cross, before

He went to the scourging post and bore our diseases, before He was even arrested, He first shed His blood for us in the garden of Gethsemane.

The Gospel of Luke records what happened: "And being in agony, He prayed more earnestly. Then His sweat became like great drops of blood falling down to the ground" (Luke 22:44). Doctors tell us that it is possible for the capillary blood vessels that feed the sweat glands to rupture when one is under conditions of extreme physical or emotional stress, causing them to exude blood. This condition is known as *hematohidrosis*.[1]

I believe that the first place our Lord Jesus shed blood from was the brow of His head. Now, why is this significant? Because what the first Adam brought about in the first garden had to be finished off in another garden by the last Adam. When Adam fell, God said to him, "By the sweat of your brow you will eat your food" (Gen. 3:19 NIV). So Jesus sweating great drops of blood from His brow means that we are redeemed from stress in our minds! Hallelujah! We are redeemed from stress, anxiety, and from every oppressive thought and crippling lie that torments our minds!

In Hebrew, the word for *sweat* is *ze'ah*. The root word of *ze'ah* is *zuwa'*, meaning "to tremble, quiver, quake, be in terror," or "to agitate (as with fear)," or "vex."[2] In other words, sweat involves agitation and being vexed. Even if you are not physically trembling, you could be quaking in your mind. You could be lying awake at night, vexed, and worried about the future and wondering, *What if?* This is sweat in your thinking and this is the *first area* Jesus has redeemed us from through His blood-mingled sweat falling from His brow.

There is a redeeming quality in the blood of Christ. The moment the sweat of the Son of God mingled with His blood, He redeemed all of us from the curse of sweat. I'm not referring to physical sweat. I'm talking about laboring that is full of stress and trouble but with no results. I'm talking about toiling and struggling. We can work but be relaxed! Let the world sweat it out. Let the world join the rat race. You can labor without stress and enjoy your Savior. Don't sweat it!

> *We can work but be relaxed. We can labor without stress and enjoy our Savior.*

The Bible also says that His blood fell to the ground. We read in the book of Genesis that the ground in the garden of Eden was cursed (see Gen. 3:17). But when the blood that redeems fell to the ground in another garden (Gethsemane), the ground was redeemed from the curse for those who believe in Him. Therefore, the ground you step on is redeemed ground, blessed ground, grace ground!

A Word for Those Believing God for a Child

If you are believing God for a child, I want to share this with you: When the Lord visited Abraham and Sarah, He said to Abraham, "I will return to you about this time next year, and your wife, Sarah, will have a son!" (Gen. 18:10 NLT). Sarah was eavesdropping from the tent door and she laughed within herself, saying, "After I have grown old, **shall I have pleasure**, my lord being old also?" (Gen 18:12, boldface mine).

The Lord said that Sarah would have a baby. She should have said to herself, "Shall I have a baby at this age?" But she didn't say that. She said, "Shall I have pleasure?" You see, she wasn't worried about producing a baby anymore. She was more interested in the *process*. For years, Abraham and Sarah tried to have a baby, but there was no result. However, when Sarah was no longer focused on producing and was more interested in having pleasure with her husband, her breakthrough came.

A renowned gynecologist who attends my church in Singapore shared with me how many couples who are trying to conceive end up making the marriage act laborious and stressful. These couples monitor their "fertile periods" so closely that they put themselves under a lot of pressure. Something that was given by God to be precious, intimate, and beautiful becomes laborious "sweat," and often there are no results.

But many a time, when these couples stop being stressed about conceiving a child and forget about scrutinizing monthly cycles—for instance, when they go on a holiday and enjoy each other's companionship without the stress of producing a baby— they come back and discover that they have conceived!

Blessed with a Baby Boy

Allow me to share with you this precious praise report that Felicia from Canada sent to me:

After three years of marriage, my husband and I started believing God for a baby. In our fourth year, we found out that I was pregnant. However, I suffered a miscarriage and was devastated.

Friends around me were bearing children and the enemy would put negative thoughts in my mind: Will it ever be my turn? Just forget about having a child, it is not in my destiny. How could the God I worship do this to me? These thoughts would run a loop in my mind, and I would tear up.

One day, I read Pastor Prince's Daily Grace Inspiration for the day and learned this phrase: I cannot, but God can. It helped direct my worries, anxieties, and fears to the One who could do something about my situation.

Whenever negative thoughts came, I would say, "I cannot, oh Lord, only You can. Help me have children for Your glory." After that, the good Lord saw me through my next pregnancy and the successful delivery of a blessed baby boy.

I am grateful to God and for how the Daily Grace Inspiration for the day would inspire, encourage, and strengthen me whenever I go through a challenge!

Beloved, I know that it can be very discouraging if you have been trying for a baby for some time. Perhaps you have tried every method you know but your situation has still not changed. Felicia shared that she directed her worries, anxieties, and fears to the One who could do something about her situation. Can I encourage you to do what Felicia did? Can I encourage you to stand still and see the salvation of the Lord?

Instead of being stressed about your situation, meditate on how the precious blood of Christ has redeemed you from stress. Let go of your cares and anxieties to the Lord. The Lord loves you. You don't have to fight—you have a God who fights for you! Even if something devastating has happened to you in the past as it did for Felicia, do not let your fear hold you back from putting your trust in the Lord. Do not let your past cripple you from stepping into His promises for you today. The Lord says to you:

Do not remember the former things, nor consider the things of old. Behold, I will do a new thing, now it shall spring forth; shall you not know it? I will even make a road in the wilderness and rivers in the desert.

—Isaiah 43:18–19

Don't let your past cripple you from stepping into His promises for you today.

Whatever may have happened in the past, whatever hurts or disappointments you may have experienced, I pray that He will give you the grace to forget the former things because He is getting ready to do a *new* thing in your life.

Perhaps it is not a physical baby you have been believing for, but you have a dream that you are waiting to see happen—having your own car, a life partner, a start-up, a ministry that God has placed on your heart. Whatever you are trusting God for, stand still and keep your eyes on the Lord Jesus. And don't wait till you see the manifestation of your promise to rejoice. "Sing, O barren!" the Bible declares (Isa. 54:1). Rest and rejoice in His finished work, even when the bills are still staring you in the face, even when you still see that negative report. Break forth into singing and praising God even when you have not seen your desired results yet! Then get ready for your miracle. God is about to make roadways in the wilderness and bring forth rivers in the desert for you. He will make a way where there seems to be no way!

BECOMING A PERSON OF REST

If you are involved in building anything, whether it's the local church, a business, or your own family, I believe this chapter will bless you. It will give you fresh insights into the Lord's heart for you as you build and show you from the Word what the Lord prioritizes for His people. If you have been pushing yourself to the limit, not allowing yourself any respite because of the great work that you see ahead of you, the Lord has a word for you in this chapter.

My friend, He loves you so much. He doesn't want to see you running yourself ragged, thinking that the only way for you to succeed is to work harder and put in more hours. He has a higher way and He has paid the price for you to walk in it. As you read on, I pray that the truths here will refresh you and set you up to build your ministry, your career, or your personal life in His strength and in the power of His might (see Eph. 6:10).

Most Important Factor in Building God's House

Do you know what the most important quality in building God's house is? It is not hard work, tenacity, or resourcefulness, even though these may all be important qualities. To answer the question, let me show you a powerful truth that we can learn from the life of King David.

David was a man after God's heart (see Acts 13:22), but God did not choose David to build Him a temple because David was *a man of war*. Instead, God told David that he would have a son who should be called Solomon. Solomon would be *a man of rest*, and he would build God's temple. See how David explains this to Solomon:

> *My son, as for me, it was in my mind to build a house to the name of the LORD my God; but the word of the LORD came to me, saying, "You have shed much blood and have made great wars; you shall not build a house for My name, because you have shed much blood on the earth in My sight. Behold, a son shall be born to you, who shall be **a man of rest**; and I will give him rest from all his enemies all around. His name shall be Solomon, for I will give peace and quietness to Israel in his days."*
>
> *—1 Chronicles 22:7–9 (boldface mine)*

Because David had "shed much blood" and "made great wars," God did not appoint David to build Him a house. Instead, He wanted someone who was *a man of rest* to build His house. God told David He wanted someone whose life was marked by peace and quietness. And so He chose David's son, Solomon, whose name in Hebrew, *Shelomoh*, means "peace."[1]

So, what is the number one quality to successfully building God's house?

Rest.

This principle applies whether you are involved in building God's house or you are building something else. People of war—people who are always fighting and striving—will struggle to build God's house. They will also struggle to build their own houses. Whether you are involved in building a business, negotiating contracts, entering a new partnership, or raising a family, remember this: God has called you to be a person of rest.

The Lord Builds the House and Guards the City

Take a look at this powerful portion of Scripture below:

> *Unless the* LORD *builds the house, they labor in vain who build it; unless the* LORD *guards the city, the watchman stays awake in vain.* It is *vain for you to rise up early, to sit up late, to eat the bread of sorrows;* for so *He gives His beloved sleep.*
> —Psalm 127:1–2

God does not want you to waste your time wringing your hands being worried, eating the bread of adversity and sorrows. Don't stay up past midnight every day or keep pushing yourself to work long hours without any rest. Stop being anxious and stressed out about your family, troubled about your job, or fretting over the tasks that you have ahead of you. Stay in His rest and win the battle over insomnia. The Bible tells us that He gives His beloved sleep. And not only does He give you sleep, but He also gives to you what you need *while* you are sleeping.

God gave Solomon wisdom as he slept. Don't be so busy being anxious and stressed and trying to accomplish more by giving up your sleep at night. Solomon's other name was "Jedidiah" (see 2 Sam. 12:25), which means "beloved of Jehovah (Yahweh)."[2] My friend, you are God's beloved and He wants to give you sleep. Don't stay up and stay stressed out—let Him who neither slumbers nor sleeps take over (see Ps. 121:4). Go to sleep when it is time for bed because that is faith in action. You can rest because *the Lord* is building the house and the Lord is guarding the city. The Lord is building your business, your ministry, your career, your family, and your health! If you are struggling today with a sleeping disorder that is induced by stress, I pray that from tonight you will experience sweet and uninterrupted sleep as you rest in His love for you.

> Don't stay up and stay stressed out—let Him who neither slumbers nor sleeps take over.

Unless the Lord Builds, We Labor in Vain

Think of it this way: If the Lord isn't building, then we would be laboring in vain anyway. That's the attitude of faith I've held toward my church and ministry, as well as the other areas of my life. I have made a decision to remain in His rest and not miss one night of sleep worrying about my life because God is the one building the ministry and guarding my family, and you know what? He wants to build and guard every area of *your* life too.

Whatever we are involved in, we can apply this principle of being a person of rest and holding with a loose hand instead of choking the Lord's supply by holding on with our own strength. The world's way is to hold on tightly to whatever position, advantage, or title they can grab. But when you know that every good thing in your life comes not from man but from God (see James 1:17), you don't have to be worried about losing out. Whether you are negotiating a contract, working out the terms of a new partnership, or raising your children, the same principle applies. Let go and have a good opinion of God. Trust that He is the God who goes before you and is your rear guard. If something does not work out—a relationship, a job opportunity, the purchase of a house you had been eyeing—then let's believe that the Lord is setting you up for something greater!

> *If something does not work out, believe that the Lord is setting you up for something greater!*

Holding Things with a Loose Hand

In the early 2000s, it became clear that our church needed a bigger venue to accommodate our growing congregation. An exciting opportunity to bid for the right to build a large facility from the ground up in an ideal location for our church arose in my city, but it would have literally taken a miracle for us to be awarded the tender in land-scarce Singapore.

Throughout the whole process, those involved in our building committee were diligent to stay in the Lord's peace and rest, and I encouraged them to hold all negotiations with a loose hand. Praise the Lord, everything eventually fell into place despite hiccups and challenges along the way, and our miracle happened. Today, we hold weekly services in what is now known as the Star Performing Arts Centre,[3] an award-winning arts and cultural venue. It cost us about $400 million U.S. to build, but by the amazing supply and grace of God this building project is already fully paid for.[4] Hallelujah! The Lord truly builds the house!

Sit Still—the Man Will Not Rest Until This Matter Is Settled

How could we hold such a massive project with loose hands? I believe the Lord first prepared us by teaching us to trust Him in other areas and smaller undertakings. In the early years of New Creation Church, we were like the children of Israel, wandering in the wilderness. We started in the cramped apartment of one of our members and moved from one meeting venue to another as the church grew. One of the venues that we used was right next to a massage parlor, and sometimes our ushers would end up mistakenly greeting people heading next door! We were desperate for a permanent location to call our own, as we could not afford to be at a loss as to where our next service would be held.

There was such a strong concern in my heart, and I remember asking the Lord, "Lord, what shall I do?" At that time, the Lord gave me a beautiful verse from the book of Ruth. With this verse, I fought all the battles of anxieties, worries, and cares that I had about securing a meeting venue and learned to rest in Him. And all glory to God, in just a short time after I received this verse, we were told that we had been awarded the lease for a prime space in which we built our first permanent home as a church—the Rock Auditorium. The mall that the space was in had originally planned to build an indoor amusement park, so they had built an elevated ceiling, not knowing that they were preparing the perfect space for us to worship the Lord in. Hallelujah!

This was the verse from the book of Ruth that put an end to all my worries and cares:

> *Sit still, my daughter, until you know how the matter will turn out; for the man will not rest until he has concluded the matter this day.*
>
> —*Ruth 3:18*

The Lord was literally telling me that if I would rest, He would not until He had concluded the matter for me.

Just to give you some background, Naomi was talking to Ruth about Boaz, the wealthy man who owned the fields of Bethlehem. Because Naomi's family had moved away from Bethlehem for many years, her right to the land belonging to her husband, Elimelech, had been forfeited. Boaz was a kinsman redeemer for Naomi's family. This means that he was a relative who *could* redeem their forfeited land, restore their full community rights, and redeem them from slavery if they had been sold into slavery.[5] But in accordance with Jewish laws and customs during that time, Boaz would also have to marry Ruth in order to fulfill his duties as a kinsman redeemer. Doing so could jeopardize his own inheritance (see Ruth 4:6), because Ruth was from Moab, a nation whose people were disqualified from entering the assembly of the Lord (see Deut. 23:3).

The night before, Ruth had gone to Boaz at Naomi's advice and had said to Boaz, "Take your maidservant under your wing, for you are a close relative" (Ruth 3:9). But Ruth was not sure if Boaz would redeem her. And that's when Naomi told Ruth to *sit still*, because Naomi knew that Boaz had fallen in love with Ruth and he *would not rest* until he had concluded the matter to his satisfaction. And we know how the story ends. Boaz marries Ruth and they became the great-grandparents of King David and became a part of the natural ancestry of our Lord Jesus. I have taught a whole series on this beautiful story called *The Love Story of Ruth*.[6]

Boaz is a picture of our Lord Jesus, who came as a man so that He could be our kinsman Redeemer (see Eph. 1:7). Beloved, whatever you are going through today, you can put your trust in your Redeemer. You can sit still because He will not rest until He has redeemed you from that trouble.

God told the children of Israel, "I will redeem you with an outstretched arm" (Ex. 6:6), and that is literally how our Lord Jesus redeemed us, with His arms stretched out on the cross to redeem us from the slave market of sin, poverty, and curses. Praise His name!

Can I share with you one more truth from the story of Ruth? After they had returned to Bethlehem, Naomi said to Ruth, "Shall I not seek **rest** for thee, that it **may be well with thee**?" (Ruth 3:1 KJV, boldface mine). I want you to really catch this important insight: As we stay in His rest, the Lord will cause all things to go well with us!

> *As we stay in His rest, the Lord will cause all things to go well with us.*

Word for Those Building the House of God

I hope you don't mind if I take some time to address church builders, pastors, leaders, and volunteers who are building a local church or serving in a ministry. I wasn't planning on writing specifically to church and ministry builders, but I believe that there is someone reading this now who needs to hear this word. As the senior pastor of a local church, I know that at times, the demands can be extremely overwhelming.

If you feel like you are running on empty today, the Lord says to you, "Let go of your cares and let Me fill you up! Stand still and let Me be your rest and your peace." When your own strength, your own wisdom, and your own hand of diligence have failed, the Lord says to you, "Rest in Me and I will command My blessings upon you in your ministry, in your health, in your marriage, in your parenting, and in your relationships. Don't lean on your own wisdom and your own strength. You want to build My house. But I declare to you that I will establish a house for you!" (see 2 Sam. 7:11 NIV).

When David told the prophet Nathan of his desire to build God a house, God was pleased with David's heart for Him. And God told Nathan to tell David, "You want to build Me a house? I will build *you* a house." My friend, the Lord sees your desire to build Him a house. But you know what? He wants to build *your* house. The Lord delights in blessing you. He delights in raining down His grace and showing you His goodness. Why? Because He loves you.

> *The Lord delights in blessing you because He loves you.*

When You Rest, He Works

I know it's not easy to stay at rest. The enemy does not want you to be at rest, and he is battling to take control of your mind. Sometimes, when I simply want to do nothing but enjoy my family, I hear accusatory voices saying things like, "How can you rest? There are so many things waiting to be done." "Do you know how many people are awaiting your counsel?" "Do you know how many people are waiting to hear from you?" It's almost as if the taskmasters converge on me with their whips the moment I try to rest. Have you ever been there? Have you ever felt guilty for daring to take even one day of rest because there is work to be done and appointments to be kept? No wonder Hebrews 4:11 (KJV) tells us to *labor to enter the rest!*

We saw in an earlier chapter how no one was more active and accomplished more in a day than our Lord Jesus, and yet no one was more at rest and filled with peace than Him—He could speak to the raging storm and still it. Our Lord Jesus could accomplish so much because He rested in His Father. Throughout the gospels, we see how He often withdrew from the crowds to pray (see Mark 6:46; Luke 5:16, 11:1) and to be with His Father. The Bible even records how He would go up to the mountains and spend a whole night in prayer (see Luke 6:12) and how it was His habit to go to the Mount of Olives to pray (see Luke 22:39–41).

This same Lord Jesus wants you to cast all your cares on Him, for He cares for you (see 1 Pet. 5:7). Kneel before Him and put all your troubles in His hands—His hands are bigger. The more you rest in Him, the more He works. Stop striving for the "good life" and stop struggling in the rat race. Work hard, of course, but inwardly, don't be a man of war. Focus only on one labor—entering the rest! Come to a place of quietness and of knowing that when you sit still, the Man will not rest until He has concluded the matter!

I've found in my own life that when I rest, He shows me from among *all* the things that I have to do, that one appointment to keep, that one text to respond to, or that one thing I need to focus on that will bring success to the church, the individual involved, or to my family. I pray right now that the Lord will rest and refresh you in the midst of all that you need to do. If you need greater wisdom, let's learn from Solomon. Solomon was a man of rest and peace, and he abounded with the wisdom of God. We cannot flow in God's supply of wisdom unless we rest in Him. As you put your trust in Him, may the Lord cause you to be divinely sharp and accurate in all that you need to accomplish, and bless all that you set your hands to!

> We cannot flow in God's supply of wisdom unless we rest in Him.

Born to Preach Rest

Pastor Prince, why do you keep talking about rest?

My friend, I keep preaching and writing about rest because I believe I was born to preach about rest. For those of you who study Scripture numerics, you would know that 5 is the number of grace. The fifth time Ruth's name is mentioned in the book of Ruth, we find her saying to Naomi, "Let me now go to the field, and glean

ears of corn after *him* in whose sight I shall find grace" (Ruth 2:2
KJV). The fifth time Noah's name is mentioned in the Bible, we find
it saying, "Noah found grace in the eyes of the LORD" (Gen. 6:8).

Now, 5 multiplied by 3 is 15. The number 15 is the number
of rest. The Jews celebrate several feasts and holidays each year
according to the Jewish calendar. They celebrate Purim on the
fourteenth and fifteenth days of the twelfth month of Adar.[7]
Purim is a Jewish holiday that commemorates the saving of the
Jewish people from Haman, whose evil plot to exterminate them
was thwarted. The fourteenth and fifteenth days are to be celebrated "as the days on which the Jews had rest from their enemies" (Esther 9:22).

The Jews also celebrate the Feast of Passover, which begins
with a day of *rest* on the fifteenth day of the first month of Nisan,[8]
while the Feast of Tabernacles begins with a day of *rest* on the fifteenth day of the seventh month of Tishri.[9] The Bible says that
both these days are rest days in which no laborious work is to be
done (see Lev. 23:7, 39 AMP).

I believe it is by no coincidence that Israel came back as a
nation against impossible odds and celebrated its first day as
a nation on May 15, 1948, following its declaration of independence. Fifteen years from then, a child was born on May 15, 1963.
That child was born to preach rest—and you probably know by
now that this child I am referring to is me!

I believe I was born to preach about rest so that *you* might find
rest in your life. I was called to build Him a house together with
other men and women of rest. God told me to never stop preaching rest until Jubilee explodes in your life and His commanded
blessing descends upon every area of your life. Rest is built on
rest, is built on rest, is built on rest. And that's why I'm writing a
whole book on rest. That's why I'm preaching it and preaching it
until you step into your promised land of rest!

The Greatest Rest Was Accomplished at the Cross

I want to show you a powerful picture of the greatest rest that was accomplished for us. Our Lord said, "Foxes have holes and birds of the air *have* nests, but the Son of Man has nowhere to lay *His* head" (Matt. 8:20). By Him all things were created (see Col. 1:16), yet He had nowhere to lay His head.

Do you know that the greatest rest He came to give was the rest that He accomplished at the cross for all of us? And that was when He cried out after hanging for six long and agonizing hours on the cross, "It is finished!" (see John 19:30). What is finished? His work of qualifying us, the punishment of all our sins, delivering us from the power of darkness, and redeeming us from the curse of the law. It is all finished. He has done it all for us. And right after He said that, the Bible says He "bowed his head and dismissed his spirit" (John 19:30 TLB). The Greek word for "bowed" here is *klino*[10]—the same, seldom-used Greek word for "lay" when He said that the Son of Man has nowhere to "lay" (*klino*) His head (see Matt. 8:20). Our Lord Jesus finally found His rest in saving you, in finishing the work for you. He found His rest in qualifying you by His blood for every blessing of God. Today, you can rest. You don't have to earn healing, or blessings, or rest—you only have to receive them!

Christ Will Rest You

Are the taskmasters still in your head? Have you been working and working, and feeling guilty every time you try to rest? Have you been pushing yourself nonstop, thinking that you have not done enough to "deserve" rest?

If that describes you, I want to invite you to enter into His rest today. When you rest, your work will take on a higher quality. Your mind works best when you are at rest. And rest comes from our Lord Jesus. In fact, when He said, "Come unto me…and I will give you rest" (Matt. 11:28 KJV), the original Greek text for "I will give you rest" actually says, "I will rest you."[11] In other words, when you come to Jesus, He Himself will *rest* you. With all the things that you need to look into in the days ahead, I pray that you will follow the Lord and let Him lead you into becoming a person of rest in every situation in your life.

15.

HEAR YOUR WAY
TO VICTORY

I believe this is one of the most important chapters I have ever written because it contains a message that will keep giving to you. In the days to come, I believe the Lord will use this message to help you in your marriage, your parenting, your health, your business, and your finances. He is going to bring you freedom from bondage and depression. He is going to impart peace to you and give you rest from the challenges that distress you. He is going to help you and He is going to build you.

And yet, this message is so simple. If you are thinking, *Pastor Prince, I've read what you've said about letting go, about His peace, and about entering into His rest. I want all that for myself, but I don't know what to do!* then let me invite you to keep on reading. This is also going to be a very practical chapter filled with examples that will help you to live the let-go life, and I cannot wait for you to get started!

Why the Gospel Does Not Benefit Some

Do you know that it is possible to hear the gospel and yet not benefit from it? This means that it is possible to hear the good news and yet the good news is not useful to us and does not positively change us. It is possible to hear the good news about what our Lord Jesus has done for us on the cross and yet not walk in any of the blessings He paid for us to enjoy. I don't know about you, but I don't want to be numbered among those for whom the gospel makes no real difference in their lives! Let's see what the Word of God says:

> *Therefore, since a promise remains of entering His rest, let us fear lest any of you seem to have come short of it. For indeed the gospel was preached to us as well as to them; but the word which they heard did not profit them, not being mixed with faith in those who heard it. For we who have believed do enter that rest.*
> *—Hebrews 4:1–3*

This Scripture passage is referring to an entire generation of Israelites who heard the good news that God was bringing them into a land where they would drink from wells they did not dig, eat from vineyards they did not plant, and live in houses they did not build. They were on the brink of entering the land, and they had even seen the luscious fruit of the land that their spies had brought back (see Num. 13:23–26). But still, they failed to enter the promised land and this was the reason: "the word which they heard did not profit them, not being mixed with faith in those who heard *it.*"

This verse tells us that the word they heard was "not mixed with faith." My friend, everything that we receive from God is by faith. We were saved by grace through faith (see Eph. 2:8). We are healed by faith in the name of Jesus (see Acts 3:16). Our Lord Jesus Himself told many of those whom He had healed, "your faith has made you well" (see Mark 5:34, 10:52; Luke 17:19). In fact, the Bible tells us that without faith, it is impossible to please God (see Heb. 11:6).

How Faith Comes

Perhaps you are reading this and you are thinking to yourself, *What if I don't have faith?* Well, don't stay without faith or simply lament that you don't have faith. The Word of God tells us so clearly how faith comes: "faith *comes* by hearing, and hearing by the word of God" (Rom. 10:17). If you study the word "God" here, you will see that it is translated from the Greek word *Christos,*[1] meaning Christ. In other words, faith comes by hearing the word of *Christ.*

Faith doesn't come when we hear about the law. It doesn't come when we hear a list of dos and don'ts that we have to fulfill, or how we have fallen short of the law's perfect requirements. Faith comes when we talk about the person and work of our Lord Jesus. Faith comes when, despite knowing that we have failed, we hear that we can still receive the abundance of grace and gift of righteousness through Christ (see Rom. 5:17) and begin living the victorious life. Jesus is the author and finisher of our faith (see Heb. 12:2). Don't try to get faith by focusing on faith. Faith comes by *hearing and hearing*—hearing and hearing and hearing and hearing the word of Christ! God wants us to focus on hearing.

> *Faith comes by hearing and hearing the word of Christ! God wants us to focus on hearing.*

Now, how do we keep hearing the word of Christ? In the context of this verse, it's not talking about God speaking to us in our hearts. Just a few verses earlier, it says, "How then shall they call on Him in whom they have not believed? And how shall they believe in Him of whom they have not heard? And how shall they hear without a preacher?" (Rom. 10:14). Do you see that? The Bible makes it clear that faith comes by hearing a *preacher* who brings the word of Christ.

Look at 1 Corinthians 1:21 (KJV) with me. It says that "it pleased God by the foolishness of preaching to save them that believe." The words *to save* are translated from the Greek word *sozo*, which means to "save, heal, preserve, rescue."[2] The methodology seems so simple and foolish, doesn't it? And yet, the delivery system that God chose for us to receive His blessings and miracles is by the foolishness of preaching. A preacher simply preaches the gospel of grace and the result is this: People are saved. A preacher preaches Jesus, and faith is imparted as the people listen. A preacher preaches the power of the cross, and people are healed from their afflictions. They are set free from anxiety attacks and rescued from addictions that have bound them—as the Word goes forth!

No wonder people followed Jesus everywhere to hear Him. Luke 5:15 tells us that "great multitudes came together to **hear, and to be healed** by Him of their infirmities" (boldface mine). They came to hear, and then be healed. That is the blueprint of God. We hear teaching and preaching, and we are healed. The Bible tells us, "And Jesus went about all Galilee, teaching in their synagogues, preaching the gospel of the kingdom, and healing all kinds of sickness and all kinds of disease among the people" (Matt. 4:23). Beloved, it doesn't matter what your affliction is or what challenge torments you. They all have to bow before the name of Jesus because He is "far above all principality and power and might and dominion, and every name that is named"

(Eph. 1:21). As you keep hearing preaching about our Lord Jesus, get ready for your miracle to happen!

During biblical times, the people had to follow the preacher to hear God's Word. Great multitudes followed Jesus everywhere. But in these last days, I believe God can use all kinds of mobile devices to contain the incorruptible seed of His Word. We can bring a preacher of His Word along with us everywhere. Whether we are exercising, commuting, or eating, we can keep hearing and hearing the word of Christ preached!

The Importance of Hearing

But what if I don't have a habit of listening to sermons?

If you don't have a habit of listening to sermons, first, can I tell you that you have been robbed? The Lord has given us such a simple but powerful way of receiving His blessings. If we don't make use of it, we are allowing ourselves to be robbed!

But it's never too late to start. You can ask God for something that Solomon, the wisest man who ever lived, asked for. First Kings 3:9 tells us that Solomon asked God for an "understanding" heart. In the original Hebrew, it is actually a *shama* or hearing heart—a heart that listens.[3] Solomon did not ask for health or riches. Of all the things he could have asked for, he asked God for a hearing heart. And this pleased the Lord so much that He not only gave Solomon what he had asked for, but He also gave him what he had not asked for: "both riches and honor" (1 Kings 3:13). Likewise, when you ask God for a wise and hearing heart today, God will give you a wise and hearing heart and much more!

Our Lord Jesus Himself also emphasized the importance of

hearing. Over and over again, the Gospels record our Lord Jesus saying, "He who has ears to hear, let him hear!" (see Matt. 11:15, 13:9, 13:43; Mark 4:9; Luke 14:35). Earlier in this book, we also saw how Jesus had gone to the home of Martha and Mary, where Martha complained about her sister to Jesus. Jesus responded by saying, "Martha, Martha, you are worried and troubled about many things. But one thing is needed, and Mary has chosen that good part, which will not be taken away from her" (Luke 10:41–42). When we do the *"one thing"* that is needful, we will not be like Martha—worried and troubled about *many things*. But what exactly is the "one thing" that Mary chose? The Bible tells us that Mary "seated herself at the Lord's feet and was *continually* listening to His teaching" (Luke 10:39 AMP). What was Mary doing? She was *hearing and hearing* the Lord's teaching!

Faith comes by hearing and hearing (present continuous tense), not by having heard (past tense). This brings me back to Hebrews 4:2. Why did the children of Israel fail to enter the promised land? We saw how the word that they heard was not "mixed with faith." But I want to highlight something else that Hebrews 4:2 tells us. It says that "the word which they heard did not profit them." Notice that the word *heard* is in the past tense? It is not enough to have *heard*. We need to be hearing, and hearing, and hearing—present continuous tense.

If you are wondering why you are not *getting* (present continuous tense) healing, blessings, miracles, and deliverances, may I submit to you that you might not have been hearing and hearing (present continuous tense) the word of Christ? If you feel like you don't have the faith to believe for the breakthroughs that you desperately need, it's not too late, my friend. Start hearing sermons that are full of Jesus and I promise you faith will come!

Don't make the mistake of thinking that because you have

heard a few sermons about God's grace you know all about it. It is not enough to have *heard*. I have received so many testimonies from people who have received tremendous breakthroughs as they listened to the gospel of grace over and over again. Each time they hear a message, they get fresh revelations. As they hear, their faith is being built, as there is food for their faith.

Just as you cannot live on the memory of what you ate last week, and you have to keep eating, food for your faith comes by hearing and hearing. If a particular sermon spoke to you, get that message and listen to it again and again. The more you listen to that sermon, the more you meditate on it, the more you will get out of it. You will miss things when you listen to a sermon only once. I've had people tell me time and again that as they listened to a recording of a service that they had attended, they heard things that did not register in their minds when they first heard them in the service!

> If a particular sermon spoke to you, get that message and listen to it again and again.

Understanding How the Enemy Operates

Would you like to see how the enemy operates when it comes to the Word of God? In the parable of the sower, our Lord Jesus tells us what happens when we hear a message preached:

> *The sower sows the word....When they hear, Satan comes immediately and takes away the word that was sown in their hearts.*
>
> —Mark 4:14–15

Notice the word *immediately*. The moment a person hears the Word of God, Satan comes immediately to take away the Word that was sown. He does not want God's Word to stay in our hearts for even one day because he knows how powerful the seeds of God's Word are once they take root. As long as the Word does not take root, look what happens when trials come our way:

> *When tribulation or persecution arises for the word's sake, immediately they stumble.*
>
> —Mark 4:17

This is why the Bible tells us to "fight the good fight of faith" (1 Tim. 6:12)! This fight is not against Satan directly but is the fight to believe that God has given to us. We fight to walk by faith and not by sight! When we are in faith, the devil is defeated. Every temptation to snare us back into stress and worry is an attempt to knock us from our place of faith in Christ. Fear causes us to focus on all the problems we can see—in the news, in our lives, at our place of work. Faith helps us to focus on what God sees—beyond the bad news, the physical symptoms, and any giants in front of us. The Word of God tells us that "the things which are seen *are* temporary, but the things which are not seen *are* eternal" (2 Cor. 4:18). Can you see that negative financial report, that situation in your marriage, or that tumor in your body? Then I have good news for you: It is temporal!

> *Every temptation to snare us back into stress is an attempt to knock us from our place of faith in Christ.*

If you are under attack, fight back with "the sword of the Spirit, which is the word of God" (Eph. 6:17)! If you are battling anxiety or doctors have diagnosed you with a debilitating condition, it is not enough to have heard that "by His stripes we are healed" (Isa. 53:5). If you are going through a financial difficulty or your business is struggling to stay afloat, it is not enough to have heard that "the blessing of the LORD makes *one* rich, and He adds no sorrow with it" (Prov. 10:22). We need to keep hearing and hearing until His promises take root in our hearts. And when that happens, we shall "produce a harvest of thirty, sixty, or even a hundred times as much as had been planted" (Mark 4:20 NLT)!

How to Keep Hearing

It does not matter what your area of need may be. If your mind is weighed down by worries and cares, the best thing you can do is to saturate yourself with the Word of God. Keep on hearing and hearing. As you are heading off for lunch, while you are eating, or as you are waiting for someone, plug in your earphones and listen to Christ-filled sermons. Pop a sermon CD into your car and listen as you make your way to work. Record sermons on television and play them over and over again as you clean the house or prepare a meal for your family.

> *If your mind is weighed down by cares, the best thing you can do is to saturate yourself with the Word of God.*

Sometimes when I have trouble sleeping, I play sermons really softly throughout the night on my speakers, and that becomes my "sleeping pill." With modern technology, we really have no reason why we can't keep hearing and hearing the Word of God.

Recently, my heart was overwhelmed with a lot of cares. I had never been a fan of audiobooks, but I decided to give them a try. As I listened to my book *The Prayer of Protection* and heard praise report after praise report on God's protection, all my anxieties began to dissipate. Ever since that experience, I have become hooked on audiobooks that are full of the person of Jesus!

The other thing I really cherish is the mobile app[4] that my team developed to archive all the messages I have preached over almost two decades. To keep myself in the atmosphere of faith each day, I search for a message, plug in, and go for my evening walk. There is something powerful and anointed about the preached Word. When our Lord Jesus is preached and unveiled, faith, strength, and courage are imparted even if the sermon I am listening to has no direct application to the challenge that I might be faced with. If you are wondering why I listen to my own sermons, it's because many times, when I am preaching, the Teacher takes over and I am just His delivery boy. So when I listen to my own sermons, I hear words of life that are beyond human wisdom and receive for myself strength and nourishment from hearing Him preached.

It's the same when I listen to recordings of my dear minister friends from around the world. I love to listen to their preaching of Jesus because I walk away filled with hope, charged with audacious faith, and greatly strengthened by His love!

Whether we are pastors, businesspersons, lawyers, or homemakers, we need to be washed daily by the water of the Word. It is a fight to make time daily because all of us have demands and distractions pulling at us. But I have settled in my heart that *one thing* is needful, so I make sure I prioritize my time with Him. As we take time to wait on Him, just see what happens:

But those who wait on the LORD shall renew their strength;
they shall mount up with wings like eagles, they shall run
and not be weary, they shall walk and not faint.

—*Isaiah 40:31*

As you take time to listen to and wait on the Lord, may He renew your strength and cause you to run and not be weary, to walk and not faint!

God Works Miracles by the Hearing of Faith

Perhaps you are thinking to yourself, *How is it possible to receive a miracle just by listening?*

I want to answer your question by asking you another question from the Word of God:

Did you receive the Spirit by the works of the law, or by the
hearing of faith?... Therefore He who supplies the Spirit to
you and works miracles among you, does He do it by the
works of the law, or by the hearing of faith?

—*Galatians 3:2, 5*

If you study the words *supplies* and *works* in verse 5 in the original Greek text, you will see that they carry the present tense, which means the actions are continuously ongoing.[5] In other words, you can read the verse this way: "He who is *constantly supplying* you the Holy Spirit and *constantly working* miracles among you, does He do it by the works of the law, or by the hearing of faith?" Wow! What a thought! What a thought to wake up to each morning and know that God is *constantly supplying* us with the

Holy Spirit and *constantly working miracles* among us—not by the works of the law, but by the hearing of faith!

Don't underestimate hearing. It may seem simple, but God works miracles by the hearing of faith. Remember the vision of the golden pipes constantly supplying blessings to the believer that I shared with you earlier in this book? God is constantly supplying us with miracles. Our part is to let go, listen to His Word, and let His supply flow.

> God is constantly supplying us with miracles. Our part is to let go, listen to His Word, and let His supply flow.

Perhaps you are thinking, *Simply hearing can't help me. My situation is hopeless!* Well, let me tell you about a man in Lystra whose situation looked hopeless. He was "a cripple from his mother's womb." He might have even given up hope of ever being able to walk, since the Bible tells us that he was "without strength in his feet" and "had never walked" (Acts 14:8). But do you know what happened? Read it for yourself:

> This *man heard Paul speaking. Paul, observing him intently and seeing that he had faith to be healed, said with a loud voice, "Stand up straight on your feet!" And he leaped and walked.*
>
> —*Acts 14:9–10*

The apostles Paul and Barnabas were preaching *the gospel* in Lystra (see Acts 14:7), and the man *heard* Paul speaking. The word *heard* here is in the imperfect tense in the original Greek text. This means that the man was a "habitual hearer of Paul's

preaching" and "heard *repeatedly* the teaching of the Gospel."[6]
He kept on hearing. And hearing. And hearing. He kept on hearing as Paul preached the gospel. Then one day, as he was listening to Paul, Paul discerned that "he had faith to be healed" such
that when Paul said to him, "Stand up straight on your feet!" the
man immediately got up. In an instant, he received his miracle. In
fact, even though Paul told him to stand up, the man didn't only
stand—he leaped and walked!

We all want to be at Acts 14:10, at the place where our miracle
happens. We all want to be at the place where the bodily condition is no more, the tumor is gone, the debt is paid. But let's take
a step back. How did the man have the faith to be healed? By now
you know that "faith *comes* from hearing, and hearing by the
word of Christ" (Rom. 10:17 NASB). We don't know how he did it.
He didn't have MP3 or CD players like we do today. Maybe Paul
stood near him preaching the same sermon over and over again,
and as he sat there he just kept hearing until the faith to be healed
was imparted. Or maybe he got his friends to carry him to wher-
ever Paul was preaching in Lystra so he could keep hearing. All we
know is, he kept on hearing. If you have not received your breakthrough yet, just keep on hearing until your heart is full of faith!

Would you like to know what this man heard? We know
that he heard Paul preach the gospel, but Acts 14:3 gives us more
insight:

> *Therefore they stayed there a long time, speaking boldly in
> the Lord, who was bearing witness to the word of His grace,
> granting signs and wonders to be done by their hands.*

Paul and Barnabas were preaching "the word of His grace,"
and God was bearing witness to what they preached, granting

signs and wonders to be done by their hands! As you keep on hearing, make sure you are hearing the word of His grace. And as you keep on hearing like that crippled man at Lystra, get ready to receive your miracle!

Make sure you are hearing the word of His grace.

Perhaps you are in a situation that looks impossible. Perhaps you have lived with a physical condition in your body for so long you have given up hope of ever being healed. Or maybe you are not suffering a physical condition, but you have always been extremely shy and crippled in your communication. Maybe you have been emotionally and mentally crippled by an oppressive depression that you have lived with for so long you have no more strength to fight it. Whatever your circumstances, there is a miracle for you with your name on it. And it'll come to you as you keep on hearing the word of Christ!

Delivered from Cancer

Leah from Georgia, United States, wrote to share with me what the Lord did for her:

> *Pastor Prince, Jesus has used your ministry to bless me. I have been watching you on television for about six years and became a partner three years ago. Through your daily broadcast on TV and your sermon CDs, the Word of God became alive to me. I embraced the gospel of grace and felt in my heart that it was pure truth. I grew in grace and was able*

to face the greatest challenge of my life when I was diagnosed with uterine cancer.

I would listen to your CDs on the way to and from the doctor, and in my house—morning, noon, and night. This helped me to understand the Bible more and more, and the Word of God became a living Word to me. I came to understand the full meaning of the finished work of Jesus on the cross. The way you explained the truth of the gospel reached my heart and I know I could trust what you were teaching because every word was confirmed when I read the Bible.

I also read your book Health and Wholeness through the Holy Communion. *I learned that I am a royal priest and did not have to be in a church service to partake of the Holy Communion. So I started partaking of the Communion daily and my love for my Father God grew and grew.*

I had to receive chemotherapy and radiation but I saw that as what the Lord wanted to use to bring about His healing in the physical realm. During those treatments, I was kept by the Word of God and the Holy Spirit comforted me. Today, by Jesus' stripes, I have been completely delivered from cancer. But I still continue to partake of the Holy Communion at least twice weekly, as I feel in my heart that I need to do this as a way of life.

Pastor Prince, I believe God has raised you up for such a time as this to build His church. You preach the pure gospel not a mixture. Your teaching about Daddy God went deep into my heart. I now know the love of God that surpasses knowledge.

Leah didn't just hear the preached Word once. Every day, she listened to the word of His grace "morning, noon, and night." I pray that you too will cultivate the habit of listening to messages that are full of Jesus and hear your way to faith and victory.

16.
THE ONE THING THAT BRINGS SUCCESS IN EVERY AREA

Do you know what is one thing you can do that will bring success in every area of your life? Meditating on the Word of God. It is something that the Lord taught me to do even when I was a teenager, and by the grace of God, I believe it has made my life what it is today. Even before I learned about grace, the Lord taught me to meditate on His Word. In fact, I think meditating on the verses that the Lord had highlighted to me when I was younger is one of the reasons I could understand grace when He began to really open my eyes to it. Listening to the Word is so important, but don't stop there. As you hear, get hold of what speaks to you, meditate on it, and make it yours.

When reading the Word of God, one of the things I enjoy most is meditating on the faith pictures that the Bible so eloquently articulates for us. In the world we live in, the news, social media, medical reports, and other information sources tend to paint negative images of sickness, death, poverty, terror, and darkness. But praise the Lord, we may be in this world, but we are not *of* this world (see John 17:11, 16). In Christ, we have been redeemed from the curse and don't have to live in fear and hopelessness. As the world gets darker and darker, the church (that includes you and me!) is getting brighter and brighter (see Isa. 60:2). So don't allow the news media to paint images that suffocate your heart with fear. Look for God's faith images in His eternal, everlasting, and unshakable Word that will establish and stabilize your heart!

> *In Christ, we have been redeemed from the curse and don't have to live in fear and hopelessness.*

Have a Faith Image from His Word

One of my all-time favorite faith images is found in Psalm 1. Would you read it with me right now? As you read it, may the Lord paint a picture of faith in your heart of the blessings that you are meant to enjoy in Christ!

> *Blessed* is *the man who walks not in the counsel of the ungodly, nor stands in the path of sinners, nor sits in the seat of the scornful; but his delight* is *in the law of the* LORD, *and in His law he meditates day and night. He shall be like a tree planted by the rivers of water, that brings forth its fruit in its season, whose leaf also shall not wither; and whatever he does shall prosper.*
>
> —*Psalm 1:1–3*

Instead of seeing the negative depictions of the world, you can see yourself like a tree planted by the *rivers* of water. We're talking about *many* rivers, not just one. What a beautiful picture of constant provision, with *rivers* of water sustaining and refreshing you all the time. Even if one river runs dry, there are other rivers flowing. You do not have to fear the reports about new strains of diseases, terrorist attacks, and economic downturns because whatever may be happening around you, even if there is drought in the rest of the land, *you* are that tree planted by rivers of fresh, flowing water. And don't miss this detail—you did not just randomly *grow* by the river. Someone *planted* you! Surely the One who planted you will also tend to and take care of you!

The psalm goes on to say that you will bring forth fruit in season. See yourself not being barren in any way, but fruitful in every area, including in your finances, in your body, and in your ministry. See yourself with leaves that shall not wither; instead, they shall be perennially green, fresh, and full of sap. What this speaks of is that you will always be young, strong, and full of life and energy. The Lord will cause your youth to be renewed like the eagle's (see Ps. 103:5). Leaves in the Bible also speak of healing. In Revelation 22:2 it says, "The leaves of the tree *were* for the healing of the nations." This means your health will be evergreen; it will not fail you!

But Psalm 1:1–3 doesn't stop there. It goes on to say "whatever he does shall prosper." What a powerful promise! Whether you are a judge, nurse, homemaker, businessperson, student, or banker, whatever you do shall prosper! Even if you make a mistake, the Lord can cause it to prosper!

Don't you love the Word of God? In just a few verses, it has given you a picture of the blessings He has for you. Whatever challenging circumstances you might be facing in the natural, let His eternal Word replace every negative expectation of evil with a positive expectation of good because of what Christ has done for you!

The Key to Walking in His Blessings

So what is the key to being the blessed man planted by rivers of water? Psalm 1:2 tells us that "his delight *is* in the law of the LORD, and in His law he meditates day and night." His *delight* is in the Word of the Lord—he savors and enjoys the Word of the Lord. Spending time in the Word is not something he does legalistically, but because he does it with revelation, it gives him delight, or "great pleasure" and "a high degree of gratification,"[1] such that he meditates on God's Word day and night!

Let's look at the word *meditates* in Psalm 1:2. It is translated from the Hebrew word *hagah*, which means to utter or mutter, to speak in a low voice as is often done by those who are musing.[2] God's way of meditation is not just to think in your head but to also mutter with your mouth.

In the last chapter, we saw how important it is to hear God's Word through a preacher. But the miracle of meditation is this: As you meditate on and mutter God's Word to yourself, you are being a preacher to yourself! As you speak out the verses, do you know what you are doing? You are hearing yourself preach about the Lord Jesus. You are hearing yourself preach life into your situation. And as we saw in the last chapter, faith comes as you keep hearing and hearing the word of Christ!

Look at what God tells Joshua when he first takes over the reins of leadership from Moses:

> *This Book of the Law shall not depart from your mouth, but you shall meditate in it day and night, that you may observe to do according to all that is written in it. For then you will make your way prosperous, and then you will have good success.*
>
> *—Joshua 1:8*

Notice that God tells Joshua that the Book of the Law shall not depart from his *mouth*—it's your *mouth*, not so much your mind, that you use in meditation. Take a word of Scripture and mutter it under your breath day and night "that you may observe to do according to all that is written in it. For then you will make your way prosperous, and then you will have good success."

Don't you think it's interesting that meditation and prosperity in every area are linked in both Psalm 1 and Joshua 1? I want to be clear that when I use the word *prosperity*, I'm not talking about finances only. True prosperity is holistic. It touches every area of your life, including your relationships, your family, your peace of mind, and your health. I also think it's interesting that the Bible specifies that you will have *good* success. This implies that there is *bad* success. If you are financially "successful" but have no time to enjoy being with your family, have alienated your friends, and are always working and don't get to do the things you enjoy, that doesn't sound like good success to me. By the way, in the Old Testament, they meditated on the Torah or the law of God. How much more blessed would you and I be when we meditate on the perfect, finished work of our Savior today under the new covenant!

Perhaps you are thinking to yourself, *I don't know how to meditate on God's Word, let alone meditate on it day and night!* Let me ask you this: Do you know how to worry? If you know how to worry—if you can think about the negative things that could happen to you, fear all the things that could go wrong, or see a bleak future—then you know how to meditate. The truth is, we are all meditating on *something* day and night. Many are meditating on their work troubles, their health conditions, or their financial challenges.

Our heavenly Father is showing us a better way. He is showing us how to live the let-go life by letting go of our worries and replacing them with His Word. And as we do that, we will be like the fresh and flourishing tree described in Psalm 1! You may not have time for many things, but you can't afford not to have daily time in the Word. It really doesn't take long for you to read and memorize just one verse and meditate on it throughout the day. Can I encourage you to give it a try today?

> *We live the let-go life by letting go of our worries and replacing them with God's Word.*

Power to Overcome Our Challenges

Psalm 1 is very special to me because there was a period when I had to handle several issues at the same time. During this time, our church was also faced with the challenge of having to raise funds to pay for our new premises at The Star. I was beset with demands, and I knew that in and of myself I did not have the capacity to do what was required. Over this trying period, instead of worrying and running around trying to solve all the problems, I decided to stay still and rest in the knowledge that the battle was not mine but the Lord's.

I started meditating on the Word more than ever before, and the passage that the Lord led me to study was Psalm 1:1–3. What I have shared with you about this passage hardly skims the surface of what you can discover when studying it. In spite of the challenges we were facing in the natural, I kept seeing myself as the blessed man, and I claimed the promise that whatever I touched would prosper. By God's amazing supply of grace, The Star building project is completely paid off today. Truly, except the Lord builds the house, our labors are in vain. Meditating on His Word gives us the power to let go of our cares to Him.

Seeing Ourselves Planted by the Waters

When I visited Israel with my pastors that year, the Lord made it such a special time for us. He was speaking to us about meditating on His Word throughout our time there. For instance, I really wanted to visit a place called Tel Dan even though it was out of the way. When we got there, I knew why God put that desire in my heart.

Many places were hot and dry during that season, but when we arrived at Tel Dan, we found ourselves in a beautiful and refreshingly cool oasis of lush greenery, with trees planted by flowing rivers. It was a place of tranquility and of thriving, vibrant life amid the arid landscape surrounding it. I simply had to get one of the guys to take a photograph of me by the waters. It was as if the Lord had brought me there so I could literally see myself as that blessed man planted by the rivers of water!

Ruminating on the Word

During that trip to Israel, we also went up Mount Arbel, one of the highest mountains in Galilee. My pastors and I then decided that since we were all macho men, we would try going down from the steep side of the mountain instead of using the route taken by most tourists. I'm not sure that was a good idea—the next day, we were all sore from using muscles we had never used before!

But during that descent, I believe the Lord divinely arranged things so that I could see something that He was speaking to me about. As we slowly made our way down, we came across a huge cave. And guess what was staring at us in that cave in the middle of the treacherous incline? A cow! I don't know how it got there, but as it sat there nonchalantly chewing and chewing its cud, I was jolted by the realization that I was looking at a picture of meditation!

The cow, like the sheep and goat, is a ruminant, which means it is able to acquire nutrients from plant-based foods by breaking down the food it eats in a specialized four-compartment stomach before digestion.[3] In the first two compartments, saliva and bacteria help break down the food into layers of solid and liquid material. The solids clump together to form cud and the partially fermented cud is then regurgitated and chewed slowly. The process of rechewing the cud to further break down plant matter and aid digestion is called *rumination*. Incidentally, the word *ruminant* comes from the Latin *ruminare*, which means "to chew again."[4] The food material then passes into the next chamber of the stomach, where water and many of the mineral elements are absorbed into the bloodstream. Next, the food is moved into the last chamber, where further digestion takes place.

Meditation is very much like rumination. After we read God's Word, we can bring it up and chew on it again and again. During the day, there are always pockets of idle time when we could be waiting for someone, answering the call of nature, standing in line, or stuck in peak-hour traffic. We can always bring up verses that can feed us all over again. We can feed on verses like "The LORD *is* my shepherd; I shall not want" (Ps. 23:1) or "A thousand may fall at your side, and ten thousand at your right hand; *but* it shall not come near you" (Ps. 91:7), ruminating on the Word until we have obtained all the nutrients and extracted all the water from it. While others are bored or feeling frustrated, we could be having a personal revival and having church all by ourselves! That's what God wants us to do—ruminate on His inexhaustible Word throughout the day and continuously feed on His truths until we have extracted all the nourishment we can from even a single verse.

> *Meditation is like rumination. After you read God's Word, bring it up and chew on it again and again.*

How to Meditate on God's Word

Would you like to learn how you can meditate on His Word? There are other ways to go about doing it, of course, but let me share how I started. When I was going through military training as a young man (it is mandatory for all men in my nation to serve in the military), I used to keep index cards with Bible verses in the pocket of my camouflage uniform. During our occasional breaks, I would pull out the cards and read one or two verses. I did not have time to read the Bible then, but I sure had time to read at least one verse, and it amazes me how much nourishment you can get out of ruminating on even one verse. Each time I chewed on a verse, the Lord gave me strength, changed my perspectives, and gave me rest and peace in place of worry.

Nowadays, you don't need to write out verses on index cards to have them with you. With Bible apps freely available today, many people literally walk around with Bibles in their pockets. You might even have several Bible apps in your smartphone. Why not try meditating on a verse when you have pockets of time during the day, instead of spending all your free time checking your social media feeds? I can guarantee that meditating on His Word will benefit you more than finding out what your friends ate for lunch or what their pets are up to. For instance, if you are going through a financial situation and your thoughts are causing you to have panic attacks, stop holding on to your worries. Let go and counter those fears by muttering His promises to yourself throughout the day!

When you are being attacked by worrisome thoughts, meditating on His Word is the best remedy. Every time the enemy keeps you awake with fearful thoughts, simply say, "Since you want to keep me awake, I'll meditate on the Word!" That's what I learned from David, who said, "I meditate on You in the *night* watches" (Ps. 63:6). I take a verse and I quote it to myself a few times, chewing on it over and over again. Many times, I fall asleep and wake up feeling so rested the next day. I don't think it's a natural rest, but a supernatural rest because of the power of God's Word!

> *When you are being attacked by worrisome thoughts, meditating on His Word is the best remedy.*

Power in Meditating on One Verse

Let me show you how meditating on just one verse can bless you:

> *He who did not spare His own Son, but delivered Him up for us all, how shall He not with Him also freely give us all things?*
>
> —Romans 8:32

A verse like this can last you a whole week at least. Don't rush through it. Break it into portions and take your time to meditate on each portion, turning them around to allow every truth in them to speak to your heart and nourish you. For example, meditate on "He who did not spare His own Son." Whom did God not spare? His own Son. Not an angel or a person, but His own Son. The word *own* is so precious. It tells us that God was personally and deeply affected. He did not send someone else's son; He sent His own. He did not spare His own Son—His only Son, the Son whom He loved. Doesn't that remind you of another father in the Bible who got to spare *his* son? Genesis 22:12 records how God had withheld Abraham's hand from sacrificing his son as a burnt offering. But God did not withhold His hand when it came to His own Son. Why did God not spare Jesus? *So that you and I could be spared.* Who are we that God Almighty would do this for us!

You can also chew on how God "delivered Him up for us all." God *delivered up* His own Son. He gave Jesus up into the hands of the ruthless soldiers to be cruelly scourged, beaten, stripped, mocked, and, finally, nailed to the cross, suspended between heaven and earth for six agonizing hours. Our Lord Jesus was not taken by the soldiers. His Father delivered Him into their hands. Can you imagine how God the Father must have felt as He gave up Jesus, knowing what His Son would have to go through as our sin offering? Knowing that He would have to turn away from His own Son when He became sin on the cross?

And God delivered Him up "for us all." He gave Jesus up, not for angels, but for *us*. And not for those who deserve it or who have lived perfect lives, but for us *all*. His love for us is unqualified and completely undeserving. He died for us while we were yet sinners. We had nothing to offer Him except our brokenness, our shame, and our failures. Yet, God chose to deliver our Lord Jesus up for *us all*! Oh, amazing grace that saved a wretch like me!

Ruminate also on the portion that says, "how shall He not with Him also freely give us all things?" When we know how much God has done for us, the enemy has no way of selling his lies to us successfully. When the enemy tries to plant the lie that God will not supply that financial need that you have or heal that symptom in your body, you can declare, "How shall He not!" And meditate on how God answers prayers not with a miserly hand or with conditions attached, but *freely*! God gives freely! Doesn't that make you want to jump up and sing? If God already gave us His best when He gave us Jesus, what is the rest to Him? What is a job opportunity, a child, favor with a client, healing for your body, wisdom for your exams, or a life partner to Him? Hallelujah!

> *If God already gave us His best when He gave us Jesus, what is the rest to Him?*

Is faith already bursting forth in your heart like it is in mine? All we have been doing is meditating on *one* verse. Now that you have seen how meditating on just one verse can yield such rich truths, I pray you will start making it a daily habit to meditate on God's Word, one verse at a time!

Meditation in the New Testament

Earlier, we looked at Psalm 1 and Joshua 1, which gave us a picture of how the Lord blesses us as we meditate on His Word. Let's look at what the New Testament has to say about meditation:

> *Meditate upon these things; give thyself wholly to them; that thy profiting may appear to all. Take heed unto thyself, and*

unto the doctrine; continue in them: for in doing this thou
shalt both save thyself, and them that hear thee.
                                        —1 Timothy 4:15–16 KJV

As you meditate upon teaching and doctrine and give yourselves wholly to them, the Scripture passage above us says that you will see "profiting" in your life. What you have on the inside will be manifested on the outside so that it becomes obvious to everybody—your profiting is demonstrated to all. The passage goes on to say, "in doing this thou shalt both save thyself, and them that hear thee."

Now, Apostle Paul was writing to Timothy, who was already saved. So why did Paul say that Timothy would *save* both himself and those who heard him? It's because the word *save* here is translated from the Greek word *sozo*, and as we have learned, *sozo* is a very rich word that also means to heal, preserve, and protect. In this context, it is not referring to being saved from hell. Paul was telling Timothy, "If you preach out of your meditation and take heed to the teaching that you've meditated on, you will both heal yourself, the preacher, as well as heal others. You will preserve yourself, as well as others. You will prosper yourself, as well as others." Amen!

By the way, if you *don't* want your way to be prosperous, can I give you some advice? Don't touch God's Word, as it has power in it to prosper your way. I don't know if you have experienced this before, but personally, when I neglect reading the Word, it seems like that day feels so short with not enough hours in it to solve my problems. In contrast, when I give time to God's Word even when many other things are calling for my attention, the day would be long but full, with so much more accomplished. This is why I believe it is so important for us to do the "one thing needful" (see

Luke 10:42 ᴋᴊᴠ). The more we need to accomplish in a day, the more we can't afford *not* to spend time with the Lord and meditate on His Word!

The more we need to accomplish in a day, the more we can't afford not to spend time with the Lord and meditate on His Word.

Set Free from Long-Term Depression

I was so encouraged when I received this praise report from Paula and I want to share it with you:

I am writing to say thank you to Pastor Prince for pointing me to Jesus.

Even though I was taught that Jesus is my Savior, I spent many years under the works of the law. I always tried to be good but always felt there was one thing I lacked. I battled with depression constantly even as a young child—it was a chronic and powerful stronghold that kept me captive. Many hours and much money spent on professional counseling, medical doctors, alternative doctors, supplements, and medication did not help me at all.

*One day, my six-year-old happened to leave the television on when she left the room. I headed over to turn it off and that was when I heard Pastor Prince being interviewed. His words grabbed my heart like nothing I had ever experienced before. I thought to myself, "He knows my Jesus!" Immediately, I grabbed the remote control and recorded the interview. **I watched it over and over, pausing it often to***

take notes. *I began reading his book* Destined to Reign *and fell completely in love with Jesus and my Bible.* **I spent many hours reading, watching, and taking down notes daily.**

When I first heard Pastor Prince sing the words of Psalm 34 on his program, it immediately became my theme song. I sang it day and night, whenever I was troubled and gripped with fear. Sometimes, I could barely choke out the words, but I kept singing the psalm and it never failed to bring comfort.

I was privileged to attend Pastor Prince's event in Dallas, Texas. When he said that some people would be set free from chronic conditions, I believed the word was for me. I didn't feel any immediate change in my body, just a deeper faith to trust God that my breakthrough would come.

Sometime later, I suffered another round of depression marked by overwhelming feelings of hopelessness and despair. It was extremely discouraging as I had been focusing on Jesus and the gospel of grace for nearly two years, spending time in Scripture and confessing them over my life, partaking of the Holy Communion daily, praying and singing in tongues, declaring away self-righteousness in me, and doing my best to rest in Him.

I kept wondering what I was missing to break free from depression. One day as I was driving, I asked God to deliver me from being a whipping post. I even let out a big yell to let the devil know that I was done letting him steal my peace! I felt a new fire in me that I can't really explain, but I felt like I came to a whole new level of not just knowing but truly believing that my heavenly Papa wanted me free from depression. I boldly rejected depression in Jesus' name, declaring His victory for me at the cross. **I immediately felt** *the depression start to dissipate, and by evening, I was feeling much better. I also talked to my heavenly Papa about the evil day that I felt had lasted way too long, and boldly declared my desire to see the good days His Word has promised.*

I am writing because I feel such an urge to spread hope to others with chronic strongholds. I would say to them that no matter how long it takes, no matter how hopeless you feel, keep believing, stay focused on Jesus and His victory at the cross, and never give up. I believe the devil tries to hit the hardest when you're closest to your victory, so hang in there! **God's grace will do for you what you can never do for yourself. Keep confessing the righteousness you have as a gift and believe you are loved no matter how you feel. Depression is not from God!**

Trials and emotions still come on some days, but I have confidence inside that I am not alone and they will pass **as I keep praising Him and professing His Word. This way, I don't fall hopelessly into depression anymore.**

Thank you so much, Pastor Prince and your team, for sharing your passion for Jesus! I love you all!

Did you see how Paula spent time daily to read, watch sermons, and take down notes on what she was hearing? She sang the words of Psalm 34 to herself day and night whenever she was troubled and gripped with fear, and kept praising God and declaring His Word. That's how she kept herself meditating on God's Word day and night. And as she kept feeding and feeding on His truths, she was set free from depression that had kept her bound for years. Whatever strongholds have bound you, I pray that Paula's testimony will strengthen and encourage you. Start by finding Scriptures that you can make your "theme song" and mutter those Scriptures to yourself over and over again until you are strengthened from the inside. If you would like to watch a video of our church worshiping with Psalm 34 on the very program Paula was referring to, please visit the resource section at JosephPrince.com/LetGo. As you keep meditating on the Word of God, His Word promises that whatever you do shall prosper!

Don't Gobble—Ruminate on God's Word!

Feeding on God's Word is not like going to the drive-through or wolfing down fast food. There is nothing wrong with listening to sermons while you are commuting. In fact, I encourage you to do that! But can I also encourage you not to just gobble down God's Word on the go, but take some time each day to really meditate on the verses that you hear or read?

> *Don't just gobble down God's Word; take some time each day to really meditate on the verses that you hear or read.*

You can start with just one verse a day. It's not about how many chapters you read, but the depths that you plunge into, and how deeply you go to really digest and think about the words that the Holy Spirit chose, and why He phrased it the way He did. Take time to be like a cow ruminating on the Word, turning it around and around in your mouth and savoring it until the essence of one verse becomes such a truth that it drowns out the facts that could be staring you in the face.

It may be a fact that there is a troubling symptom in your body. But you know what? The truth of God declares, "But if the Spirit of Him who raised Jesus from the dead dwells in you, He who raised Christ from the dead will also give life to your mortal bodies through His Spirit who dwells in you" (Rom. 8:11). It may be a fact that the amount you have in the bank is dwindling. But the truth is that "God *is* able to make all grace abound toward you, that you, always having all sufficiency in all *things*, may have an abundance for every good work" (2 Cor. 9:8). It may be a fact that your doctor has said it is not possible for you to have children. But the truth is, "You shall be blessed above all peoples; there shall not be a male or female barren among you or among your livestock" (Deut. 7:14).

Light and darkness cannot exist in the same space. Meditate on His Word and let it drive out all fear and stress. As you make a decision to prioritize and meditate daily on His Word, His truths will overshadow every negative fact! May you become like the blessed man planted by the rivers of water, always bringing forth fruit in season. May whatever you do prosper in the mighty name of Jesus. Amen!

17.
EXPERIENCING BLESSINGS IN MARRIAGE

We have been studying how to live the let-go life together, and I pray that it has made a difference to you and helped you to live in greater freedom from fear, stress, and anxiety than ever before.

If you're married but you and your spouse are constantly quarreling and getting upset with one another, it is hard to live the let-go life. That's why in this chapter, I want to look at God's heart for your marriage and how you can invite the Lord Jesus into your marriage so that you can live the victorious, let-go life as a couple. Don't try to deal with all your stress and anxieties on your own—learn to live the let-go life as a couple. Together, put into practice whatever you might have learned from this book.

For instance, make it a game to catch one another being anxious and remind each other not to let your hearts be troubled. Decide that both of you will always be quick to forgive one another and to let go of any hurts to the Lord. Find Christ-centered messages that you can listen to together and share the portions that spoke to you with your spouse. If you are going through a health or financial challenge, find promises in God's Word that you can meditate on as a couple. Ask the Lord, who is always for you, to help you both keep Him in your conversations and to always keep Him in the center of your marriage.

There is such power when you and your spouse are in agreement. Our Lord Jesus said, "If two of you agree on earth concerning anything that they ask, it will be done for them by My Father in heaven" (Matt. 18:19). Together, you can agree to cast all your cares to the Lord. Cast every care about providing for your family, about your children's education, and about the bills to be paid, because He cares for you and your family. Together, you can agree to stay in rest instead of being stressed out and flustered. Remind each other that the Lord Himself fights your battles against any chronic sickness, any lack of time for one another, and against any addiction that has put a strain on your marriage. As you keep focusing on the Lord Jesus and His finished work instead of focusing on each other, I believe He will draw you closer to your spouse and cause your marriage to be stronger than ever before!

Days of Heaven in Your Family Life

Do you want to know what God promised would happen if you keep on remembering His goodness and listening to His Word? In the book of Deuteronomy, God tells the Israelites to "hearken diligently" to His commandments (Deut. 11:13 KJV). If you study the verse in Hebrew, "hearken diligently" is made up of *shama shama*, which literally means "listen, listen."[1] A few chapters ago, we looked at how important listening is because the blessings of God come by us listening. When we *shama shama*, this is what the Lord promises us:

That your days may be multiplied, and the days of your chil-
dren, in the land which the LORD *sware unto your fathers to*
give them, as the days of heaven upon the earth.
                                        —*Deuteronomy 11:21* KJV

The promise that we can have "days of heaven upon the earth"
is in the context of family life. Do you want to experience "days of
heaven" in your marriage? Do you want to have a marriage that
is full of love and affirmation, instead of strife and contention?
Then keep on listening to His Word together!

Maybe you are thinking, *But my marriage feels more like hell*
than heaven on earth! I know that with all the pressures and stress
that you face on a daily basis, your family life and marriage may
not always feel like heaven on earth. But it is a promise that you
can cling to, and I pray that every person reading this book will
walk in a greater and greater measure of this wonderful promise
in the days to come.

To have "days of heaven upon the earth" is a promise
we can cling to and walk in a greater measure of in the
days to come.

Pressures on Marriages

God ordained marriage to be a powerful covenant. The Bible
declares that one can chase a thousand, but two can put ten thousand to flight (see Deut. 32:30). There is exponential power in a
marriage. It comes as no surprise then that the enemy wants marriages to fail. Attacks on marriages come from various fronts. I
read that the top reasons that marriages fail include dealing with

financial problems; lack of communication; rifts stemming from the stress of raising children; the quality of physical intimacy; infidelity; problems related to addictions such as drugs, alcohol, and gambling; physical or emotional abuse; incompatibility in personalities; unrealistic expectations; and a lack of quality time spent together.[2] Perhaps many of these reasons sound familiar to you, and you are currently experiencing them in your own marriage.

Perhaps you are reading this and you are crying out in your heart because your marriage is not in a good place. Maybe you can't remember the last time you and your spouse spoke nicely to one another, let alone held hands. Intimacy has been out of the question because of the constant tension between you and your spouse. Deep down, you believe you still love your spouse, but every conversation you have tried to have has ended with raised voices, angry words, and wounded hearts.

Or perhaps you feel like you are living a lie. On the outside, everything in your marriage looks fine. You live in a nice house, you do things as a family, and financially, you are doing okay. But inside, your heart has grown cold, and it feels like your spouse is just your roommate or worse—a stranger. Maybe you are wondering, *Where is God's supply and grace in all this?* My friend, I want you to know that God cares. He cares about your family and He cares about your marriage. Don't give up. I believe God has a word for you in the next few pages that can supernaturally turn your marriage around!

Your Marriage Is Important to God

Family was God's first priority. Long before God ordained a church, God ordained the institution of the family in the garden of Eden. I don't believe it was by coincidence that the very first miracle Jesus performed when He walked on earth was at a wedding feast. Before He healed anyone who was sick, before He ever multiplied bread and fish to feed the hungry, before He even raised the dead to life, our Lord started His ministry by turning water into wine at a wedding. Doesn't that give you a wonderful insight into God's heart for your marriage? God's Word is so full of truths about His supernatural supply for your marriage and I pray that as you read on, He will cause you to step into a whole new level of intimacy in your relationship with your spouse.

No matter how wonderful the man you married is or how amazing your wife is, there will be times when you *will* go through valleys in your marriage. And whether you are in a valley right now or not, there are so many truths that we can learn by studying what our Lord Jesus did at that wedding in Cana, and I want to start by highlighting this: Human love can run out. Just like the couple ran out of wine at their wedding feast in Cana, many marriages run out of love when they are built solely on human love. If you are a divorcée or divorcé, please know that, in Christ, there is therefore now no condemnation (see Rom. 8:1). God loves you, and I pray you will experience His restoration and supply of grace in every area of your life.

You and I know that it is not our heavenly Father's heart for our marriages to be marked with strife, stress, and the loss of love. Just observe what our Lord Jesus did when He was a guest at a wedding and the wine ran out: He turned water into wine. In fact, the resultant wine was so good that when the master of ceremonies tasted it, he marveled that the bridegroom had kept the "best wine" for the end (see John 2:1–11 NLT). Perhaps the wine has run out in your marriage. Once upon a time, there was excitement and romance, but demands piled up and the wine ran out. Babies came. There were diapers to be changed and mouths to feed, and the wine ran out. There were bosses to please, deadlines to meet, and the wine ran out.

Demands, stress, and burdens can have a negative impact on our relationships and marriages. Worries can cause you to become short-tempered and irritable and lead you to start taking your stress out on each other. Your anxiety can put a large strain on your marriage and even affect intimacy.[3] This is why it is so important for us to live the let-go life that is more conscious of God's abundant supply for us than the demands placed on us.

If it feels like the wine has run out, please know that every marriage needs a "third party" in order to thrive. His name is Jesus. The Bible tells us that "a threefold cord is not quickly broken" (Eccl. 4:12). When you invite Him to take center place in your marriage and you each draw from Him instead of constantly making withdrawals from each other, your marriage can be strengthened instead of becoming depleted—even when demands pile up.

> *Every marriage needs a "third party" in order to thrive. His name is Jesus.*

When you put your spouse in a place where all your happiness depends on your spouse, you will be disappointed. Only the Lord can take that place. Your spouse cannot be God. When you keep your eyes on the Lord instead of each other, you can minister to each other out of His unlimited strength and grace, instead of drawing from each other. When you invite Him to take center place in your marriage, He can cause that which is tasteless and bland to become sweet and intoxicating. He can infuse your marriage with more passion and love than when your marriage first started. He will ensure that the wine never runs out and that you are supplied exceedingly, abundantly, above all that you ask or think (see Eph. 3:20)!

Pastor Prince, you don't understand. It has been too long. Too many hurtful words have been exchanged for too long. I've neglected my spouse for too long. Our marriage is beyond repair.

Beloved, let me share something with you: When Jesus turned the water into wine, He was showing that He is the Lord of time. It takes years for high-quality wine to be produced, but He compressed time and in an instant produced the best wine. He can do in a short time what takes years through human effort. One moment of His favor can turn your whole marriage around. Right now, I speak His supernatural favor over your marriage. May you find favor in each other's sight and experience a new excitement and love for one another in Jesus' mighty name. Even if it has been years since there has been love in your marriage, the Lord can redeem the years that have been wasted. As you invite Him into your marriage, He declares to you today, "I will restore to you the years that the swarming locust has eaten" (Joel 2:25)!

> One moment of His favor can turn your whole marriage around.

Ask God for More Grace

One of the reasons marriages break up is that one of the spouses has been unfaithful. Adultery is destructive, and as a pastor and counselor, I have personally seen too many families torn apart by the painful betrayal of adultery. My heart has been broken by the tears, the unanswered questions, and the intense anger that infidelity leaves in its wake. I have seen the impact it has on children, who end up blaming themselves when they see their parents' marriage crumble before their eyes. The consequences are devastating and far-reaching.

Adultery is wrong, and I want to be clear that I do not in any way condone it. If you have fallen in this area, I pray that you will have a fresh revelation of all that our Lord Jesus has done for you and receive the grace and the strength to get out of that adulterous relationship. As for your marriage, I believe it is never too late for the Lord to work a miracle. Lazarus had been dead for days, but our Lord Jesus brought him back to life (see John 11:38–44). Even if it feels like your love for one another has died, His healing and restorative power can still flow into your marriage and resurrect whatever is dead.

We can learn from the story that the Bible records of a man who fell into adultery. King David had many wives and concubines. Yet, he was not satisfied. If you think that your spouse is not good enough for you and that you would be happy if you had another spouse, learn from David. Having another person does not mean you will be satisfied. Satisfaction comes from the Lord!

When David saw how beautiful Bathsheba was, he committed adultery with her and she became pregnant. To cover up what he had done, he arranged for Bathsheba's husband to be killed. Isn't that so characteristic of the destructive nature of sin, which always takes you further than you want to go? God then sent the prophet Nathan to correct David. I want you to pay attention to what Nathan said:

> *Thus says the LORD God of Israel: "I anointed you king over Israel, and I delivered you from the hand of Saul. I gave you your master's house and your master's wives into your keeping, and gave you the house of Israel and Judah. **And if that had been too little, I also would have given you much more!**"*
> —2 Samuel 12:7–8 (boldface mine)

Nathan reminded David of how God had supplied him abundantly in other areas. But David had not asked God to supply what he needed in the area of his marriage. Many times, people have the mistaken idea that God is concerned with more "important" things like salvation and they fail to bring more "mundane" areas like their marriage to the Lord. If that describes you, I pray that once and for all, you will see that God cares for your marriage and He wants to supply His grace for your marriage. Don't forget, our Lord Jesus chose the first day of a marriage as the setting for His first miracle. Your marriage is important to Him! When you try to provide for yourself, you will end up in a deeper problem.

Today, if you are not satisfied with your marriage—the passion has run out and there is no more joy in your relationship—ask the Lord for more of His grace in your marriage. But let's be clear that He won't give you a relationship outside of your marriage. He will give you and your spouse a fresh desire for one another and infuse that which has become bland with His sweet love!

> *If you are not satisfied with your marriage—the passion and joy has run out—ask the Lord for more of His grace in your marriage.*

Receive the Gift of a Blessed Marriage

Pastor Prince, you don't know how I have failed. I don't deserve to have a good marriage.

My friend, even if you have failed, the Lord can still turn things around. You may not deserve a good marriage, but the Lord can still bless your marriage because of His grace! As you experience His undeserved and unmerited love, I believe the

Lord can cause you to be an even better spouse than ever before. You don't deserve it, but at the cross, He paid the price for you to experience His blessings in your marriage. He was your trespass offering, bearing every punishment that you deserved so that you can walk in every blessing that He deserved (see Eph. 2:4–7). In the Old Testament, wine was referred to as "the blood of the grapes" (Deut. 32:14). Jesus Himself took a cup of wine and said, "This cup *is* the new covenant in My blood, which is shed for you" (Luke 22:20). Jesus' first miracle in Cana was a picture of His blood being poured out abundantly, resulting in celebration.

> As you experience His undeserved and unmerited love, I believe the Lord can cause you to be an even better spouse than ever before.

The only reason you and I can celebrate today is because of His shed blood, which is the basis for every blessing we receive from God. The law was given by Moses. Grace and truth came by Jesus Christ. The first miracle that Moses performed under the law was to turn water into blood, resulting in death. Jesus' first miracle of grace was to turn water into wine, resulting in joy and festivity. Aren't you glad Jesus came? Beloved, it is time to let go of condemnation and receive His grace for your marriage today.

Let His Supply Flow in Your Marriage

Every challenge that you can face in your marriage has been borne by your Savior at the cross. Your part is to let go of all your trying, all your worrying, and all your regrets. Let go and rest in His finished work. I am believing with you that as you put your trust in Him instead of all your efforts, His miracle working power will begin to flow and you will see Him do a new thing in your marriage. Now, romance, paying attention to each other's needs, communicating with one another, and other pragmatic aspects of cultivating a healthy marriage are important and have their place. In fact, I have taught a whole series on how the Bible is full of practical guidelines on how we can have successful marriages.[4] But the cross needs to take center place. May He build roadways where you see wilderness and cause rivers of love to spring forth in the deserts of your hearts (see Isa. 43:18–19), just as He did for this brother from my church in Singapore:

My relationship with my wife turned really bad after the birth of our second child. As young parents we were not able to cope with two young children who were a year apart. Things got worse when we became stressed at work. We quarreled frequently and had less time with each other. Our lives seemed to revolve around the children and work.

We finally separated and engaged lawyers to end the relationship. My wife and children moved to stay with my in-laws. At this darkest point in our lives, God divinely arranged for us to attend New Creation Church without each other's knowledge. When I found out that my wife and children were attending the same church as me, I suggested fetching them to church every week.

Though things were still gloomy, both my wife and I chose to fix our eyes on Jesus as our only way to salvation. **Weeks of hearing and learning about what Jesus has done for us slowly set us free from stress and anger. We began to love each other again with Jesus in our midst.**

By the grace of God my wife and I eventually reconciled and
our relationship is now better than ever before.

   *Our third child was born within four years after we had
separated, and my wife has found a new job that offers better
work-life balance. She was also promoted within two years,
and in the third year she was transferred to the department
of her choice, where the work is easier to manage. Indeed
with Jesus, everything is possible!*

Don't you love how the Lord works in such supernaturally
natural ways? This couple was not trying to solve the problems
in their marriage. In fact, they had already engaged lawyers to
end their marriage. But as they kept on hearing about what Jesus
had done for them, the water turned into wine. Love returned to
their marriage and their relationship became better than it was
before! My friend, if God can do it for this couple, He can do it for
you too!

I speak Jesus' blood of protection over the marriage of anyone reading this book. For those who are married, may you never
have to walk through the pain of a broken marriage because Jesus
has paid the price for you to have a blessed marriage and family
life. If you are single or divorced, you can also experience days
of heaven on earth by listening and listening to the words of our
Lord Jesus. Let His Word wash over you daily, washing away every
fear and every burden that you find so hard to let go of.

Beloved, as you listen to Him, healing is imparted. As you listen to Him, He is cleansing you and renewing your mind. Keep
looking to our heavenly Bridegroom, who showed us what love
truly is and laid down His life to redeem us. And may you walk in
a greater and greater measure of His promise that we can experience days of heaven on earth!

18.
STRESS-FREE
PARENTING

Down through the years, I have counseled and received many emails from parents who have shared with me that while they desire to live the stress-free, let-go life, what causes them to become all strung up is their kids.

I am not just talking about having young babies with endless diapers to change and the stress of adapting to parenthood. I am talking about the whole spectrum—from dealing with tantrum-throwing toddlers, to handling rebellious teenagers, to managing young adults who have walked away from the church and are dealing with complex relationships and addictions. If this describes what you are going through today, I want you to know that you are not alone. The stress of parenting is very real. It is especially challenging for single parents or parents with children who have been diagnosed with behavioral disorders and developmental disabilities. Making the decision to let our hearts not be troubled when it comes to our own lives is already difficult—how much more mammoth of a feat it is when it involves our kids!

As we have seen in the previous chapter, God desires for us to experience *days of heaven upon the earth* and this speaks of blessings over our households, our marriages, as well as our children.

Do you want to see your children successful, stress-free, healthy, and flourishing in the house of God? How much more does our Father in heaven desire that for them!

> *Our Father in heaven desires to see our children successful, stress-free, and healthy.*

How Your Children Can Enjoy Days of Heaven on Earth

Let's look once again at Deuteronomy 11, where God talks about how our days and the days of our children can be multiplied. I want you to see how the Lord not only wants us to have long life but also wants to give to us and to our children days that are "as the days of heaven upon the earth." What an amazing promise for our children to be blessed! Let's look at what the Lord said:

> *Therefore shall ye lay up these my words in your heart and in your soul, and bind them for a sign upon your hand, that they may be as frontlets between your eyes. And ye shall teach them your children, speaking of them when thou sittest in thine house, and when thou walkest by the way, when thou liest down, and when thou risest up. And thou shalt write them upon the door posts of thine house, and upon thy gates: That your days may be multiplied, and the days of your children, in the land which the LORD sware unto your fathers to give them, as the days of heaven upon the earth.*
> —*Deuteronomy 11:18–21 KJV*

God wants us to lay up His words in our hearts and souls—to meditate and to chew on His words over and over again until they sink into our hearts and souls. He wants us to bind them to our hands, to really lay hold of His promises, and to put them as frontlets between our eyes, to always look to His words and to remember all that He has done to save us. Not only that, but also He wants us to teach our children about His words, and He teaches us how we can do that in our daily lives—by talking about His words whether we are sitting down in our own house or walking along outside, when we are getting up and when we lie down. *Why* does He want us to do all that? So that our days and the days of our children may be multiplied, and *be like days of heaven on earth.*

> *God wants us to teach our children about His words so that our days and their days may be like days of heaven on earth.*

Notice that God tells *us* to lay up His words in *our* hearts and souls before He tells us to teach them to our children. As we spend time personally meditating on His Word and "muttering" them in the presence of our children, that's how they will learn! This applies especially for younger children. As you meditate on God's Word, let them hear you say, "The Lord is my Shepherd, I have everything that I need." Tell them, "What does a shepherd do for his sheep? He lets them lie down in green pastures where they have plenty to eat, and leads them to still waters where they can safely drink. Do you know that God does that for us? He provides for us and He takes care of us. When we are tired, He gives us rest. He goes before us to prepare the way for us. Isn't He good?" Your children will learn through your meditation on the Word. And because of your example, they will come to know of the goodness of God!

Teach Your Children about Jesus

If you study Deuteronomy 11:19 in Hebrew, you'll find out *what* you should speak to your children about when the Bible says, "And ye shall teach them your children, speaking of them when thou sittest in thine house, and when thou walkest by the way, when thou liest down, and when thou risest up." Look at the first line, bearing in mind Hebrew reads from right to left:

אֵת   אֹתָם   לִמַּדְתֶּם

(untranslated)   them   And you shall teach

The Hebrew word that is left untranslated is actually two alphabets, *Aleph* and *Tav*.[1] Do you know what that is? That's the signature of our Lord Jesus. *Aleph* is the first letter of the Hebrew alphabet, while *Tav* is the last letter. In the book of Revelation, Jesus told John, "I am the Alpha and the Omega, *the* Beginning and *the* End" (Rev. 1:8). Alpha is the first letter of the Greek alphabet while omega is the last. But Jesus wouldn't have spoken Greek or English to His fellow Jews. He would have spoken in Hebrew, and this is what He would have said, "I am *Aleph* and I am *Tav*."

So what should you speak to your children about when you sit down in your house, when you walk by the way, when you lie down, and when you rise up? Teach them Jesus!

When good things happen, tell them, "Jesus did this for us." When they are fearful, tell them, "Don't worry, Jesus will take care of you." When they are crying over a broken toy, tell them, "Jesus has something better for you." Sing songs about Jesus. Use the name of Jesus throughout the day. As you meditate on the shadows in the Old Testament that point to Jesus' finished work, tell your children. Tell them how the Lord rescued His people from Egypt and how He can help us today even when it seems like there is no way. Tell them how it blessed you to see that because of Jesus, you can be like that blessed man or woman planted by rivers of water in Psalm 1. Let them see how the Word of God is so much a part of your own life. As you drive them to school, share with them how the Bible says that Joseph was a successful man because the Lord was with him, and tell them that their success is not dependent on their grades or their popularity on social media, but on the Lord.

What I'm trying to say is, make Jesus a part of your everyday life. You don't have to be a Bible teacher or insist that your children memorize Scripture for them to learn about Jesus. Every child and every family is different, and the Holy Spirit will show you what works for yours. However, if your children are able to memorize Scripture, by all means, encourage them to do so! Justin was just four years old when he told me he wanted to recite Psalm 23 for everyone. He was really adorable (of course every father thinks his own son is cute), and you can watch him reciting Psalm 23 in front of our congregation at this link if you want: JosephPrince.com/LetGo. But I didn't make him sit down every day and recite the psalm to me before he would be allowed to drink his milk or anything like that. When I was meditating on Psalm 23, I would simply speak it over him every night before he slept, and he would hear me during the day when I was meditating on it, and unconsciously he memorized it himself.

Sandwich Your Family in His Anointing

As you keep speaking of the Lord Jesus, praying over your children, meditating on the Word in front of your children, sharing testimonies of breakthroughs with them, and playing anointed psalms, hymns, and worship songs or sermons in the background at home, do you know what you are doing? You are sandwiching your children in His anointing. Remember what the Shunammite woman did when her son died? She put him on Elisha's bed, which was soaked with the anointing (just like how even the hem of Jesus' garment was filled with anointing and could heal the woman with the issue of blood). Later, Elisha stretched himself out on top of the child, putting the boy in a divine anointed sandwich—anointing below and anointing upon—and the boy was brought back to life (see 2 Kings 4:32–35).

I believe that gives us a picture of how covering our loved ones with the anointing and surrounding them with the Word of God can cause them to become spiritually alive. Even if they don't look like they are listening, trust that seeds are being planted in their hearts. You may not see fruits immediately, but in due season, they will bear fruit! Don't be discouraged even if your children don't look like they are interested in God's Word. By faith, keep on telling them about your wonderful Jesus, who loves them unconditionally even when they fail. Keep on bringing them to church, even if they don't understand the teachings. Our Lord Jesus said, "For where two or three are gathered together in My name, I am there in the midst of them" (Matt. 18:20). He is in the midst of your children—and His presence will guide and guard them.

> *Keep on telling them about your wonderful Jesus, who loves them unconditionally even when they fail.*

Grace for Wayward Children

Sometimes, it's hard to be carefree and to live the let-go life when it comes to our children, especially when it feels like we have lost control of them. Our instinct is to hold on even tighter. But the best thing we can do for our wayward children is to let go of them and release them into the Lord's arms of love.

> The best thing we can do for our wayward children is to let go of them and release them into the Lord's arms of love.

I remember when a precious lady in my church came to me and asked that I pray for her daughter. Her daughter was a talented and highly accomplished athlete who started representing Singapore at international swimming meets at the age of eleven. However, this lady was very worried for her daughter, as she had fallen into bad company, become rebellious, and was caught up in a lifestyle of wild partying. We prayed for her teenage daughter and asked God to touch her and turn her around. This lady was afraid that it was too late for God to do anything, but I encouraged her to trust the Lord and cast all her cares about her daughter to Him.

In just a matter of months, her daughter, Joscelin, came to church and was *gloriously* saved. And not only did Joscelin leave her partying days behind, but she also fell in love with Jesus and got involved in ministering to and counseling people in our church when she retired from competitive swimming!

Would you like to hear from Joscelin about how the Lord wooed her and saved her from a life that was on the path to destruction? This is what she shared with me:

> I was talented in swimming and joined the national swim team when I was eleven. Very quickly, I became successful. But the success exposed me to people and environments that I was not ready for.

At eleven, I began clubbing and, with that, smoking and drinking. I was lost, depressed, and suicidal. I cut myself because hurting myself with physical pain would momentarily distract me from the mental and emotional pain I was feeling. While I appeared successful, I was really a mess on the inside.

When I turned fifteen, I moved overseas to swim and study. That helped me feel better for about a year, but soon, the emptiness and hollowness on the inside just took over. By sixteen, I was partying hard four to five times a week and had seen every vice associated with that lifestyle.

I was at such a low that I would do anything to feel good about myself. My life was a mess, and I didn't know how to get out of it. Even though I was born into a Christian family, I felt I couldn't turn to God for help because I thought I had broken every one of God's laws and honestly believed I was eternally doomed.

When I returned to Singapore for a short holiday, my family shared with me the testimonies they had heard at church. I listened but was unmoved. My older brother also invited me to attend church with him. After turning him down numerous times, I finally agreed to go. But both times I went, I fell asleep even before the praise and worship sessions began. However, on both occasions, I woke up during the altar call and experienced something very odd—I felt compelled to raise my hand each time.

The first time I felt that compulsion, I ran out of the service. The second time, I could almost hear the testimonies that my family had shared with me ringing at the back of my head. I thought, "What if this God can save me from my toilet-bowl life?" So at the very last moment, when Pastor

Prince gave the final call, I raised my hand and walked all the way to the front to pray the sinner's prayer. That was the turning point in my life. As I continued attending church, hearing the gospel, and understanding more about grace, I began to live the life more abundant that Jesus came to give me. Friends from my past could barely recognize me.

I am so thankful for my loving Savior who has redeemed my life from destruction. Thank you, Pastor Prince, for preaching the good news that Jesus took the punishment for my sins and that I am now the righteousness of God in Christ. This is the truth that has set me free from the cycle of sin and condemnation to live a life of favor, blessing, and goodness that Christ died to give me.

I trust that you will be greatly encouraged by Joscelin's testimony. She is one of the most successful competitive swimmers in our nation, having won a record forty Southeast Asian Games gold medals, as well as represented Singapore in four Olympic Games. Today, she is a mother, and she is happily married to a pastor in my church. Know this: It is *never* too late for God to turn things around in the lives of your children.

It is never *too late for God to turn things around in the lives of your children.*

Your child could have strayed into bad company as Joscelin did. Or perhaps you are faced with different issues. Maybe your son shows no interest in his studies at all and is spending hours on computer games or on social media. Maybe you have a daughter who is obsessed about how she looks and is struggling with anorexia. Maybe your child is going from one bad relationship to another. You have tried your best to scold, nag, manipulate, or bribe your children, but you find that the more you try, the worse it becomes. What can you do? Stand still! Stop trying by your own efforts to change your children. The Lord loves your children more than you ever could. Let go, and put your trust in the Lord. Unless the Lord builds the house, we labor in vain (see Ps. 127:1). The Lord is building your house today. Stand still, and see the salvation of the Lord. You can rest. You can trust Him!

When Our Children Go through Challenges

What if your children are not being willful, but your heart is burdened because they are going through challenges, and you don't know how to help them? What if your child has been diagnosed with a medical condition? What if your child is going through anxiety attacks and meltdowns because of the pressures he faces at school? What if your child does not seem to fit in and is very affected because she can't seem to make friends? What if your young child is not developing as fast as he should, or your teenager is struggling with esteem issues?

My friend, whatever challenge your children may be going through, the greatest thing you can do for them is to surrender them to Jesus. I know it's hard—I'm a father. But as you focus on laying up God's Word in your heart and teaching your children all about Jesus, let's believe that the blessing of experiencing days of heaven upon the earth will come upon your children. Apply the cross to whatever challenges your children are faced with—every sickness, every rejection, every struggle was put on the body of Jesus on the cross. Keep on meditating on His finished work and pointing them to Him. There is only so much you can do in the natural, and you have probably already done it all. Now it is time for you to do what Moses' mother, Jochebed, did.

> *The greatest thing you can do for your children is to surrender them to Jesus.*

When the children of Israel were in Egypt, the Egyptians were afraid of them because they were fruitful, they multiplied, and grew exceedingly mighty (see Ex. 1:7). The Egyptians forced them into slavery, and the king of Egypt decreed that every newborn boy was to be killed (see Ex. 1:22). But by faith, Jochebed was not afraid of the king's command and hid Moses for three months (see Heb. 11:23). When she could no longer hide him, she "took an ark of bulrushes for him, daubed it with asphalt and pitch, put the child in it, and laid *it* in the reeds by the river's bank" (see Ex. 2:3).

Notice that Jochebed did not hide Moses because she was afraid. She hid him by faith! Is your faith today in the decrees of doctors, teachers, or psychologists who may have put a "death" sentence on your child? Perhaps "experts" have told you there is no hope for your child. Are you going to put your faith in their words? Or are you going to put your faith in the One whose words will not return to Him void? (see Isa. 55:11).

Jochebed then went on to put baby Moses into an "ark" that was made waterproof with asphalt and pitch, and laid it in the reeds by the river's bank. Where do you think she got the idea for the ark? Perhaps she had been meditating on how God had instructed Noah to build an ark that was covered with pitch (see Gen. 6:14) to save his household. When you keep on chewing and meditating on His Word, God can give you ideas and lead you to do things that can save your children!

What is the ark a picture of? It is a place of salvation, safety, and deliverance. When you let go of your cares about your children, you are not releasing them into treacherous waters. You are letting your children go and placing them into the Ark. Those who were in Noah's ark were saved from the waters of judgment, so the ark is a picture of our Lord Jesus! You are letting go of your cares about your children and putting your children into the hands of Jesus, who will *never* fail.

Even if negative things have happened to other children with a similar diagnosis or in similar situations, you can trust that your children are safe in His arms. Pharaoh had ordered every newborn Hebrew boy to be cast into the river (see Ex. 1:22). It is very likely that the bodies of other baby boys already taken by the Egyptian soldiers were in that river. But in this same river, what happened to Moses when his mother chose to put her trust in the Lord? Pharaoh's own daughter found Moses and decided to raise him as her own. When you put your children in His hands, He can cause them to be at the right place at the right time and save them from destruction. He can bring the right people into their lives who will take care of them, teach them, and provide for them as if they were their own children! But God did not stop at saving Moses' life. Jochebed was paid to take care of her own son, and Moses was sponsored by the treasury of Pharaoh, the same man who had ordered his death. You have to read the story for yourself:

> *And Pharaoh's daughter said to her, "Go." So the maiden went and called the child's mother. Then Pharaoh's daughter said to her, "Take this child away and nurse him for me, and*

I will give you your wages." So the woman took the child and nursed him.

—*Exodus 2:8–9*

> God can cause your children to be at the right place at the right time and save them from destruction.

Parents, this is our God! Let go. Put your children in His hands and whatever the devil meant for evil, God will turn it around and cause *all* things to work together for their good and to His glory (see Gen. 50:20, Rom. 8:28)!

Great Shall Be the *Shalom* of Your Children

There is another powerful promise found in Isaiah 54 that I want to share with you today:

All your children shall be taught by the LORD, and great shall be the peace of your children.

—*Isaiah 54:13*

The Bible says that our children will be taught by the Lord. Wow! We started this chapter by looking at how we can teach our children about God and about the finished work of Christ. How much better it is when the Lord Himself teaches them! When He teaches them, the Word of God tells us that not only shall they have peace, but their peace shall also be great! The Hebrew word for "peace" here is *shalom*, and as we saw earlier in this book, *shalom* is a very rich word, which also means completeness, soundness, welfare, and peace. Today, whatever your children may be going through, you can stand on this promise that your children can be completely healthy, whole, and well. You can lay hold of this truth that they can walk in supernatural peace—even if the circumstances around them may not look good.

Keep Our Eyes on the Cross

Do you know *why* our children can walk in this amazing promise of having great *shalom*? Because Isaiah 54 and its promises come after Isaiah 53, and Isaiah 53 is all about the work of our Lord Jesus at the cross. Would you take some time to meditate on Isaiah 53 today?

> *He is despised and rejected by men, a Man of sorrows and acquainted with grief. And we hid, as it were, our faces from Him; He was despised, and we did not esteem Him. Surely He has borne our griefs and carried our sorrows; yet we esteemed Him stricken, smitten by God, and afflicted. But He was wounded for our transgressions, He was bruised for our iniquities; the chastisement for our peace was upon Him, and by His stripes we are healed.*
>
> *—Isaiah 53:3–5*

Some of you might be blaming yourself for some of the things that your children are going through. Perhaps you are angry with yourself for not spending enough time with them when they were younger, not taking enough vitamins when you were pregnant with them, or maybe for losing your temper too often with them. Maybe you blame yourself for their behavioral problems because your marriage ended in divorce. Beloved, whatever may have happened in the past, do not remember the former things. Forget the things of old. Behold, He will do a new thing (see Isa. 43:18–19)!

Whatever you have done or failed to do, your children can have an intimate walk with the Lord and be taught by Him. They can be blessed with great *shalom* in every area of their lives. It has nothing to do with you, but everything to do with what our Lord Jesus did on the cross. He was despised and rejected so that they can be loved and accepted. He bore their griefs and carried their sorrows so that they will never have to bear them themselves. He was oppressed so that they need never come under any mental oppression or tormenting stress. The chastisement for their peace was upon Him, and by His stripes, they are healed.

Parents, your hands are too small. There is so much you cannot do for your children. That is why the most important thing you can do for them is to point them to the Lord Jesus and let Him take care of them. Today, you can live the let-go life in your family life because God Himself builds your house and watches over your children. I pray your heart will be more and more established in knowing that because of what Jesus has done on the cross, your children can be blessed in every area of their lives. Just as the children of Israel experienced supernatural light in their dwellings when all of Egypt was enveloped in darkness (see Ex. 10:23), may you and your children also experience the Lord's protection and supernatural light even in these dark times we're living in. In Jesus' mighty name, I speak blessings upon you and your household and declare that your days and the days of your children shall be as days of heaven upon the earth!

19.

LET GO AND LIVE LONG

Some of you reading this book may have been told by doctors that your days are numbered, that you only have a few years or maybe even months to live. Or perhaps your parents passed on when they were still young, and you are fearful that you too will die young. With all due respect to doctors (thank God for doctors, who are on the same side fighting against sickness and disease), the things that are impossible with man are possible with God. Whatever doctors have told you, I want you to know that the eternal Word of the living God declares that with *long life*, He shall satisfy you (see Ps. 91:16). So let's stand in faith together on this promise from the Word of God.

This chapter is all about God's desire for you to live a long, healthy life, a let-go life free to fully enjoy the blessings that He has prepared for you. I believe the Lord has hidden secrets to health in His Word that will bless you, especially when you see how it is all linked to what we have been talking about throughout this book. And as you read on, I pray that the Lord will establish your heart with His promises and drive out every fear in your life.

A Heart at Peace Gives Life to the Body

This chapter is so vital because I am going to show you how living the let-go life, living stress-free, and walking in His *shalom*—all the things that we have been talking about in this book—have an impact on our health. Do you want life to be released in your body? The Bible tells us how. Let me show you a few different translations of Proverbs 14:30 so we can see more clearly what the Holy Spirit meant:

> *A heart at peace gives life to the body, but envy rots the bones.*
>   —*Proverbs 14:30* NIV

> *A peaceful heart leads to a healthy body; jealousy is like cancer in the bones.*
>   —*Proverbs 14:30* NLT

> *A tranquil heart is life to the body, but passion is rottenness to the bones.*
>   —*Proverbs 14:30* NASB

Isn't it amazing to read all these translations together? When you are meditating on a verse, this is one way you can really dig deep to chew on the truths in a single verse. Let's look at the New King James translation of this verse:

> *A sound heart* is *life to the body, but envy* is *rottenness to the bones.*
>   —*Proverbs 14:30*

The Hebrew word for "sound," describing the heart in this verse, is the word *marpe*, which means "a healing" or "cure."[1] So what does all this tell you? When your heart is at peace, when it is tranquil and peaceful, it becomes a healing heart that gives life to your body! In other words, if you want to live long, have a relaxed attitude. Let your heart not be troubled, neither let it be afraid (see John 14:27)!

> *If you want to live long, let your heart not be troubled, neither let it be afraid.*

Secrets of Healing in the Hebrew Language

Can I take some time to show you some more secrets to supernatural health hidden in the Hebrew language? This is what *marpe* looks like in Hebrew:

מַרְפֵּא

Remembering that Hebrew reads from right to left, when you remove the first letter, *mem* (מ), to get to the root word of this noun, you will get the word *rapha*:

רְפֵא

Rapha means "to heal,"[2] and this is the same word the Lord uses to refer to Himself as our *Jehovah Rapha*, "the LORD who heals you" (Ex. 15:26). Now, if we go just one step deeper, we'll see that *rapha* is closely related to the root verb *raphah*, which means "to relax, to let go."[3,4]

In other words, in Hebrew, *healing* is closely tied to the act of *relaxing*. I find this very interesting. Relax. Doesn't this remind you of what I have been sharing with you about letting go of your worries, relaxing your grip, and allowing His supply to flow through those pipes from heaven? Doesn't this also remind you of the unforced, effortless rhythm of grace? It also confirms the connection we just read about in Proverbs 14:30, between having a peaceful heart and how that gives life to our bodies.

There are more truths hidden in the word *rapha* that I want to show you. Each Hebrew letter has a corresponding picture or idea.[5] Reading from right to left, the first letter of *rapha* is *resh*, the letter in the middle is *pey*, and the last letter is *aleph*. The picture associated with *resh* is a head. That's what we use to think and to meditate with. The picture that corresponds to *pey* is that of a mouth—what we use to speak with. Finally, the picture linked to the letter *aleph* is the sacrificial ox.

Hebrew letter	א	פ	ר
Name	*aleph*	*pey*	*resh*
Pictogram	sacrificial ox	mouth	head

Putting them all together, what do you see? Healing comes when the head and mouth speak of the sacrifice! The more we meditate on and speak about the sacrifice that our Lord Jesus made on the cross, the more we will walk in the health that He paid for us to possess. If you are trusting the Lord for healing today, keep on thinking and speaking of His sacrifice. Keep on meditating on verses that speak of His finished work. Declare by faith that *surely* He has borne all your sicknesses and carried all your sorrows (see Isa. 53:4). Thank the Lord for all His benefits. Praise Him for forgiving all your iniquities, for healing all your diseases, and for redeeming you from destruction (see Ps. 103:2–4).

God's Words Are Health to All Your Flesh

Let me show you another portion of Scripture:

> *My son, give attention to my words; incline your ear to my sayings. Do not let them depart from your eyes; keep them in the midst of your heart;* **for they** are **life to those who find them, and health to all their flesh.**
>
> —*Proverbs 4:20–22 (boldface mine)*

What does God tell us to do? He tells us to give attention to His words and to incline our ears to His sayings. He exhorts us to not let His words depart from our eyes. This means we are to keep our focus and attention on *His* words. Whatever negative reports or diagnosis we may have received, let's keep our eyes on His words and never lose sight of them. Let's allow His promises to penetrate deep into our hearts. And when we do that, the Bible declares that His words "*are* life to those who find them, and health to all their flesh." By the way, the Hebrew word for health here is *marpe*. God's Word is healing to *all* our flesh. It is healing to our eyes. It is healing to our kidneys. It is healing to our bones. It is healing to our skin. It is healing to our lungs. It is healing to *all* our flesh! Not a single part of our bodies will be left untouched by the healing power of God's Word!

Many treatments work in one area of your body but may result in negative side effects in other parts of your body. For instance, some medications might keep tuberculosis from attacking your lungs but could cause you to suffer dizziness.[6] Another treatment could arrest the cancer cells but cause you to lose your appetite and suffer from anemia.[7] If you are going through such treatments today, can I encourage you not to let God's Word depart from your eyes? Even as you listen to your doctor's advice, hide God's Word in the midst of your heart and counter any possible side effects of your medical treatment with the sword of the Spirit, which is the Word of God! Keep reading, hearing, and speaking about our Lord Jesus, who went about "healing all kinds of sickness and all kinds of disease" (Matt. 4:23). Keep declaring that His Word is health to *all* your flesh. Receive the *shalom* that our Lord Jesus bequeathed to you and keep meditating on how it brings *life* to your whole body!

> *If you are going through medical treatment today, counter any possible side effects with the Word of God.*

But, Pastor Prince, can't you see how big this growth is? Can't you see this X-ray? My friend, can I encourage you to keep your eyes on the written Word of God? In fact, it says, "Do not look at the things which are seen, but at the things which are not seen. For the things which are seen *are* temporary, but the things which are not seen *are* eternal" (2 Cor. 4:18). That blood test and cancer marker reading are temporal; God's Word is eternal. That medical report and CT scan are natural; God's Word is supernatural. Man is subject to failures and mistakes; God never fails. Amen? The more you think and speak forth His Word, the more you will experience His supernatural healing!

Delivered from Cancer in the Bladder

Let me share with you a powerful testimony from Dana, who stood on the Word with her husband and saw the Lord deliver him from cancer in the bladder. When her husband first discovered he was bleeding during urination, they went to see a doctor who told them he had a prostate condition. But as the bleeding continued to worsen, Dana tuned in to my program one day and heard me teach on the Holy Communion and standing on the Word of God for our healing, health, and wholeness. She shared what she'd heard with her husband and they began to partake of the Holy Communion together. They also began getting ahold of healing Scriptures and confessing Psalm 91 and 1 Peter 2:24 over him and his condition.

They held on to the Word and practiced partaking of the Lord's Supper as they had read in the Word, even as they received news from her husband's doctor that the bleeding was caused by an aggressively malignant tumor in his bladder. Despite having it removed, they were told that the cancer had spread to the inner wall of the bladder and that her husband had to have his bladder removed. But I want you to see what Dana said about how she and her husband responded to the news and what happened next:

Although this was a disheartening report, we continued to believe the Lord Jesus by confessing His Word and partaking of the Holy Communion.

When we went for the biopsy the doctor arranged for my husband, the results showed that no traces of cancer and no new tumors were found in my husband's bladder. Thanks be to Jesus for the victory and His finished work! All glory to Him!

Praise the Lord! What an uplifting testimony of the power of God's Word to bring health and life to our bodies. The symptoms may not go away immediately, but as you keep believing, meditating on, and declaring His Word, that Word will not return void!

Receive Your Healing

Beloved, as you hold on to His Word, whatever your condition might be, I am believing with you for your complete healing too in the mighty name of Jesus. Be still. Cease striving and know that He is God. Stand still and see the salvation, the help, and the deliverance of your God. He has not forgotten you. At the name of Jesus, every knee bows. Whatever disease, whatever sickness, whatever condition you might have, it bows to Jesus. So in the name of Jesus, be healed. Right now, that same Holy Spirit that raised Jesus Christ from the dead quickens your body. Receive that infusion of strength. Receive renewal of youth like the eagle's and restoration of strength in Jesus' name!

God Wants to Satisfy Us with Long Life

Do you know that God wants you to enjoy a long, fulfilling, and healthy life? It is a blessing to live to see our children's children (see Ps. 128:6). But our heavenly Father doesn't just want us to live long. As we saw in the earlier chapters, He also wants us to enjoy days of heaven on earth in every area of our lives (see Deut. 11:21), and this means that even as we advance in age, it is not God's will for us to live with sickness and pain.

> God wants you to enjoy a long, fulfilling, and healthy life.

Have you heard people say things like "I must be getting old—I'm so forgetful nowadays," or "Age is catching up to me—my body doesn't work as well as it used to"? My friend, do not accept the lie

that your body has to deteriorate as you grow older. Don't accept
that it is "normal" to become weak or to have any age-related disease! It may be true for the people of the world, but as for you, child
of God, Christ has redeemed you from every curse (see Gal. 3:13)!

You can trust God to be like Caleb, one of only two spies
who made it into the promised land because he chose to believe
God's promises instead of looking at the giants in the land. At the
age of eighty-five, Caleb asked Joshua for a mountain filled with
giants and he went on to conquer it together with his sons. Caleb
declared, "I *am as* strong this day as on the day that Moses sent me;
just as my strength *was* then, so now *is* my strength for war, both
for going out and for coming in" (Josh. 14:11). Forty-five years had
passed since Moses first sent him to spy out the land, but the Lord
had not only kept him alive (see Josh. 14:10), He had also kept him
robust, healthy, and just as strong *for war*! You can also trust God
to be like Moses, who was 120 years old when he died, "yet his eye-
sight was clear, and he was as strong as ever" (Deut. 34:7 NLT).

Ladies, the Bible calls you daughters of Sarah (see 1 Pet. 3:6).
When Sarah was in her sixties, the Bible tells us that the Egyptians
saw "that she *was* very beautiful" (Gen. 12:14) and took her for
Pharaoh's harem. This happened to Sarah again when she was in
her nineties, with Abimelech, king of Gerar, also taking her for his
harem (see Gen. 20:2). Now, these were heathen kings who had
their pick of the most beautiful women in their land. What does
that tell you? God renewed her youth. You can trust God to be like
Sarah and for your youth to be renewed like the eagle's (Ps. 103:5)!

George Müller's Secret to Long Life

One of my heroes from the 1800s is George Müller. Over the course
of his life, Müller established 117 Christian schools ministering to

about 120,000 young people. He distributed over 285,000 Bibles, over 1.4 million copies of the New Testament, and over 240,000 other religious books and pamphlets. He funded over four hundred missionaries, including Hudson Taylor, to varying degrees. In 1875, at the age of seventy, he began a seventeen-year period of missionary travels where he preached in almost forty countries, including the United States, India, Australia, Japan, and China. He was able to preach in English, French, and German. He was also well versed in Hebrew, Greek, and Latin.[8]

In the year that he would turn ninety-three, he visited two of his friends, who were about ten years younger than he was. He noticed that he was much stronger than they were and could still actively serve the Lord, whereas they could no longer do so. After those meetings, he remarked, "I came away from both these beloved brethren feeling that I was quite young by comparison as to strength, though so much older. Oh, how very kind and good my heavenly Father has been to me! I have no aches or pains, no rheumatism, and now in my ninety-third year, I can do a day's work at the orphan houses with as much ease and comfort to myself as ever."[9]

What a wonderful faith picture for us—to be serving the Lord in our nineties and to experience no aches and pains at all! When Müller passed on later that year, he simply took off to be with Jesus. He had led a prayer meeting at his church one evening and his body was found in his study the next morning, completely without any sickness. I believe that's how all believers should leave. When we are satisfied, we simply head off to be with the Lord without any pain or suffering!

When he was asked the question, "What's the secret to your long life?" Müller, who read the Word every day, attributed it to three causes, one of which was the love he felt for the Scriptures and the constant recuperative power they exercised upon his whole being.[10] There's a reviving, purifying, resuscitating, reju-venating, and prospering power in God's Word! This is why the enemy does not want you to spend time in the Word, but don't let him stop you from reaping the wonderful benefits that the Lord meant for you to enjoy!

> *There's a reviving, purifying, resuscitating, and rejuvenating power in God's Word.*

Let Go and Live Long

There is another reason I am sharing with you about the life of George Müller. I believe he lived a long, significant life and was used mightily by God because he truly lived the let-go life that we have been talking about throughout this book. I believe he lived in the reality of Philippians 4:6–7, which says:

> *Be anxious for nothing, but in everything by prayer and supplication; with thanksgiving, let your requests be made known to God; and the peace of God, which surpasses all understanding, will guard your hearts and minds through Christ Jesus.*

Müller said, "For more than seventy years I have not been anxious."[11] Can you imagine him living life without anxiety? And he didn't live a life without anxiety because he was holed up in a mountain somewhere with no demands on him. His life was very full, and apart from many other achievements, he was responsible for providing for and taking care of over *ten thousand* orphans during his lifetime.[12] Some of us are overcome by stress when we have two or three children to look after. Can you imagine the demands that come with housing, feeding, clothing, and educating ten thousand children? And yet, this is what he said: "It is the great privilege of the child of God not to be anxious. And it is possible to attain to it even in this life; yea, in the midst of great difficulties, great trials."[13]

Do you know how Müller was able to not be anxious? He said, "I have rolled my burdens on the Lord, and He has carried them for me. The result of that has been that 'the peace of God, which passeth all understanding,' has kept my heart and mind."[14] You and I are children of God. Like Müller, we have the great privilege of not letting our hearts be troubled even when we are faced with challenges. We have the great privilege of casting our cares into the hands of the One who loves us and of enjoying the peace that our Lord Jesus came to give us!

How to Enjoy Length of Days

So many studies have been done on centenarians and longevity is always depicted as something you can "achieve" if you do the right things, like watching your diet and exercising. A number of years ago, Wendy and I saw a television documentary in which two scientists had studied the centenarians in Okinawa, Japan, for over three decades. They concluded that the longevity of the centenarians could be attributed to several factors, including genetics, diet, an active lifestyle, as well as a relaxed attitude to life. Many of the centenarians apparently have a common saying in their culture: "Don't worry, it will work out." We agree that these things are important, of course. But all these are natural means. Would you like to hear God's supernatural prescription for long life?

*I have set before you life and death, blessing and cursing; therefore choose life, that both you and your descendants may live; that you may love the L**ORD** your God, that you may obey His voice, and that you may cling to Him, **for He is your life and the length of your days**; and that you may dwell in the land which the L**ORD** swore to your fathers, to Abraham, Isaac, and Jacob, to give them.*
—Deuteronomy 30:19–20 (boldface mine)

Did you see that? The Bible says that the Lord is your life and the length of your days. The length of your days is a person—Jesus! Our longevity and the blessings we can enjoy are not based on what we need to do but dependent on He who is all-powerful, all-knowing, and best of all, all-loving! Because of Him, we can have a security that is unshakable, a joy unspeakable, and peace that surpasses understanding!

> *Our longevity is not based on what we need to do but dependent on Jesus, who is all-powerful, all-knowing, and all-loving.*

Let me show you another powerful passage of Scripture:

*Because he has set his love upon Me, therefore I will deliver him; I will set him on high, because he has known My name. He shall call upon Me, and I will answer him; I will be with him in trouble; I will deliver him and honor him. **With long life I will satisfy him, and show him My salvation.***
—Psalm 91:14–16 (boldface mine)

The secret of long life is found in the last line, which says, "With long life I will satisfy him, and show him My salvation." Do you know what is the Hebrew word for "salvation" in this verse? It is *yeshua*,[15] the name of Jesus in Hebrew. In other words, the verse can be read as, "With long life I will satisfy him, and show him My *Yeshua*," or "With long life I satisfy him by showing him My Jesus." The more of Jesus you see in the Word, the more you will live long. And God gives you long life so that you can see more and more and more of His Son. Why? So that you can share the good news of His Salvation with people who don't know the glories of His Son!

> *The more of Jesus you see in the Word, the more you will live long.*

When Jesus rose from the dead, He appeared to two disciples on the road to Emmaus. But the Bible tells us that Jesus restrained their eyes so that they couldn't recognize Him in His resurrected form. Then, "beginning at Moses and all the Prophets, He expounded to them in all the Scriptures the things concerning Himself" (Luke 24:27).

Until they had seen Him in the Bible, our Lord Jesus restrained their eyes from recognizing Him. I asked the Lord once, "Why did You restrain their eyes from seeing You? Wouldn't it have been better for them to have seen You physically?" His answer floored me. I have never heard anyone share or preach on this. He said, "It was more important for them to see Me in the Scriptures than to see Me in person." *It was more important for the disciples to see Him in the Word than to see Him in person.* This gives all of us hope because while we may not see Jesus physically today, we can all see Him in the Scriptures. Long life is connected to seeing Jesus in the Word of God, and that is why I love expounding on truths concerning my Lord Jesus in the Bible. I believe my job as a preacher is to magnify the loveliness of Jesus Christ and to proclaim His finished work. Jesus is "the bread of life" (John 6:35). He is our "living water" (John 4:10). He is "the resurrection and the life" (John 11:25). May we all see Jesus and feed on Him because when we do, we partake of His resurrection life, His divine health, and His promise of a long, good life!

20.
YOU ARE NOT ALONE

Don't be too hard on yourself when you find yourself bogged down with worries and your heart loaded with anxieties even after learning about the let-go life that God wants you to live. More often than not, I have to deliberately remind myself to let go, be conscious of the Lord's provision, and trust Him for the supply to flow into my areas of stress. Living the let-go life is a daily journey of faith. Every day, there is a battle for our minds. New issues can arise and we can find ourselves faced with multiple challenges coming at us from different fronts.

But whether you are dealing with a serious medical condition, a crisis at home, or a frustrating situation in your workplace, you have a choice. You can choose to allow your mind to go into overdrive, stressing out over all the possible worst-case scenarios you can think of and holding on to your cares with as much strength as you can muster. Or you can choose to step into the river of faith and start practicing the let-go life.

Life can be overwhelming. Things don't always happen the way we want them to happen. Despite our best efforts, we can fail. There are times when we look at the results we are getting and wonder why we even bother to try. Maybe it feels like the breakthroughs we are waiting for may never come. Or things happen to us or to our loved ones and there is just no answer to the question "Why?"

If you are in that place of despair right now, would you allow me to share this psalm with you?

> *When my heart is overwhelmed; lead me to the rock that is higher than I. For You have been a shelter for me, a strong tower from the enemy. I will abide in Your tabernacle forever; I will trust in the shelter of Your wings.*
>
> *—Psalm 61:2–4*

Even if everything around you seems to have been shaken, I want you to know that there is an unshakable Rock that is higher than you. His name is Jesus. His everlasting love toward you will *never* fail. He is the strong tower you can run to when your enemies surround you. In the shelter of His wings, you can safely rest.

He is the strong tower you can run to when your enemies surround you.

He Knows and He Cares

In writing this book, my desire was for you to be led to the Rock that is higher than you and me. If you can walk away from this book knowing that you have someone watching over you whose hands are so much bigger and who continues to work miracles for you today, then the time and effort that have gone into writing this book would have been worth it. My friend, I prayed that this book would find you. I prayed that in your day of adversity, this book would lead you to the Lord and that you would have such a deep revelation of the length, the breadth, the depth, and the height of His exceeding love toward you. You can let go of all your cares to Him because He—the God who hung the stars in the heavens and marked out the foundations of the earth—loves *you*.

Perhaps you have been waiting for results in a certain area of your life, and, like David, you are asking the Lord, "How long, O LORD? Will You forget me forever?" (Ps. 13:1). Maybe you see breakthroughs happening for other people but not for you and you are asking, "Will the Lord cast off forever? And will He be favorable no more?" (Ps. 77:7). Beloved, He numbers the very hairs on your head—He knows exactly what you are going through right now (see Luke 12:7). He knows the thoughts in your mind. He knows the secret struggles that have left you discouraged and battered. He knows the things that you don't even share with your spouse. He knows them all. And, my friend, He loves you. He doesn't get offended because you have those thoughts and questions. Trust in His love for you, no matter what challenges may surround you. I believe God has given me a word of encouragement that is going to set you free.

> *Trust in His love for you, no matter what challenges may surround you.*

God Is in Control

I want to share with you the story of a man in the Bible who was depressed and suicidal—Elijah. I believe the Holy Spirit placed his story in the Scriptures to show us that God can even use someone who gets disheartened. And more importantly, I want you to see God's heart of tenderness toward Elijah when he was at his lowest moments. I believe we can learn from Elijah, because he wasn't some mighty man of God with no weaknesses. The

Bible tells us he was a man with a nature like ours, with the same physical, mental, and spiritual limitations and shortcomings (James 5:17 AMP).

There was a dark period in Israel's history, when Ahab, the king then, "did evil in the sight of the LORD, more than all who *were* before him" (1 Kings 16:30). Ahab married Jezebel, a Phoenician princess. Ahab went on to worship her gods, Baal and Asherah, even building a temple for Baal in Samaria and leading the nation to worship them (see 1 Kings 16:32). Jezebel was an evil woman who massacred the prophets of the Lord and who raised up four hundred fifty prophets of Baal and four hundred prophets of Asherah as her advisers (see 1 Kings 18:4, 19). It is at this point Elijah came onto the scene. He went before Ahab and declared, *"As the* LORD *God of Israel lives, before whom I stand, there shall not be dew nor rain these years, except at my word"* (1 Kings 17:1). And from the time that Elijah spoke, there was no rain for three and a half years. In fact, the Bible records that there was a "severe famine" in Samaria (see 1 Kings 18:2). Baal worshipers believed that it was Baal who provided rain, blessed their crops, and controlled the weather.[1] God sent Elijah to demonstrate that Baal could do nothing and was of no effect in the midst of the famine.

But God took care of Elijah throughout the famine. First, He told Elijah to hide by the Brook Cherith, where he could drink from the brook. God commanded ravens to feed him there, bringing him bread and meat every morning and evening (see 1 Kings 17:3–6). When the brook dried up because there had been no rain in the land, God told Elijah to go to Zarephath, where He had commanded a widow to provide for him. The widow only had a handful of flour in a bin and a little oil in a jar. But God multiplied the flour and oil and they did not run out, feeding Elijah as well as the widow's household throughout the famine until God sent rain again (see 1 Kings 17:14). And even when Elijah was in hiding, God used him mightily. During the time Elijah was staying with the widow, her son became sick and died. But God used Elijah to bring the boy back to life (see 1 Kings 17:17–23)!

God Shows that He Alone Is God

Finally, three and a half years after the drought had started, God told Elijah to present himself to Ahab. Elijah did so and told Ahab to gather all the Israelites as well as all the prophets of Baal and Asherah on Mount Carmel. He then issued a challenge to prove once and for all if Baal or God was the true God. He told the prophets of Baal to choose one bull, cut it in pieces, and lay it on the wood, but put no fire under it. He would prepare another bull and do the same. Then he told the prophets of Baal to call on the name of their god and he would call on the name of the Lord. He then boldly declared, "The God who answers by fire, He is God" (1 Kings 18:23–24). The Bible records how the prophets of Baal then "called on the name of Baal from morning even till noon, saying, 'O Baal, hear us!' But *there was* no voice; no one answered" (1 Kings 18:26). All day, they leaped about the altar that they had made, prophesied, and cut themselves as was their custom until blood gushed out. But still, no one answered.

When it was Elijah's turn, Elijah took twelve stones according to the number of the tribes of Israel. With the stones he built an altar in the name of the Lord and made a trench around the altar. After he had cut the bull into pieces and laid it on the wood, he got the people to pour water all over the sacrifice and wood over and over again. Twelve pots of water were poured over the sacrifice, until water ran all around the altar and filled the trench.

At the time for the offering of the evening sacrifice, Elijah prayed, and the fire of the Lord fell and *consumed* the sacrifice, the wood, the stones, the dust, and even all the water that was in the trench. When the people saw this, they fell on their faces and said, "The LORD, He *is* God! The LORD, He *is* God!" In Hebrew, they cried out, "*Yahweh*, He is *Elohim!*"[2] The true name of God was proclaimed. Elijah then executed all the prophets of Baal and told Ahab to get ready, for rain was coming. And in that same day, heavy rain poured down, ending years of drought (see 1 Kings 18:30–45).

What a powerful demonstration of the power of God! The whole nation of Israel must have been shaken. There had been a showdown, and God established beyond the shadow of any doubt that He alone was God. Elijah had called down fire from heaven. The prophets of Baal were dead. It was a resounding victory for Elijah. So when Jezebel found out what had happened and sent a message to Elijah saying that she would kill him, you would think that Elijah would have said something like, "Oh yeah? Go ahead. Make my day!" But that's not what happened. The Bible tells us that "when he saw *that*, he arose and ran for his life" (1 Kings 19:3).

Win over Discouragement

Why did Elijah run for his life? After everything that God had done through him, why was he suddenly afraid? I submit to you that it was because Elijah *saw*. Elijah—the man of faith—started to walk by sight. When we see our finances dwindling, we get discouraged. When we see the economy on a downtrend, we get dejected. When we see the letters chasing us for the debts we have to pay, we get dismayed. When we see the lump growing in our bodies, we despair. We get snared by the visible things that are temporal and we lose sight of the invisible God, who is eternal.

Elijah forgot the God who led him to Cherith. He forgot who brought the ravens that fed him by day and by evening. He forgot about the widow whom God commanded to feed him. And he forgot about the barrel of meal that never ran out and the jar of oil that never ran dry. He forgot the God of the resurrection who raised the boy from the dead through him. He forgot the God who answered by fire and the rain that followed. Why? Because in just one moment, any of us can lose sight of a good God. Even if we walked in the greatest faith yesterday, we can go back to sight today.

What else happened to Elijah? The Bible tells us that Elijah went a day's journey into the wilderness, sat under a tree, and prayed that he might die, saying, "It is enough! Now, LORD, take my life, for I *am* no better than my fathers!" (1 Kings 19:4). He wasn't only fearful; he also became depressed and suicidal.

God Ministers to Us in Our Depression

Perhaps like Elijah, you just want to give up. Perhaps you are feeling discouraged and you feel like all that you have done with your life has amounted to nothing. Maybe you have poured your life into your ministry or into your family and it feels like you have nothing left to give. Maybe you feel like you have failed—failed as a minister, or as a husband, or as a mother. I am writing to believers who are suffering depression and discouragement and to those of you who are disappointed with God. I am writing to those who feel like your best years are behind you. I am writing to *you*, my friend. I want you to see what God did for Elijah because I believe that it will lift you out of the darkness that has surrounded you.

The Bible tells us that as Elijah lay and slept under the tree, an angel touched him and said to him, "Arise *and* eat." He looked around and there by his head was some bread baked over hot coals and a jar of water (see 1 Kings 19:6 NIV). He ate and drank and then lay down again. And the angel of the Lord came back the second time and touched him, and said, "Arise *and* eat, because the journey *is* too great for you." So he got up and ate and drank. Strengthened by that food, he traveled forty days and forty nights until he reached Horeb, the mountain of God (see 1 Kings 19:7–8).

My friend, there are so many things from this passage that I believe the Lord wants to show you today. Maybe when you look at the commitments that you have in front of you, the payments you have to make, and the deadlines that stretch before you, all you can say is, "the journey is too great." I want you to know that God knows how you feel.

When you find "the angel of the LORD" in the Old Testament, in most instances it refers to the pre-incarnate appearance of Christ. Doesn't the "bread baked over hot coals" remind you of another meal? The Gospel of John records how the resurrected Jesus cooked breakfast for His disciples. They were fishing, and when they got back to shore, "they saw a fire of coals there, and fish laid on it, and bread" (John 21:9). The Lord Jesus will provide for you practically. He prepared coals of fire to keep His disciples warm and He fed them because they were hungry. The same Jesus who so tenderly told His disciples, "Come *and* eat breakfast" (John 21:12), had appeared to Elijah. And I believe that right now, the same Jesus is reaching out to you and saying to you, "Arise and eat, because the journey is too great for you." My friend, He loves you, and He cares for you intimately and practically. Never doubt that.

God loves you, and He cares for you practically.

In the natural, your journey may be too great, but you have food from heaven that can strengthen you and sustain you. Elijah went on the strength of the food that the angel of the Lord gave him for forty days and forty nights. I want to encourage you to keep feeding on His Word. Keep partaking of Jesus in the Word. Keep eating of the bread of life. See the Lord Jesus breaking bread for you and saying to you, "Take, eat; this is My body" (Matt. 26:26). One word from God can cause you to go in His strength.

There's something else I want to highlight to you: Elijah slept. You may not realize that all of us are subject to bouts of depression. And sometimes, what the Lord does for us is, He gives His beloved sleep. If you have not been sleeping, please allow yourself to rest, and allow Him to take over your burdens. If you feel like you can only go on if you had supernatural strength, then God wants to give you supernatural food and supernatural sleep!

Our Ever-Present Help

I used to have the impression that if I were discouraged, God would not hear my prayers. After all, I was in no state to pray the prayer of faith and to say with no doubt in my heart to any mountain, "Be removed and be cast into the sea" (Mark 11:23). I don't know where I got that idea. But I was so wrong. Do you know what the Bible records? If you forget everything else, don't forget this: *In the day of Elijah's faith, ravens fed him and the widow sustained him. But in the day of his depression, angels waited on him, and God Himself fed him.* What a God! His mercies fail not. They are new every morning!

God will not forsake us in our day of depression. In fact, He seeks us out to strengthen us during our time of discouragement and right now, that is what the Lord is doing for you. He could be speaking to you through the pages of this book. He could be sending a friend to write a note of encouragement to you. He could be whispering to you through His Word. By whatever means He chooses, He wants this message to get to you: "Be strong and of good courage, do not fear nor be afraid of them; for the LORD your God, He *is* the One who goes with you. He will not leave you nor forsake you" (Deut. 31:6).

> God seeks us out to strengthen us during our time of discouragement.

When Elijah spent the night in a cave at Horeb, God said to him, "What are you doing here, Elijah?" (1 Kings 19:9). Now, for God to say, "What are you doing here?" it means that God was also there with him. Beloved, God will *never* ever leave you nor forsake you, even if the journey you took was your own. Even if you are on a long journey because you fled from someone who was angry with you, even if you went by the visible instead of the invisible, God has *not* forsaken you. He is on the journey with you!

You Are Not Alone

One of the reasons we get discouraged is when we look around us, we think like Elijah did: "I alone am left" (1 Kings 19:10). We think that God has left us all alone and we have to fight for our own survival. The enemy wants you to feel isolated and alone. He wants you to think that God doesn't care about you. It is easy to keep you in the bondage of stress when you feel isolated. And it is easy to keep you bound with the spirit of discouragement and despair when you believe the lie that God is against you and doesn't care about you. My friend, I announce to you that you are not alone.

Do you want to know how God responded to Elijah's outcry? God told Elijah, "I have reserved seven thousand in Israel, all whose knees have not bowed to Baal" (1 Kings 19:18). Wow. Elijah was not alone by any measure, but he didn't know it because he did not *see* those seven thousand. My friend, when you can't see, trust. Trust in the invisible, infallible God who loves you! Jesus said, "I am with you always, *even* to the end of the age" (Matt. 28:20). The Lord Jesus Himself is with you. Always. Right now.

> When you can't see, trust. Trust in the invisible, infallible God who loves you.

Where Is God?

Before God told Elijah about the seven thousand, Elijah had had a powerful encounter with the Lord. God told Elijah, "Go out, and stand on the mountain before the LORD." And behold, the Lord passed by, and a great and strong wind tore into the mountains and broke the rocks in pieces, but the Lord was not in the wind. After the wind there came an earthquake, but the Lord was not in the earthquake. After the earthquake, there was a fire, but the Lord was not in the fire. And after the fire, there was a still, small voice (see 1 Kings 19:11–12).

Sometimes, we are looking for spectacular signs to tell us that God is with us. But you know what? The Lord was not in the earthquake, the wind, or the fire. He was in the still, small voice. If you study this verse in Hebrew, this refers to a calm whisper of gentleness.[3] What's that? It's the ministry of grace. Don't look for God in outward manifestations. He is in the gentle whisper that speaks right to your heart.

Talk to Jesus, the Friend You Can Always Depend on

David wrote these lines in a beautiful psalm: "My heart has heard you say, 'Come and talk with me.' And my heart responds, "Lord, I am coming" (Ps. 27:8 NLT). The Lord is the still, small voice that is talking to you right now and saying to you, "Come and talk with Me." Whatever cares or anxieties might be weighing you down, Jesus wants you to talk with Him and to tell them to Him. You don't have to craft perfect prayers or follow some religious formula when you talk to Him. Just talk to Him like a friend.

As you tell Him about your worries, do you know that you are actually casting your cares to Him? Do you know that simply by talking to Him you are exercising your faith? It doesn't have to be a mountain-moving, Mark 11:23 prayer, although there definitely is a place for such prayers. But when you are feeling despondent and have no faith, just tell it to Jesus, as the words of this hymn so beautifully put it:

Tell It to Jesus

Are you weary, are you heavyhearted?
Tell it to Jesus,
Tell it to Jesus;
Are you grieving over joys departed?
Tell it to Jesus alone.

Tell it to Jesus, tell it to Jesus,
He is a friend that's well-known;
You've no other such a friend or brother,
Tell it to Jesus alone.

Do the tears flow down your cheeks unbidden?
Tell it to Jesus,
Tell it to Jesus;
Have you sins that to men's eyes are hidden?
Tell it to Jesus alone.

Do you fear the gath'ring clouds of sorrow?
Tell it to Jesus,
Tell it to Jesus;
Are you anxious what shall be tomorrow?
Tell it to Jesus alone.

Are you troubled at the thought of dying?
Tell it to Jesus,

Tell it to Jesus;
For Christ's coming kingdom are you sighing?
Tell it to Jesus alone.[4]

> When you are feeling discouraged and have no faith, just tell it to Jesus.

As you simply tell it to Jesus, you will realize He truly is your Friend—and what a friend we have in Jesus! Talking to Him is like spending time over coffee with a dear friend. Hours can pass before you know it as you pour out your heart to Him. I like going on evening walks and talking to Him, telling Him all the concerns on my heart. And as I talk to Him, somehow strength is imparted, and I walk away so much more conscious of His golden pipes flowing with supply toward me than of the challenges I have to deal with. As I tell Him my burdens, they are lifted from my shoulders, and I am reminded afresh that I have a heavenly Father who loves me. If He takes care of the birds of the air and the lilies of the field, how much more will He take care of me!

Freedom from Depression and Discouragement

Jesus said, "Come to Me, all *you* who labor and are heavy laden, and I will give you rest" (Matt. 11:28). If you are heavy laden, the Lord is asking you to come to Him. Come to Him with all your hurts, your disappointments, and your failures. Come to Him with all your bitterness and all your pains. He wants to give you His rest. He wants to give you His peace.

As you come to the close of this book, I pray you have

encountered Jesus in a deep and intimate way. I declare that today, you shall experience your Jubilee. Even right now, I believe there's an anointing that's releasing people from depression, from discouragement, from self-pity, from anger, and from resentment. Elijah heard the sound of the abundance of rain (see 1 Kings 18:41). I hear the sound of prison doors being unlocked and flung open. I see people being set free from years of depression. Free from discouragement. Free from anger. Free from stress. Free from a life of self-pity, from a life of being angry with people around them.

In the mighty name of Jesus, I command the spirits of depression and discouragement to loose you and let you go. Know that you are loved. Know that even when the troubles are of your own making, He will not leave you nor forsake you. Even if you had willfully chosen a path that has taken you to the valley of the shadow of death, He is with you. He will not leave you. He will not forsake you (see Ps. 23:4).

Whenever you get discouraged, tell Him. Whenever you are feeling down, tell Him. He is a wonderful friend who sticks closer than a brother (see Prov. 18:24). And as you learn to cast your cares to Him every day, may you begin to live the let-go life, free from fear, stress, and anxiety!

CLOSING WORDS

My dear reader, it has been my privilege to share with you what the Lord has revealed to me through the years about living a life free from crippling cares, anxieties, and stress by depending on His love and grace. It's my prayer that as you have taken this wonderful journey with me, you have begun to experience a deeper inward rest and *shalom*-peace grounded on God's unshakable Word.

We live in a world where we're surrounded by fears, uncertainties, responsibilities, and demands 24/7. This is why it's so important for us to be established in how God's grace is all about supply. When you feel the chokehold of a demand mind-set starting to claim your heart, remember the picture of the golden pipes constantly bringing fresh supply from heaven into every area of need. Begin to practice letting go of your worries. Relax your grip, and allow His supply to flow.

Beloved, you are of immense value to the Father, who gave up His Son, heaven's darling, for you. His love for you didn't end there but is still giving to, healing, and delivering you in all the practical ways you need Him to. I pray that as you learn to stand still and let Him fight your battles, you will begin to enjoy days of heaven upon the earth and walk in new levels of victory!

I would love to personally hear from you if this book has been a blessing to you. Please don't hesitate to send me your praise reports at JosephPrince.com/testimony.

Grace always,
Joseph Prince

NOTES

CHAPTER 1: *Let Go*

1. Retrieved February 24, 2017, from www.mayoclinic.org/healthy-lifestyle /stress-management/in-depth/stress/art-20046037?pg=1.
2. Charles R. Swindoll, *The Mystery of God's Will: What Does He Want for Me?* (Nashville: Thomas Nelson, 1999).

CHAPTER 3: *Experience His Quality Life and Health*

1. American College Health Association, *American College Health Association— National College Health Assessment II: Reference Group Executive Summary Spring 2016* (Hanover, MD: American College Health Association; 2016); American College Health Association, *American College Health Association—National College Health Assessment II: Reference Group Executive Summary Spring 2000* (Baltimore, MD: American College Health Association; 2000); American College Health Association, *American College Health Association—National College Health Assessment II: Reference Group Executive Summary Spring 2010* (Linthicum, MD: American College Health Association; 2010).
2. American Psychological Association, *Stress in America: Paying with Our Health*, 2015 survey.

CHAPTER 4: *The Way to Living Worry-Free*

1. Retrieved March 10, 2017, from www.merriam-webster.com/dictionary /worry.

CHAPTER 5: *The Rhythm of Rest*

1. OT: 1369, Joseph Henry Thayer, Francis Brown, Samuel Rolles Driver, and Charles Augustus Briggs, *The Online Bible Thayer's Greek Lexicon*

and Brown Driver & Briggs Hebrew Lexicon. Copyright © 1993, Woodside Bible Fellowship, Ontario, Canada. Licensed from the Institute for Creation Research.

2. Retrieved August 18, 2017, from www.formula1.com/en/championship/inside-f1/rules-regs/Power_Unit_and_ERS.html.
3. Retrieved August 18, 2017, from www.government-fleet.com/channel/fuel-management/article/story/2015/10/gas-vs-diesel-the-bad-investment-only-fleet-managers-know-about.aspx.
4. Retrieved March 24, 2017, from http://biblehub.com/hebrew/5146.htm.
5. Retrieved March 27, 2017, from www.blueletterbible.org/lang/lexicon/lexicon.cfm?Strongs=H5117&t=NKJV.
6. Retrieved March 24, 2017, from www.mayoclinic.org/healthy-lifestyle/stress-management/in-depth/stress/art-20046037.
7. Retrieved March 24, 2017, from www.health.harvard.edu/mind-and-mood/relaxation-techniques-breath-control-helps-quell-errant-stress-response.
8. Retrieved March 24, 2017, from http://msue.anr.msu.edu/news/understanding_cortisol_the_stress_hormone.
9. Silvan S. Tomkins, *Affect Imagery Consciousness* (New York: Springer, 1962).
10. Retrieved March 24, 2017, from https://en.wikipedia.org/wiki/Giant_tortoise#Life_expectancy.

CHAPTER 6: *Walking in the Rhythm of Grace*

1. NT: 142, James Strong, *Biblesoft's New Exhaustive Strong's Numbers and Concordance with Expanded Greek-Hebrew Dictionary*. Copyright © 1994, 2003, 2006 Biblesoft, Inc. and International Bible Translators, Inc.
2. Retrieved March 27, 2017, from http://biblehub.com/hebrew/6428.htm.
3. Retrieved March 27, 2017, from http://biblehub.com/greek/2508.htm.

CHAPTER 7: *Rest Brings God's Commanded Blessings*

1. Retrieved March 29, 2017, from www.biblestudytools.com/dictionary/seven.
2. OT: 6942, Joseph Henry Thayer, Francis Brown, Samuel Rolles Driver, and Charles Augustus Briggs, *The Online Bible Thayer's Greek Lexicon and Brown Driver & Briggs Hebrew Lexicon*. Copyright © 1993, Woodside Bible Fellowship, Ontario, Canada. Licensed from the Institute for Creation Research.

3. Retrieved March 29, 2017, from https://en.wikipedia.org/wiki/Lord%27s_Day.

4. Retrieved March 29, 2017, from www.aish.com/jl/hol/o/48944546.html.

5. Retrieved March 29, 2017, from www.jewishvirtuallibrary.org/what-is-shabbat-jewish-sabbath.

6. Retrieved March 29, 2017, from https://en.wikipedia.org/wiki/List_of_Jewish_Nobel_laureates.

7. Retrieved March 29, 2017, from www.inc.com/melanie-curtin/want-a-life-of-fulfillment-a-75-year-harvard-study-says-to-prioritize-this-one-t.html.

8. Retrieved March 29, 2017, from http://articles.mercola.com/sites/articles/archive/2013/05/25/great-plow-up.aspx.

CHAPTER 8: *Have a Throne Attitude*

1. Retrieved March 31, 2017, from www.blueletterbible.org/lang/lexicon/lexicon.cfm?t=kjv&strongs=h6061.

CHAPTER 9: *Tune In to Peace*

1. Retrieved May 29, 2017 from www.blueletterbible.org/lang/lexicon/lexicon.cfm?Strongs=G1519&t=NKJV.

2. Retrieved March 27, 2017, from www.blueletterbible.org/lang/lexicon/lexicon.cfm?Strongs=G3875&t=KJV.

3. NT: 1018, William Edwy Vine, *Vine's Expository Dictionary of Biblical Words*. Copyright © 1985, Thomas Nelson Publishers.

4. Retrieved March 27, 2017, from http://biblehub.com/text/mark/5-34.htm. Retrieved April 3, 2017, from www.preceptaustin.org/greek_quick_reference_guide.

CHAPTER 10: *All-Encompassing* Shalom

1. OT: 7965, James Strong, *Biblesoft's New Exhaustive Strong's Numbers and Concordance with Expanded Greek-Hebrew Dictionary*. Copyright © 1994, 2003, 2006 Biblesoft, Inc., and International Bible Translators, Inc.

2. Ethelbert W. Bullinger, *A Critical Lexicon and Concordance to the English and Greek New Testament* (Grand Rapids, MI: Kregal Publications, 1999).

3. Kenneth S. Wuest, *Wuest's Word Studies from the Greek New Testament, Volume Two* (Grand Rapids, MI: Wm. B. Eerdmans Publishing Co., 1973).

4. Retrieved April 5, 2017, from http://biblehub.com/interlinear/john /14-27.htm.
5. Retrieved April 5, 2017, from https://en.oxforddictionaries.com/definition /cast.
6. Retrieved April 5, 2017, from http://biblehub.com/topical/s/shalem.htm.
7. Retrieved April 5, 2017, from www.bible-history.com/past/flagrum.html.

CHAPTER 11: *Above All Things, Guard Your Heart*

1. OT: 5341, Joseph Henry Thayer, Francis Brown, Samuel Rolles Driver, and Charles Augustus Briggs, *The Online Bible Thayer's Greek Lexicon and Brown Driver & Briggs Hebrew Lexicon.* Copyright © 1993, Woodside Bible Fellowship, Ontario, Canada. Licensed from the Institute for Creation Research.

CHAPTER 12: *Peace in Your Conscience*

1. Joseph Prince, *Destined to Reign* (Tulsa, OK: Harrison House Publishers, 2007), pp. 89–98.
2. NT: 1391, William Edwy Vine, *Vine's Expository Dictionary of Biblical Words.* Copyright © 1985, Thomas Nelson Publishers.

CHAPTER 13: *Stand Still*

1. Retrieved April 11, 2017, from www.ncbi.nlm.nih.gov/pmc/articles /PMC2810702.
2. Retrieved April 11, 2017, from www.blueletterbible.org/lang/lexicon/lexicon .cfm?Strongs=H2111&t=KJV.

CHAPTER 14: *Becoming a Person of Rest*

1. OT: 8010, Joseph Henry Thayer, Francis Brown, Samuel Rolles Driver, and Charles Augustus Briggs, *The Online Bible Thayer's Greek Lexicon and Brown Driver & Briggs Hebrew Lexicon.* Copyright © 1993, Woodside Bible Fellowship, Ontario, Canada. Licensed from the Institute for Creation Research.
2. OT: 3041, Joseph Henry Thayer, Francis Brown, Samuel Rolles Driver, and Charles Augustus Briggs, *The Online Bible Thayer's Greek Lexicon and Brown Driver & Briggs Hebrew Lexicon.* Copyright © 1993, Woodside Bible Fellowship, Ontario, Canada. Licensed from the Institute for Creation Research.

3. Retrieved April 13, 2017, from http://thestar.newcreation.org.sg/birth-of -the-star.php.

4. Retrieved April 13, 2017, from www.straitstimes.com/singapore/new -creation-churchs-500m-centre-fully-paid-for.

5. Retrieved April 13, 2017, from www.biblegateway.com/resources/dictionary -of-bible-themes/7388-kinsman-redeemer.

6. Retrieved April 13, 2017, from www.josephprince.com/audio-albums /the-love-story-of-ruth.

7. Retrieved April 13, 2017, from https://en.wikipedia.org/wiki/Purim.

8. Retrieved April 13, 2017, from https://en.wikipedia.org/wiki/Passover #Date_and_duration.

9. Retrieved April 13, 2017, from www.hebrew4christians.com/Holidays /Fall_Holidays/Sukkot/sukkot.html.

10. NT: 2827, James Strong, *Biblesoft's New Exhaustive Strong's Numbers and Concordance with Expanded Greek-Hebrew Dictionary.* Copyright © 1994, 2003, 2006 Biblesoft, Inc., and International Bible Translators, Inc.

11. NT: 373, Joseph Henry Thayer, *Thayer's Greek Lexicon* (electronic database). Copyright © 2000, 2003, 2006 by Biblesoft, Inc. All rights reserved.

CHAPTER 15: *Hear Your Way to Victory*

1. Retrieved April 20, 2017, from http://biblehub.com/interlinear/romans /10-17.htm.

2. Retrieved April 20, 2017, from http://biblehub.com/greek/4982.htm.

3. OT: 8085, Joseph Henry Thayer, Francis Brown, Samuel Rolles Driver, and Charles Augustus Briggs, *The Online Bible Thayer's Greek Lexicon and Brown Driver & Briggs Hebrew Lexicon.* Copyright © 1993, Woodside Bible Fellowship, Ontario, Canada. Licensed from the Institute for Creation Research.

4. Retrieved April 20, 2017, from http://app.josephprince.com.

5. Retrieved April 20, 2017, from http://biblehub.com/text/galatians/3-5.htm. Retrieved April 21, 2017, from www.preceptaustin.org/greek_quick_reference _guide.

6. Retrieved April 21, 2017, from http://biblehub.com/commentaries/acts /14-9.htm.

CHAPTER 16: *The One Thing that Brings Success in Every Area*

1. Retrieved April 24, 2017, from www.merriam-webster.com/dictionary /delight.

2. OT: 1897, Joseph Henry Thayer, Francis Brown, Samuel Rolles Driver, and Charles Augustus Briggs, *The Online Bible Thayer's Greek Lexicon and Brown Driver & Briggs Hebrew Lexicon*. Copyright © 1993, Woodside Bible Fellowship, Ontario, Canada. Licensed from the Institute for Creation Research.

3. Retrieved April 24, 2017, from https://en.wikipedia.org/wiki/Ruminant.

4. Retrieved April 24, 2017, from http://medical-dictionary.thefreedictionary.com/ruminant.

CHAPTER 17: *Experiencing Blessings in Marriage*

1. OT: 8085, Joseph Henry Thayer, Francis Brown, Samuel Rolles Driver, and Charles Augustus Briggs, *The Online Bible Thayer's Greek Lexicon and Brown Driver & Briggs Hebrew Lexicon*. Copyright © 1993, Woodside Bible Fellowship, Ontario, Canada. Licensed from the Institute for Creation Research.

2. Retrieved April 26, 2017, from http://divorce.com/top-10-reasons-marriages-fail.

3. Retrieved April 26, 2017, from www.healthcentral.com/anxiety/treatment-260009-5.html.

4. Retrieved April 26, 2017, from www.josephprince.com/video-albums/christ-is-the-centre-of-happy-marriages-2-dvd-album_b1r.

CHAPTER 18: *Stress-Free Parenting*

1. Retrieved April 27, 2017, from http://biblehub.com/interlinear/deuteronomy/11-19.htm.

CHAPTER 19: *Let Go and Live Long*

1. Retrieved April 26, 2017, from www.blueletterbible.org/lang/lexicon/lexicon.cfm?Strongs=H4832&t=KJV.

2. Retrieved April 26, 2017, from www.blueletterbible.org/lang/lexicon/lexicon.cfm?Strongs=H7495&t=KJV.

3. OT: 7503, Joseph Henry Thayer, Francis Brown, Samuel Rolles Driver, and Charles Augustus Briggs, *The Online Bible Thayer's Greek Lexicon and Brown Driver & Briggs Hebrew Lexicon*. Copyright © 1993, Woodside Bible Fellowship, Ontario, Canada. Licensed from the Institute for Creation Research.

4. Retrieved March 27, 2017, from www.abarim-publications.com/Meaning/Rapha.html.

5. Retrieved April 26, 2017 from www.hebrew4christians.com/Grammar /Unit_One/Pictograms/pictograms.html.
6. Retrieved April 26 April, 2017, from www.tbalert.org/about-tb/global-tb -challenges/side-effects.
7. Retrieved April 26, 2017, from www.cancer.gov/about-cancer/treatment /side-effects.
8. Retrieved April 26, 2017 from www.georgemuller.org/uploads/4/8/6/5 /48652749/george_muller_seminar_stan_murrell.pdf.
9. Arthur T. Pierson, *George Muller of Bristol: A Man of Faith and Prayer* (Harrington, DE: Delmarva Publications, 2013).
10. Retrieved April 27, 2017, from www.georgemuller.org/devotional/category /arthur-t-pierson.
11. Retrieved April 27, 2017, from www.rogersteer.com/george-muller-on-how -to-live-a-happy-life.
12. Retrieved April 26, 2017, from https://en.wikipedia.org/wiki/George _M%C3%BCller.
13. Retrieved April 26, 2017, from www.georgemuller.org/quotes/for-more -than-seventy-years-i-have-not-been-anxious.
14. Retrieved April 26, 2017, from www.georgemuller.org/quotes/rolled-my -burdens-on-the-lord.
15. Retrieved April 26, 2017, from www.blueletterbible.org/lang/lexicon /lexicon.cfm?Strongs=H3444&t=KJV.

CHAPTER 20: *You Are Not Alone*

1. Retrieved April 27, 2017, from www.bible-history.com/resource/ff_baal .htm.
2. Retrieved April 7, 2017, from http://biblehub.com/interlinear/1_kings /18-39.htm.
3. Retrieved April 27, 2017, from www.blueletterbible.org/lang/lexicon /lexicon.cfm?Strongs=H1827&t=KJV.
4. Retrieved April 27, 2017, from http://hymnary.org/text/are_you_weary _are_you_heavyhearted.

EXTRA RESOURCES

———

To hear Joseph Prince preach on the biblical principles and truths shared in each chapter of this book, please check out the following audio messages at JosephPrince.com/LetGo:

Chapter 1: Let Go

It's Time to Let Go!
Your Only Battle Today Is the Fight to Remain at Rest

Chapter 2: Just Look at the Birds

Let Go and Let God Flow
God's Rest for the Rest of Your Life
Never Alone, Always Cared For

Chapter 3: Experience His Quality Life and Health

Becoming Stress-Free and Healthy
Never Alone, Always Cared For

Chapter 4: The Way to Living Worry-Free

Becoming Stress-Free and Healthy
Live the Let-Go Life!

Chapter 5: The Rhythm of Rest

Living by the Unforced Rhythms of Grace
Rest Is the Promised Land of the Believer
Live Stress-Free by His Spirit

Chapter 6: Walking in the Rhythm of Grace

Let Go and Flow in the Vine Life

Chapter 7: Rest Brings God's Commanded Blessings

Jesus Our True Jubilee and Sabbath
Restful Increase versus Stressful Increase

Chapter 8: Have a Throne Attitude

Have a Throne Attitude—Rest Until God Makes Your Enemies
   Your Footstool
Your Only Battle Today Is the Fight to Remain at Rest

Chapter 9: Tune In to Peace

Peace Keeps What Grace Gives
Live Stress-Free by His Spirit
If It's a Miracle You Need, a Miracle You'll Get—If You Remain
   in Peace

Chapter 10: All-Encompassing *Shalom*

If It's a Miracle You Need, a Miracle You'll Get—If You Remain
   in Peace
Live the Let-Go Life!
Peace Keeps What Grace Gives

Chapter 11: Above All Things, Guard Your Heart

Rest Is the Promised Land of the Believer

Chapter 19: Let Go and Live Long

Hidden Secrets to Health in the Hebrew Language
The Health-Giving Power of a Relaxed Heart

Chapter 20: You Are Not Alone

Win Over Discouragement, Depression and Burnout

SALVATION PRAYER

If you would like to receive all that Jesus has done for you and make Him your Lord and Savior, please pray this prayer:

Lord Jesus, thank You for loving me and dying for me on the cross. Your precious blood washes me clean of every sin. You are my Lord and my Savior, now and forever. I believe You rose from the dead and that You are alive today. Because of Your finished work, I am now a beloved child of God and heaven is my home. Thank You for giving me eternal life and filling my heart with Your peace and joy. Amen.

WE WOULD LIKE TO HEAR FROM YOU

———

If you have prayed the salvation prayer or if you have a testimony to share after reading this book, please send it to us via JosephPrince.com/testimony.

SPECIAL APPRECIATION

Special thanks and appreciation to all who have sent in their testimonies and praise reports to us. Kindly note that all testimonies are received in good faith and edited only for brevity and fluency. Names have been changed to protect the writers' privacy.

STAY CONNECTED
WITH JOSEPH

—

Connect with Joseph through these social media channels and receive daily inspirational teachings:
Facebook.com/JosephPrince
Twitter.com/JosephPrince
Youtube.com/JosephPrinceOnline
Instagram: @JosephPrince

FREE DAILY E-MAIL
DEVOTIONAL

—

Sign up for Joseph's *free* daily email devotional at JosephPrince.com/meditate and receive bite-size inspirations to help you grow in grace.

BOOKS BY JOSEPH PRINCE

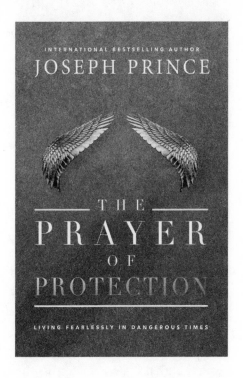

The Prayer of Protection

We live in dangerous times. A time in which terrorist activities, pandemics, and natural calamities are on the rise. But there is good news. God has given us a powerful prayer of protection—Psalm 91—through which we and our families can find safety and deliverance from every snare of the enemy. In *The Prayer of Protection*, discover a God of love and His impenetrable shield of protection that covers everything that concerns you, and start living fearlessly in these dangerous times!

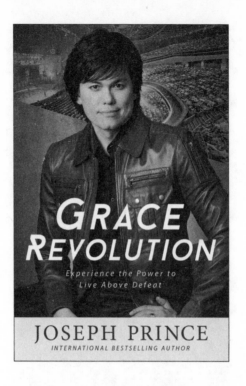

Grace Revolution

Experience the revolution that is sweeping across the world! In *Grace Revolution*, Joseph Prince offers five powerful keys that will help you experience firsthand the grace revolution in your own life and live above defeat. See how these keys can work easily for you, as you read inspiring stories of people who experienced amazing and lasting transformations when they encountered the real Jesus and heard the unadulterated gospel. Whatever your challenge today, begin to step away from defeat and take a massive leap toward your victory. Get your copy today and let the revolution begin in your life!

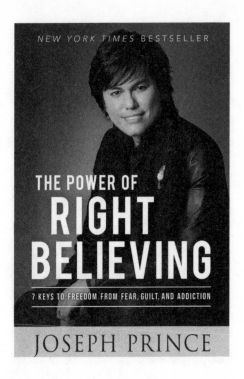

THE POWER OF
RIGHT
BELIEVING

7 KEYS TO FREEDOM FROM FEAR, GUILT, AND ADDICTION

JOSEPH PRINCE

The Power of Right Believing

Experience transformation, breakthroughs, and freedom today through the power of right believing! This book offers seven practical and powerful keys that will help you find freedom from all fears, guilt, and addictions. See these keys come alive in the many precious testimonies you will read from people around the world who have experienced breakthroughs and liberty from all kinds of bondages. Win the battle for your mind through understanding the powerful truths of God's Word and begin a journey of victorious living and unshakable confidence in God's love for you!

Destined to Reign

This pivotal and quintessential book on the grace of God will change your life forever! Join Joseph Prince as he unlocks foundational truths to understanding God's grace and how it alone sets you free to experience victory over every adversity, lack, and destructive habit that is limiting you today. Be uplifted and refreshed as you discover how reigning in life is all about Jesus and what He has already done for you. Start experiencing the success, wholeness, and victory that you were destined to enjoy!

Unmerited Favor

This follow-up book to *Destined to Reign* is a must-read if you want to live out the dreams that God has birthed in your heart! Building on the foundational truths of God's grace laid out in *Destined to Reign*, *Unmerited Favor* takes you into a deeper understanding of the gift of righteousness that you have through the cross and how it gives you a supernatural ability to succeed in life. Packed with empowering new covenant truths, *Unmerited Favor* will set you free to soar above your challenges and lead an overcoming life as God's beloved today.